What Coaching and Healing
about Deep Coa

"Deep Coaching reveals a well-articulated, precise blueprint for change that is immediately accessible, universal in application, and profound in its orientation. With simplicity and acuity, Roxanne weaves together a rich tapestry of the human experience illuminating what is possible when we reorient our clients to a truer, more expansive sense of self. Inevitable struggles become unique pathways to our client's highest aspirations and deepest knowing. Whether you are new to coaching and the Enneagram or have decades of experience, this book will not only transform your coaching but also nourish a deeper understanding and experience of compassion, joy, and true freedom."

> — **Diana Redmond, PCC, ICF Mentor Coach, Enneagram Coach and Facilitator, and Experiential Learning Leader**

"Roxanne's language in Deep Coaching helps me approach the human condition with compassion and hope as a pastor and spiritual director. She frees us from shaming framework often imposed by religion or psychology and invites deep curiosity about the ways we've been formed and why. Her work with the Enneagram lights up paths of liberation toward greater connection with ourselves, with others, and with whatever we might call the divine. It's become an essential part of both my pastoral and coaching work!"

> — **Reverend Julie Van Til, IEA Accredited Professional and DCI Certified Enneagram Coach**

"This book changed my life! Roxanne Howe-Murphy offers a compassionate, wise, and insightful book about the human experience. Educators will find the practices valuable for personal and professional development. It also changes communities. I found it incredibly useful in designing and implementing educational and therapeutic programs for individuals with autism and other developmental disabilities. Read it for yourself and for those who you serve."

> — **Irma Velasquez, LHD, Founder of Wings Learning Center and De Colores Arts and Author of *Fish Dreams: A Mother's Journey from Curing Her Son's Autism to Loving Him as He Is***

"The first edition of Deep Coaching proved an invaluable tool and guide as I moved from my physician role of treating illness to my role of guiding that same patient and client into a new relationship with their deeper knowing. This new and enriched volume, I am sure, will be as worn and dog-eared as its predecessor. Helping my consulting patients and coaching clients to look through the lens of Enneagram core type has been revolutionary. I enthusiastically urge anyone wishing to work with physical, emotional, and spiritual healing to embrace this volume."

> — **Karen A. Van Zino, MD, Deep Coaching Professional and Author of *Midnight's All a Glimmer: Poetry, Personality, and the Power to See—An Anthology***

"Deep Coaching is both profound and practical. Roxanne's wisdom and counterintuitive approach to change is powerful. Her approach described in this book has changed my life. As a result, I have increased my capacity to be more present, aware, compassionate, and choiceful. This book also provides a practical guide for using the Enneagram and deep coaching to support clients in accessing their gifts and releasing old patterns."

— **Marcia Hyatt, PCC Leadership Coach, Creator of Best of Ourselves Podcast, and Author of** *What Have I Mythed? Stories for Reflection*

"Roxanne's visionary way of teaching the Enneagram when combined with coaching offers us a powerful map for how to walk with someone into the tender territory of personal transformation. Deep Coaching opened me to the Enneagram as an embodied, heart-opening, truth-telling journey that has led to shifts in perspective and sustainable change in my life and the lives of my clients. This book is a one of a kind treasure!"

— **Devon Carter, ACC, CMT, Somatic Enneagram Coach**

"Roxanne Howe-Murphy's writings and teachings have had a profound impact on my life as an executive in state government and as a coach and human being. *Deep Coaching* is a magical combination of compassion, wisdom, insights, and clear, pragmatic, hands-on tools and practices that support personal exploration and growth through the power of presence and attention to our three centers of intelligence. The second edition of this brilliant, insightful, and very practical book has high value for leaders who seek a deeper understanding of the amazing diversity of human motivation."

— **Susan M. Hansch, MA, ACC, IEA and Deep Coaching Certified Professional and Retired Chief Deputy Director of California Coastal Commission**

"After studying the Enneagram for years with other teachers, I am grateful for both the creation and further development of *Deep Coaching: Using the Enneagram as a Catalyst for Profound Change*. Reading Roxanne's words evokes the wisdom I've always known within myself. The art of deep coaching is Roxanne's invitation to each of us to relax into who we truly are. It invites us as coaches to create an expansive container to help both ourselves and others to explore any experience from our three centers of intelligence: the sensations of the body, the emotions of the heart, and the quiet mind, revealing the mystery of ourselves as we relax our personality reactions."

— **Brian Mitchell-Walker, PCC, Riso-Hudson Certified Enneagram Teacher, IEA Former Board Member, Racial Justice Facilitator, and Certified I.D.E.A. Enneagram Practitioner**

"Roxanne's work is a brilliant discourse on how we can benefit from honoring the wisdom of the Enneagram to move our clients toward life's fullness. It is a gift to my Rosen Method bodywork practice, to my clients, and for my own journey toward living a more spontaneous life. *Deep Coaching* offers rich insights into how we can realize our own capacity to be present as we untangle the knots of our default patterns, allowing for a richer and more authentic life, free from our conditioned responses and in greater alignment with our truth."

— **Jeanie C. Williams, Senior Rosen Method Bodywork Practitioner**

"*Deep Coaching* is a groundbreaking contribution not only to the coaching field and Enneagram community but also to humanity as a whole. Human beings have the capacity to evolve, and this book is a road map for this evolution. *Deep Coaching* has been used as a guide by many coaches to support transformation and healing in the individual and collective consciousness. Through spiritual guidance such as presence and practical day-to-day instructions, Roxanne brings a radically compassionate approach to coaching, in a world that so desperately needs it. We each have the option to stay in a constricted state of being or to live into our highest potential; Roxanne not only creates a road map for the path to a wholeness and a meaningful life but also ushers you through the journey with radical honesty and deep love."

— **Lara Heller, ACC Certified Coach and Enneagram Teacher and Facilitator**

"Having spent much of my life in active addiction, I work as an addiction recovery coach and help traumatized and hurting men laden with shame rise beyond the same sort of inner pain that plagued much of my life. This work requires delicate and compassionate holding. Of all the traditional psychotherapy and training I have received, nothing landed in my heart like the coaching course where I met Roxanne and her vision for personal growth. The deep coaching methodology has become the foundation upon which I have learned to explore my own inner sanctum. Maya Angelou said, "There is no greater agony than bearing an untold story inside you." This book is a gateway to the story of who we are, and we need to explore it, speak it, own it, and live to enjoy it every day. *Deep Coaching* teaches you first to deepen your understanding of self and, on the wings of this discovery, to coach others to recognize the joy to be found by reembracing the spark of life that first accompanied them into this world. Thank you, Roxanne, for giving so much back to a world so in need of the guidance you bring through this book and through your never-ending quest to help others live free in their deserved inner truth."

— **Mark Drax, Addiction Recovery Coach, England**

"*Deep Coaching* embodies the sacred path that clients need to confidently reach their highest potential. In graceful support of this journey, Dr. Roxanne Howe-Murphy has adeptly combined an aliveness of the Enneagram with practical tools for presence. This masterful confluence illuminates the path of the seeker toward wholeness and radical acceptance of their full expression of being a messy, brilliant, beautiful, and courageous human."

> — Pamela Johnson, Transformational Life Coach, Enneagram Teacher, and Archetypal Consultant

"*Deep Coaching* is a must-read for those who are courageous enough to walk the road less traveled and who are passionate about creating profound, sustainable transformation. Roxanne's approach includes the coach as an instrument of love and interconnectedness, which spans beyond traditional coaching approaches. Her concept of shared commonalities among everyone reminds me of what we describe in South Africa as Ubuntu. Ubuntu is a Zulu term meaning 'humanity' and is roughly translated as 'I am because you are.' Hence, the ability to be seen, heard, and accepted precisely for who we are is a starting point for developing trust in the coaching relationship. This book is the best coaching guide for presence-based coaching practices and strategies to grow individuals and leaders."

> — Alicia S Pieterse, MA, Founding Member of Nurturing Growth Trading and International Leadership and Depth Coach, Johannesburg, South Africa

"I found *Deep Coaching* to be very helpful in deepening the coaching experience. As a licensed counselor, I unexpectedly found this book equally applicable in the realm of therapy. At its core, successful therapy is about connecting to people. The deeper the connection, the higher the likelihood for change and healing. The five pillars taught throughout this second edition and the elements of the iceberg model, along with all the suggested prompts and inquiries, teach us how to deepen the connection to others and approach our clients with the ability to understand, validate, and ultimately facilitate transformation."

> — Jared Bingham, Licensed Professional Counselor and Chief Operating Officer of High Country Behavioral Health

"I highly recommend *Deep Coaching* as an indispensable guide for the spiritually wired coach actively engaged in deep inner work. Roxanne's work uniquely depicts the architecture of personality structure by Enneagram types, integrates an understanding of each type's relation to the Enneagram's centers of intelligence, and intertwines deep understanding of the work of Presence. The book presents a wealth of wisdom and guidance for precisely tailored coaching to a client's uniqueness by personality type. *Deep Coaching* supports a deep, dynamic coaching engagement that potentially leads to an ongoing deepening of the coach's self-realization and subsequently actualizing such in the world through coaching with psychological and spiritual expertise."

> — **Samuel Schindler, The Narrative Enneagram Certified Teacher and Practitioner of the Diamond Approach**

"Roxanne Howe-Murphy artfully marries the science of the Enneagram with a delicious exploration of our deepest inner life experience. This book is a game changer for coaches and other professionals who seek insights into the psychological architecture and the resultant motivations, fears, and desires of each personality type. This book is key to my personal journey as well as the work I do with clients, as it offers an exciting vision of human possibility and a clear map of the nine paths supporting our transformation to our highest self-expression."

> — **Nelia Steyn, Coach, Consultant, and Corporate Trainer, Pretoria, South Africa**

Also by Roxanne Howe-Murphy, EdD

Deep Living with the Enneagram: Recovering Your True Nature, revised and updated, (2020)

*Deep Living: Transforming Your Relationship to Everything That Matters
through the Enneagram* (2013)

Deep Coaching: Using the Enneagram as a Catalyst for Profound Change (2007)

.

Second Edition

Deep
Coaching

Using the Enneagram
as a catalyst for profound change

Roxanne Howe-Murphy, EdD

Deep Coaching
Using the Enneagram as a Catalyst for Profound Change, 2nd Edition
Roxanne Howe-Murphy, EdD

Enneagram Press
Published by Enneagram Press, Santa Fe, NM

Proofreader: Jeanie Williams
Index: Maria Hypponen
Cover and Interior Design: Davis Creative, CreativePublishingPartners.com

Publisher's Cataloging-In-Publication Data
(Provided by Cassidy Cataloguing Services, Inc.)

Names: Howe-Murphy, Roxanne, author.
Title: Deep coaching : using the enneagram as a catalyst for profound change / Roxanne Howe-Murphy, EdD.
Description: Second edition. | Santa Fe, NM : Enneagram Press, [2022] | Includes bibliographical references and index.
Identifiers: ISBN: 978-0-9793847-6-9 (paperback) | LCCN: 2022911453
Subjects: LCSH: Enneagram. | Mind and body. | Personal coaching. | Change (Psychology) | BISAC: PSYCHOLOGY / Personality. | EDUCATION / Professional Development. | BODY, MIND & SPIRIT / Inspiration & Personal Growth.
Classification: LCC: BF698.35.E54 H68 2022 | DDC: 155.26--dc23

Dedication

*For all of our children and grandchildren and
the generations to come—with hope that the
powerful force of Love will be instilled in their hearts
and expressed through their beings.*

TABLE OF CONTENTS

FIGURES AND TABLES

Figures

Tables

FOREWORD TO SECOND EDITION
by Belinda Gore

When this book was first published fifteen years ago, it was a pioneering contribution introducing the Enneagram system of personality to the coaching profession. The title, *Deep Coaching: Using the Enneagram as a Catalyst for Profound Change,* makes it clear this is no ordinary approach to coaching. Not only does it explain the Enneagram and its nine personality types in concepts and language our clients can comprehend and relate to, but this book illuminates the Enneagram as a guide for spiritual transformation. The growing Enneagram community welcomed it in 2007 as an essential professional resource for coaches and as a groundbreaking foundational structure for working with a new, counterintuitive model for change. It was revolutionary then and it still is today.

Roxanne Howe-Murphy is a gifted teacher, a deeply spiritual wise woman, and my good friend. We met at an International Enneagram Association conference, introduced by our mutual friend, the late Brian Grodner. All three of us were students of Don Riso and Russ Hudson. Roxanne directed the Enneagram Institute of the San Francisco Bay Area, Brian founded the Enneagram Institute of New Mexico, and I was the founding director of the Enneagram Institute of Central Ohio. Roxanne and I became instant friends. We discovered that not only were we born just a few days apart, but we had for years considered Santa Fe a second home. Each of us was also developing an Enneagram certification program for coaches, psychotherapists, spiritual directors, and human resource professionals. In our own work with clients, we had realized what a powerful tool the Enneagram is for revealing the deep structures of our personality tendencies and how Enneagram wisdom could show a path for activating our inherent higher capacities.

While *Deep Coaching* uses the Enneagram as an incomparable tool, the approach is built on the practice of presence, that is, being awake and aligned in body, heart, and mind. In writing this book, Roxanne had gathered her years of experience as university faculty, life coach, and group facilitator, then opened to her inner guidance. It was inspired.

After writing the original edition of *Deep Coaching,* Roxanne invited me to join her in facilitating a live workshop based on her book. We have joked ever since that while she gave birth to the teaching, I was the midwife. It was a role I was honored to fulfill.

We wove together our collective experience to develop a teaching format and experiential exercises designed to bring the practice of presence to life. It was an amazing workshop, and I was immediately committed to this powerful new teaching. This groundbreaking book then grew into a school, the Deep Coaching Institute, with our new partner, Diana Redmond, joining us.

To use presence-based coaching, understanding the centers of intelligence is invaluable. George Gurdjieff (considered, along with Óscar Ichazo, a founder of the modern version of the Enneagram) taught that every human has three foundational centers of intelligence and consciousness: the belly or instinctual center (termed the moving center by Gurdjieff), the heart or feeling center, and the head or thinking center. He described the nine Enneagram types as each having a characteristic imbalance among the three. This forms a distortion that drives the overuse of one center and neglect of one or two of the others. Presence, on the other hand, is the condition of being "awake," inhabiting and being aligned in all three centers at the same time. Presence changes everything: it is a condition that fosters healing.

Throughout *Deep Coaching*, you'll discover coaching practices anchored in presence that support the awakening of each of these centers with a special emphasis on developing the underused center.

When Don Riso and Russ Hudson wrote the foreword for the initial publication of *Deep Coaching*, they recognized the significant need within the coaching field "to mature beyond the 'get ahead,' careerist mentality to become a field where deeper personal and spiritual values are accepted and openly spoken about." With this book, Roxanne challenged the profession to embrace a counterintuitive approach to coaching: being with what is here and not trying to fix anything. It was new in 2007 and is still on the cutting edge of the coaching profession today.

I am excited about this new edition of *Deep Coaching*. Roxanne has integrated layers of insights she has gained through teaching and practicing deep coaching over these past fifteen years. This is a living, dynamic teaching. I invite you to immerse yourself in it to discover what it will awaken in you. These are tumultuous times, full of challenge and the potential for transformative change. *Deep Coaching* is a guide to grasping the possibilities and flowing with unfolding promise. May you join the movement toward greater wholeness.

Belinda Gore, PhD

Author, *Finding Freedom in Authentic Relationships: A Life-Changing Exploration of the Enneagram and Object Relations*

FOREWORD TO FIRST EDITION
by Don Richard Riso and Russ Hudson

You are holding in your hands one of the first books of its kind, a book about using the Enneagram in coaching. We believe that this book will lay the groundwork for the growth and appreciation of both the Enneagram and coaching, showing the way toward greater excellence in both fields. The author, Roxanne Howe-Murphy, is uniquely suited, in both background and the depth of her personal development, to the task of synthesis and creation that she has set for herself.

The Enneagram is such an effective tool for the coaching process that it is actually surprising that this synthesis is not yet widely used by coaches. Perhaps the field of coaching needed to mature beyond the get-ahead, careerist mentality to become a field where deeper personal and spiritual values are accepted and openly spoken about. Coaches themselves needed to mature to where they feel comfortable speaking about the unseen and immeasurable world of the spirit, about higher values and broader contexts than simply about what works.

Further, clients needed to appreciate that really excellent coaching involves more than helping them to make quick fixes. The professional HR culture in general now more widely realizes that coaching is a profoundly human interaction, one that is therapeutic and healing, spiritual, and psychological. The process is deeper than people generally first thought—it is about a radical re-visioning of yourself, your work, and your relationships so that one can lead a more alive, productive, and joyous life. In short, coaching needed to become something that allowed and encouraged a depth and openness that we associate with other profound and sacred counseling and mentoring relationships. This book provides a gateway to this depth of meaning within the universe of possibilities that is the domain of coaching.

Of course, we believe that this is where the Enneagram can be helpful and where this book is a huge boon to anyone who will be coaching or guiding another. Real coaching involves radical openness, acceptance of the other where they are (that is, without our personal agenda), deep listening, the ability to make a direct and ongoing connection with the person, honesty and frankness with tact and discretion, profound humility, humor, and an honoring of limits and boundaries. A book on coaching needs to take account of all of these qualities—and more.

This book does, while giving guidance about these qualities for each of the nine types—or better, to each person, since a good coach never treats a client like a type. (Paradoxically, the Enneagram typology helps us see individuals more clearly, not as generic types.) The Enneagram-aware coach starts with the nine archetypal patterns of habitual, repetitive behaviors and identifications that the client usually thinks is who they are. The coach then helps lead the client to a new depth of insight into themselves, their lives, and the options that are available to them for more real freedom, growth, and joy. Coaching is thus an induction of the person into a richer and more meaningful life, and the Enneagram is a powerful map and source of guidance for that great journey. May all who use this book find everything they are looking for—and more!

Don Richard Riso and Russ Hudson

Authors of *Personality Types* and *The Wisdom of the Enneagram*
January 2007

PREFACE TO SECOND EDITION

I'm astonished how quickly twenty years have passed since the early inklings of this book found their way to the page. Five years after its inception, *Deep Coaching: Using the Enneagram as a Catalyst for Profound Change* found its way into the Enneagram, coaching, and other growth and healing-oriented professional communities. It seemed to resonate as users discovered the extraordinary immediacy offered by the presence-based approach to the Enneagram in meeting the breadth and depth of themselves and their clients with clarity, compassion, and courage. Now, with fifteen additional years of continued learning, teaching, mentoring, coaching, and personal deepening within the context of an ever-fluid world, the right moment for a second edition became apparent.

Built on the foundations of the 2007 book, this second edition includes over 40 percent new and revised material, including teachings not found in previous writings, more in-depth descriptions of coaching processes, and the addition of more coaching cues to support the use of the material in the professional-client relationship. The ego code and Triangle of Identity, which which I introduced in the original and revised editions of the *Deep Living* books (2013, 2020), are integrated into the descriptions of the nine Enneagram types with suggested ways they can be applied in the coaching process.

Also new in this edition is the explicit naming of five pillars of deep coaching, which are presented initially in chapter 1 and interwoven throughout the book. These intersecting pillars are the Enneagram; presence as the basis for coaching (incorporating the three centers of intelligence); the counterintuitive change process; orienting clients toward self-acceptance, love, and interconnectedness; and the inner work of the coach. This paradigm, anchored in the practice of presence, allows the practitioner to meet clients where they are, accepting the full range of their human experience. Calling upon these pillars supports the healing of inner pain, illuminates hidden obstacles and new pathways to true choice, and leads to unexpected and sometimes exceptional outcomes that could not have been predicted. I still find myself in awe as clients experience significant shifts in consciousness and states of being. They are changed.

It's important to note that with the explosion in awareness and acceptance of the Enneagram since 2007, it is sometimes approached primarily as a typology. The *Deep Coaching* approach to the Enneagram emphasizes this framework's unique value in providing insight into an individual's inner landscape and acknowledges that one's core type is actually a powerful starting place for experiencing a new relationship with oneself, expanded levels of awareness, and the transformative movement toward wholeness.

While this book was originally written for coaches who specialize in diverse areas of emphasis, readers have found use for it across many physical and mental health therapies, spiritual direction, leadership and organizational development, and other growth-oriented professions.

USING THIS BOOK

While this book is of necessity presented in sequential chapters, the principles underlying the five pillars are integrated throughout the book. I recommend starting with section 1, as it provides the framework for being with your clients. Many users find that the chapters in section 3, which further expand upon the framework, can be useful to bring into the coaching environment even before addressing the specific types found in section 2.

The Enneagram offers a wealth of wisdom and basis for presence based around the three centers of intelligence (body, heart, head). It sparks our desire for understanding and openness to insight, awakens us to our feelings and all that is experienced deeply in our hearts, and brings attention to inhabiting our physical substance that is inherently connected to Mother Earth. Thus, I encourage you to take on the worldview, the emotional landscape, and the relationship to the body for each type. In other words, I invite you to be affected by having a whole-being experience of each type to the degree possible.

As I was working with this revision for its fifteenth-year anniversary, I often felt waves of enormous sadness for the pain in the world amid extraordinary gratitude, joy, "not knowing," and an essential trust in what is brought forth here. We all know that people hurt, especially as the world becomes more turbulent and unpredictable. But much of the pain comes from the disconnection to oneself. The inner sources of individual well-being that are available right here, right now, and which can help heal this inner divide, go unnoticed.

It is my great desire that you will find *Deep Coaching* to be a deep well of guidance and wisdom for the healing so needed in the world. Every time you open the book, may you experience deeper anchoring, openheartedness, curiosity, and courage, along with compassion and gratitude for your own inner work and the transformational possibilities that you support in others. It all matters.

It's my true honor to share the second edition of *Deep Coaching* with you. It is offered with love.

Roxanne Howe-Murphy, EdD

March 2022

Being a Catalyst for Human Development and Transformation

Chapter 1

AN INTRODUCTION TO DEEP COACHING:
Integrating Coaching and the Enneagram

THE CALL TO COACHING

As coaches, we have the unique opportunity to be with human beings who are engaged in the life-altering work of committing to and realizing their desires for a fulfilling life, and at a deeper level, living with true authenticity. We do our best to show up so that our clients can do the same, meeting somewhere in the client's familiar inner world and traveling together to new territory that yields both remarkable possibilities and realities that, at one time, seemed but a distant dream.

This is no small undertaking.

What equips us to travel this journey with another human? Our natural inclinations for supporting the gifts and strengths of others, the specific skills and knowledge we have gained as part of our professional preparation, and our own psychological and spiritual development are all necessary contributors. But it is a fundamental trust in the capacity of each person to evolve into their highest nature that confirms that this is the work we are meant to do.

An expansive, yet grounded, frame of reference is available to help clients experience themselves in entirely new ways and to naturally express themselves from this new foundation in their daily lives.

There is a system that provides a robust framework for psychological and spiritual health that comprehensively and precisely describes the nature of the human condition and offers a map of not only external behaviors, but also the vast inner terrain of the human experience. This map compassionately guides the user in deepening self-understanding, becoming more conscious, and choosing options that create a more satisfying and interconnected life. The Enneagram is such a system.

WHAT THE ENNEAGRAM DOES FOR YOU AS A COACH

Within the context of consciousness, the Enneagram is a system that reveals nine dimensions of essential nature. It also illuminates nine versions of the human condition (generally referred to as personality types), each with their specific default patterns of thought, emotion, attention, behavior, and motivations.

While no system takes every aspect of human nature into account and there is no panacea to address all of life's challenges and opportunities, the Enneagram is a profound field of knowledge and guidance that brings into awareness the possibility of significant life shifts and transformation. In a world that is chaotic and often fuels distress, the Enneagram, used with presence, supports the development of mental, emotional, physical, and spiritual health and well-being.

If you are reading this book, you no doubt want to be the most effective coach that you can be. You may sense that different people require different strategies and approaches in order for them to reach their intended outcomes in a sustainable manner. Perhaps you have found ways to vary your coaching language and have experimented with modifying questions or have employed different written tools, creative exercises, or somatic strategies. Whether you are new to or experienced in your field, you might reflect upon these meta-questions: *What is the basis for selecting the approaches you use with a particular client? What are your assumptions underlying the change process itself? Through what lens do you see your client? Do you see someone who needs help? Do you take in the whole human being that has both gifts and challenges? Are you aware that this individual has likely experienced some degree of alienation from their inner self? Do you recognize that this person also is a mystery and you'll be entering the unknown together?*

The Enneagram provides a framework for answering these questions and approaching deep coaching. For now, let me share just three reasons I can't imagine coaching without a background in this powerful system of knowledge and wisdom.

First, to be effective agents of change, coaches are charged with the important responsibility of knowing themselves well. From the basic perspective of a personality typing system, knowing which of the nine Enneagram types you most resonate with is indispensable to deepening your self-knowledge. You will begin to recognize innate strengths, assumptions, obstructions, and modus operandi (or automatic patterns) that no other framework can give you as precisely. Diving deeper into this system, you will be given the gift of discovering internal, and mostly unconscious, motivations that have shaped your reactions and the ways you have coped with the demands of living in this complicated world. Continuing on your journey, you may also encounter moments when the veils fall away and the awe of this stunning moment is front and center. You know in that instant that you could not have planned for the right people and the right timing to have come together in this magical way. Something else is at work.

Thus, if you are not familiar with your type or if you haven't used the Enneagram for your own self-development work, it is incumbent on you to do so. With your own experience as a foundation, you will find the material coming alive as you bring it to your clients. It is a profound privilege to know ourselves at the deeper levels, even when we encounter uncomfortable, hidden dimensions and allow for the needed inner healing to take place. This increases our capacity for meeting clients in *their* inner world that is otherwise rarely acknowledged.

As a coach, it is important to recognize the automatic patterns associated with your personality type because they are likely to show up in your coaching style. For example, do you expect yourself to have the answers to your client's dilemmas, or expect immediate change, or take steps to make sure the client sees how helpful you are, or keep your sessions upbeat and fun? Through working with the Enneagram in ways that you'll learn about in this book, you will discover a broader and potentially more impactful range of responses available than when you rely on familiar questions and strategies. Acting upon this discovery allows you to be more attuned to yourself and to your client.

Second, as you gain awareness of each client's core type, you will gain insight into what may be going on underneath the client's spoken words or actions, become attuned to what potentially can be powerful mirroring or feedback for the client, and be able to co-create next steps that can help free your client from their own obstructions. When you're unaware of the client's default behavioral, mental, energetic, and emotional patterns, you can inadvertently reinforce the internal systems that helped the client to become stuck in the first place.

Third, while identifying your core personality type is a vital step in using the Enneagram, you will gain the most value in becoming less identified with and less driven by your type-related patterns and more present to yourself and others, which naturally leads to true compassion and greater effectiveness. The shifts from a personality-centric orientation toward your more expansive nature are supported by the inclusion of transformative conditions and processes. In addition to offering information on each of the nine personality types, this book attempts to decipher and explain these processes.

> WHILE IDENTIFYING YOUR CORE PERSONALITY TYPE IS A VITAL STEP IN USING THE ENNEAGRAM, YOU WILL GAIN THE MOST VALUE IN BECOMING LESS IDENTIFIED WITH AND LESS DRIVEN BY YOUR TYPE-RELATED PATTERNS AND MORE PRESENT TO YOURSELF AND OTHERS, WHICH NATURALLY LEADS TO TRUE COMPASSION AND GREATER EFFECTIVENESS.

By integrating the power of the presence-based Enneagram and the potency of conscious coaching, we find the real purpose of deep coaching: helping clients experience greater connection and intimacy with themselves, sustainable life shifts toward their expansive psychological and spiritual nature, and their inherent belonging to life.

WHY "DEEP" COACHING?

Deep Coaching as a book and as a professional growth initiative was borne out of two major influences that transformed how I thought about the coaching relationship. They helped me realize that coaching can go beyond a linear problem-to-solution approach to one that honors the mysteries of the human being and of life itself. Of course, one of those influences for which I am profoundly grateful is the Enneagram. The second undeniable influence is what I refer to as the "deep movement," which had been emerging for at least thirty years in 2007 when the original *Deep Coaching* book was written. It was and still is reflected in deep ecology, the science of the interconnectedness of everything; deep democracy, engaging hard-to-reach populations who are often unseen and unheard to activate new voices; deep teaching, seeing one another more deeply in learning communities as taught by Parker Palmer[1]; deep space, explored by the Hubble Space Telescope, which was designed to peer more deeply into space and has now been replaced by far more powerful, deeper space exploration technology; deep time, taught by Joanna Macy[2]; deep listening, taught by the late Thích Nhất Hạnh[3]; and depth psychology. These were all signs of an awakening consciousness and the willingness to enter into unknown territory.

Even as these forms of pioneering work were evolving, what was becoming more evident to me was the growing inner divide and disconnect humans were experiencing consciously or unconsciously. The aching divide between the content, demands, and distractions of one's outer life—which is then reflected in the face one shows to the world—and one's often-ignored hungry, remarkable, and vast inner world is revealed in every part of our culture. Another reflection of the inner divide is embedded in the many ways that humans reject large parts of themselves, resulting in damaging struggles. The cost of these divides is too great for any soul to bear, and the loss can feel irreparable.

Deep coaching embraces the person who shows up for coaching—along with their intentions, self-doubts, challenges, possibilities, and capacity for inner growth—and provides support for the integration of what can feel like separate pieces of their inner world. It acknowledges not only the personality and the messy issues that are part of the human experience, but also what lies beyond the personality and our clients' ways of perceiving themselves. Here we have the sacred opportunity to be with clients in a sliver of the mystery of who they truly are.

On a more intimate level, I think of deep coaching as a co-created trust walk. It takes courage on the part of the coach to not be an expert on the client's journey—in effect, being in the unknown. At the same time, clients are encouraged to develop enough trust in the coach, in themselves, in their own journey, and in the unfolding process to allow for change and transformation to take place.

> THE FUNDAMENTAL TRUST IS THAT ONE'S LIFE, THE INNER AND THE OUTER, CAN BE WOVEN BACK TOGETHER INTO WHOLENESS WITH ACCEPTANCE AND LOVE.

FIVE PILLARS OF DEEP COACHING

To understand what is involved in deep coaching, it is useful to name the pillars upon which it rests. Each is explored in subsequent chapters and interwoven as fundamental threads throughout the book.

FIRST PILLAR: The Enneagram

The Enneagram is a profound map for understanding the full range of the human condition. As coaches, we typically work with clients who are experiencing some obstacles to growth and development that are based in the personality structure itself. This can be difficult for clients to recognize at first. It is not uncommon for us humans to attribute our unhappiness to external factors, such as a difficult boss, disruptive children, or our childhood, as examples. Upon deeper inquiry, clients may come to recognize their own part in difficult circumstances, not from a self-blame perspective, but from an honest intention to observe, gain insights, take responsibility for their actions, and be more at-choice.

It can be shocking to see our own assumptions, obstructions, biases, projections, defense mechanisms, and strategies for coping distilled so clearly in our Enneagram personality type.

When at last we recognize that my way is simply that—just my way, which exists as a tiny fraction of the whole of life—then our perspective and experience can radically change. There is a less ardent ego to defend and to judge in ourselves and in others.

It also is stunning to recognize the blessings that are inherent in each Enneagram type. These gifts are greatly needed in our hurting families, communities, and world. This is why I call the Enneagram a map of love.

SECOND PILLAR: Presence

Presence is the basis for deep coaching. The Enneagram shows us how the activated personality structure keeps us out of contact with our depth and out of contact with the movement and unfolding of life. We have three innate centers of intelligence: body, heart, and head. The greater our capacity to come into direct contact with these three pivotal centers, the more present we can be for our clients. When we are more fully present in the coaching relationship, clients have more capacity to respond with open curiosity and kindness to current circumstances, make decisions that are aligned with their deeper guidance, and take effective next steps.

A fundamental orientation to presence applies to all life circumstances, including working through difficulties in relationships, developing an authentic sense of self, rehabilitating after an injury, living with a serious illness, working in organizations with ineffective dynamics, opening to a new career path, challenging a social injustice, or diving deeper into one's spiritual path.

THIRD PILLAR: The Counterintuitive Change Process

The change process itself is informed by presence. This counterintuitive, paradoxical approach to change allows us to meet clients where they are without judgment or a preconceived idea of what the coaching outcome should look like. This approach supports clients in developing a deeper relationship with their innate knowing that lies beyond their personality's usual ways of coping.

This approach has not been nourished in Western society, as it runs counter to approaches reflecting a linear, goal-oriented style. It is inherently open, reflective, and receptive as it supports greater access to both the client's and the coach's deeper dimensions of intelligence to guide an integrative process.

FOURTH PILLAR: Orienting Clients toward Self-Acceptance, Love, and Interconnectedness

A sense of aloneness and separation pervades the human experience. When we are wrapped up in the inner bubble of the personality, we naturally feel separate. This sense of separateness may be vague and less unconscious for some of us; for others, it may be undeniably in our faces.

The more deeply we come to understand ourselves, the more likely we are to perceive ourselves and others more accurately. With understanding comes a compassion for the human condition that we all share. Our hearts become more open and available. As our clients begin to loosen the grip of the personality, they begin to recognize that they are not as alone and separate as they had thought.

All of these shifts naturally contribute to a greater recognition of our existing and potential impact on others and on the environment. Our relationship to Mother Earth and to our own physical bodies deepens. Here, too, we make decisions from a greater realization of the choices available.

There is a quote etched at the beginning of a trail in Yosemite National Park that speaks to interconnectedness: "When we try to pick out anything by itself, we find it hitched to everything else in the universe." To feel separate is a delusion of the small self.

Through the deep coaching process, we can support the client's experience of shared commonalities with others, belonging to the greater human journey, and connecting to a higher power, sense of purpose, and/or the ground of being. In this way, coaches help illuminate that all are inherently a part of the great web of life, bringing attention to both the internal integration and external weaving of the fabric of the human community.

FIFTH PILLAR: The Inner Work of the Coach

The inner work of coaches in becoming more self-aware and oriented toward spaciousness allows for growth that supports not only our own unfolding but (in sometimes unknown ways) our clients' openings. We can best serve through engaging in our own deeper work.

By calling upon these five pillars, we tap into the power of deep coaching, leading to unexpected outcomes that the coach or the client could not have predicted.

Chapter 2

THE PERSONALITY-ESSENCE RELATIONSHIP:
The Key Factor

THE ENNEAGRAM OF GROWTH

The work of numerous Enneagram scholars, researchers, and authors describes the vast terrain of human behavior ranging from that which is healthy and effective to behavior that violates oneself and others. The body of knowledge is informed by contemporary psychological theory, findings from neuroscience research, and the ancient wisdom that is nearly universally shared by a cross section of wisdom traditions, including Christianity, mystical Judaism, Sufism, and Buddhism. Thus, we find the Enneagram's wisdom to be infused into every part of life.

When we become aware of our own type-specific patterns, we gain clarity on longtime coping strategies that are troublesome and how those strategies have impacted the quality of our lives. Often, these patterns—which *feel* like who we are—have actually limited our sense of choice. Through inner exploration, we can identify the interior dynamics underlying the patterns, and through presence-based practices, we can loosen the hold these patterns have on us. This ensuing awareness gives us access to new conscious behavioral, attitudinal, and emotional responses. As we realize that we have relied unknowingly on a narrow range of automatic responses, a deepening experience of choice and spaciousness unfolds.

The Enneagram acts like a mirror that reflects the nature of our inner personality structure, allowing us the remarkable ability to see ourselves clearly, perhaps for the first time. The Enneagram brilliantly clarifies the unique gifts of each type and highlights the pathway toward the gifts. Approaches based on presence can help us accept and manifest those gifts.

> THE ENNEAGRAM ALLOWS US THE REMARKABLE ABILITY TO SEE OURSELVES CLEARLY, PERHAPS FOR THE FIRST TIME.

Occasionally, the Enneagram has been used inadvertently to justify behavior or blame and pigeonhole people for their type. This was never the intended use of this powerful body of wisdom. Rather, approaching self-discovery using the Enneagram with compassionate honesty allows us to soften the restrictions created by the personality structure. Then, movement toward inner peace; psychological, emotional, and spiritual liberation; and behavioral effectiveness can unfold. Ultimately, the Enneagram is much more than a system for identifying one's type; it is a framework based on sacred psychology that supports transformation so that we may live from our truer nature.

THE NINE PERSONALITY TYPES

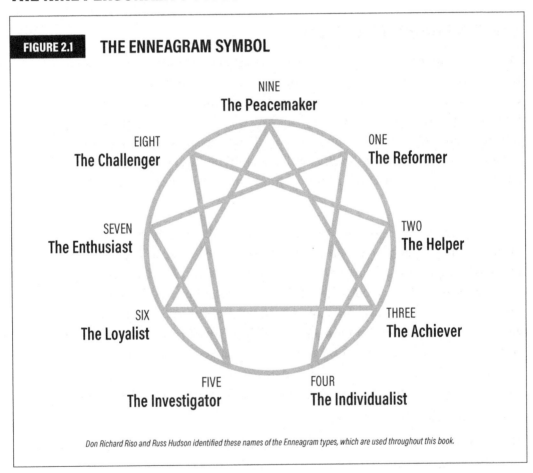

| FIGURE 2.1 | THE ENNEAGRAM SYMBOL |

NINE
The Peacemaker

EIGHT
The Challenger

ONE
The Reformer

SEVEN
The Enthusiast

TWO
The Helper

SIX
The Loyalist

THREE
The Achiever

FIVE
The Investigator

FOUR
The Individualist

Don Richard Riso and Russ Hudson identified these names of the Enneagram types, which are used throughout this book.

The Enneagram symbol identifying the nine types is shown in figure 2.1. Note that the symbol comprises three distinct and interrelated shapes:

– The outer circle. The outer circle represents the ultimate Unity and Oneness of All That Is. The nine points located on this circle can be perceived in different ways. They represent nine different facets of reality, nine dimensions of essence, nine relationships to reality, nine different worldviews, and nine variations in the human condition that are referred to as types. (Note: Throughout most of this book, I refer to Types One, Two, etc. from the perspective of personality. However, the nine points on the circle reflect the inherent connection to Unity and Oneness. When the personality structure becomes set into place, there's an enormous sense of loss of this true connection, even though it still exists in reality. So each point represents not only a specific personality type, but also a specific aspect of Unity and Oneness.)

– The inner triangle. The inner triangle, consisting of three lines connecting three Enneagram points, represents the triadic nature of reality. This runs counter to dualistic, either/or thinking that has permeated Western culture. You will notice that Types Nine, Three, and Six are located on the triangle.

– The inner hexad. The inner hexad is an irregular shape, representing the movement of the life force, of consciousness, of change itself. You may want to use your pencil or finger to follow the pattern of the types that are located on the points of the hexad: Points One, Four, Two, Eight, Five, Seven, and back to One.

These inner lines connect the types in ways that will be discussed in later chapters.

UNDERSTANDING PERSONALITY AND WHAT IT MEANS FOR COACHES

Why do clients come to you?

While the specifics of their situations differ, most clients probably will surface a concern that they feel stuck, unclear about what they want or how to realize their desires, or in need of support to create momentum.

Underneath their circumstances, your clients may feel that there is something wrong with them and want "to be fixed." They probably tend to be focused on the *content* of their lives, which is the conditioned focus in Western-based societies. And they may look to you to "fix" them. This is the personality at work, and how you respond to that explicit or even implicit agenda will significantly impact the coaching relationship. There is nothing to fix.

The constricted personality is a powerful force in life. It is that dimension of ourselves that most people identify with—the behaviors, emotions, and ideas we have of ourselves, as well as the way we experience our physicality. As coaches, we may have a self-description that feels real and right. Our clients will have the same.

The problem we face if we identify too heavily with our self-description is that it is inherently limiting. Whatever you take yourself to be limits the expression of other dimensions of yourself. This core dynamic of equating ourselves with the limited personality is one of the challenges that arises frequently in coaching because it is this identity that inherently limits perceived access to choices. It is easy to hold back from approaching life circumstances in new, more effective and satisfying ways. Identifying with the ego aspect of oneself also poses a dilemma for the sustainability of healthy families, local neighborhoods, the global community, and for the environment. There are many compelling reasons on both micro and macro levels to discover the authenticity of a more expansive identity.

The Enneagram provides a distinctive framework for understanding what the personality actually is, how it acts, and its relationship to presence and our essential nature.

For now, let's look at three functions of the personality:
- The personality as a structure of identity
- The personality as an energetic system
- The personality as a coping structure

These three perspectives of the personality are excerpted from *Deep Living with the Enneagram: Recovering Your True Nature.*[1]

PERSPECTIVE #1: The Personality as a Structure of Identity ("I Am")

Central to the Enneagram is understanding the personality as an internal blueprint that serves as the foundation for how each person expresses themselves. Just as a building's architectural blueprint comprises many different elements, including dimensions, relationship between rooms, and points of egress that provide the foundation for the form and function of the building, the blueprint of the personality provides the hidden foundation for the functioning of the personality. This blueprint comprises various elements, such as one's preferences, behaviors, attitudes, desires, primary focus of attention, fears, defense mechanisms, and other factors, many of which are not seen by the individual.

Each of the nine Enneagram types has its own characteristic version of the architectural blueprint. Each type's internal structure shapes the individual's inner commentary, perception of self, perception of the external world, and relationship to the world. In effect, the specific personality structure gives rise to one's sense of identity and leads to one's experience of "this is just who I am."

The Enneagram iceberg model, which has been updated since its introduction in the original edition of this book, is described in detail in chapter 6. It provides a template for illustrating the architecture of the personality. Briefly, the iceberg captures the behavioral (observable) characteristics of the Enneagram type in the section extending above the waterline. The motivational factors that give shape to the behaviors are shown below the waterline. See figure 2.2.

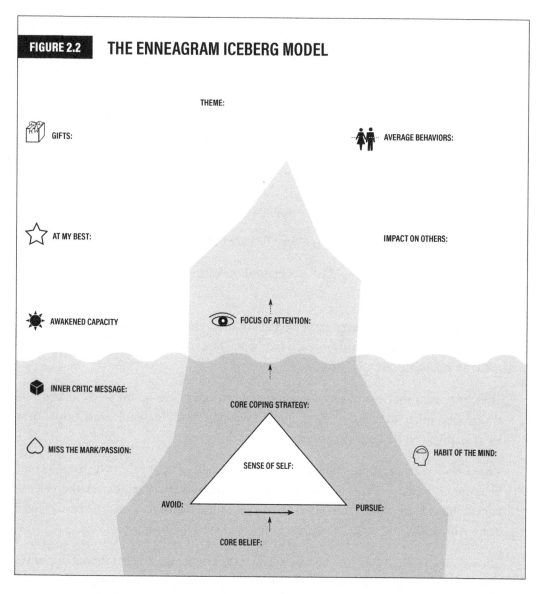

FIGURE 2.2 **THE ENNEAGRAM ICEBERG MODEL**

THEME:

GIFTS:

AVERAGE BEHAVIORS:

AT MY BEST:

IMPACT ON OTHERS:

AWAKENED CAPACITY

FOCUS OF ATTENTION:

INNER CRITIC MESSAGE:

CORE COPING STRATEGY:

MISS THE MARK/PASSION:

HABIT OF THE MIND:

SENSE OF SELF:

AVOID:

PURSUE:

CORE BELIEF:

Note that a person with a particular type may be aware of some, but not all, of the behavioral characteristics that are above the water. They may have a vague awareness of selected under-the-water motivators; however, these are typically hidden to the person.

A specific blueprint for each type is shown and described in section 2.

〰〰 Coaching Cue:

The iceberg illustration can be used as a tool for exploration with clients.

Please note that the iceberg model is meant to provide an objective lens into many of the structural elements of the personality. At the same time, it reflects a subjective dimension of the human condition and experience. It touches into very private and tender territory.

Becoming knowledgeable about the differences in blueprints allows you to step inside the inner terrain of the client with heartfulness. It is powerful to recognize the client's predictable and automatic patterns, the sense of identity, and aspects of underlying pain, as well as the client's significant strengths and expansive and awakening nature. Use with care.

PERSPECTIVE #2: The Personality as an Energetic System ("I Believe")

The personality is also an energetic system that, like any system, if closed or uninterrupted, continues to build on itself. When uninterrupted, the system allows in only selective information that reinforces its existing patterns.

Here's a description of how the energetic system of the personality works:

Each of the nine personality types has a specific core belief.

- The core belief can be thought of as a central operating principle that helps shape the developing personality.

- The core belief actively filters and selects data that reinforces itself from the vast field of information that bombards us each moment. Data that do not fit into the core belief patterns are unconsciously dismissed.

- Therefore, data that could provide another perspective are ignored. We likely don't realize that other data are present. Looking at our recurring experiences over time, we are convinced that our experience is the truth.

- When responses are predictable, they are automatic reactions. Since the reaction/behavior is based on the belief, it generates feedback that reinforces the original belief. Thus, the feedback mirrors the message of the internal voice. The core belief is again affirmed.

- The seeming truth of this core belief leads to reexperiencing early emotional responses, such as anger, frustration, fear, or emotional dependency, among others. Most often the emotional response is not fully in the consciousness, and the experience "feels like who I am."

- These patterns feel so real that we come to think of ourselves as these habitual patterns. They are almost like the air we breathe—they feel so natural that it never occurs to us to question them. We don't suspect that a belief even exists—it is just what is.

For coaching to be effective, it must address not merely superficial clusters of behaviors and attitudes, but the core beliefs and multiple ways that they are played out.

Let's take a real-life example.

- Core belief: Life is hard and unjust. It's not safe to be vulnerable.

- This powerful belief acts as a filter and finds or perceives data that reinforce the belief from the vast field of information available.

- The client sees herself as needing to be strong and in control. She is highly demanding of others, even when it is detrimental to relationships or to the effectiveness of getting things done. She finds people backing away from her. When she lets someone she cares about into her life, she hears the inner critic's warnings.

- The internal critic says, "You have to be strong and not show any weakness. Your vulnerability will be exposed, and you'll get hurt."

- The client now acts as if she cannot show her softer side and becomes even more domineering.

- Her heart feels closed. She doesn't know how to be real or close with herself or with people she loves. She doesn't understand why people are so intimidated by her. She may be asked to leave her place of employment or be put on notice of an impending separation if something doesn't change.

- She falls into the trap of feeling stuck in "this is who I am." All of her evidence supports the belief that life is unjust. Her innate sense of being rejected is further confirmed.

This is just one example of a closed personality system at work. We will discover that the content of the closed system is different for each of the Enneagram types.

One of our roles is to support the client in recognizing openings in their own inner system so that the core belief can be brought to light and addressed. In time, this can lead to a shift in internal perceptions. New behavioral, mental, and emotional responses also can be accessed.

≋ Coaching Cue:

One of the great values of coaching is the use of processes to identify beliefs and interrupt old patterns. It's important to explore this territory with caring and curiosity. For example, you might ask your client: "What do you recognize about this belief? Does it land for you? Feel familiar? Are you aware of some ways it has impacted your life?" We can gradually open and expose this previously closed system to new information.

Core beliefs become the basis for all major life beliefs. That is why it is beneficial to bring them into awareness at an appropriate time during the coaching process.

In addition, we can open our own internal systems by noticing the personality's patterns at work and creating some distance between the observer part of ourselves and the part of us that is doing the personality. With intention, the very process of nonjudgmentally observing and noticing can lead to a deepening awareness and begin relaxing our attachment to these patterns. As we do so, we notice the loosening and releasing of the constrictions over time. We sense a movement toward lightness and spaciousness as we become more open, flexible, and responsive and less reactive and compulsive.

The open personality system is dynamic and fluid. And it moves us closer to the higher qualities of our type.

PERSPECTIVE #3: The Personality as a Coping Mechanism and Protection ("I Protect")

Clients often come to coaching because at some level, they realize their usual ways of coping are no longer working or are actually contributing to their inner discomfort.

As we explore the personality as a coping or protective mechanism, we can recognize and bring more attention to healing the emotional pain that lies under the surface of the human experience. It is through a kind, compassionate attitude that healing can occur and that new forms of inner freedom and choice emerge.

Let's go back to the beginning: everyone on the planet experienced pain when they came into the world. Every one of us was an intrinsically sensitive little being who picked up the spoken and unspoken, the seen and unseen elements of our environments.

For some, there were objective forms of abuse in early years. For many, the early years may have been confusing, with little stability. For most, our unique and sensitive perspectives, especially as young children, resulted in interpreting the actions or attitudes of others as meaning something that was not actually intended. Either way, we learned how to cover our fears, anger, shame, disappointments, sense of being rejected, and feelings of being lost and all alone.

All of us learned to cope and hide a lot of those hurts. The accumulation of hurts resulted in emotional energy that we had neither the words for (many of these experiences took place before we could talk) nor the neurological or biological capacity to tolerate the hurt. Suppressing and masking these early experiences were necessary to survive as an intact person.

That was the role that the personality took on. It served as a protection from experiences that were unacceptable or simply too much to process at that moment.

Over time, our coping mechanisms crystallized. Growing into adolescence, then adulthood, those coping strategies predominated, so our inherent capacity to handle those old hurts didn't have a chance to develop.

Now, perhaps your clients have arrived at a new phase in life, and the desire for growth has outdistanced the need for all that protection.

≈≈ Coaching Cue:

At the appropriate time, a question to pose to your client might be, "What is more important to you NOW than relying on your familiar coping strategies?"

THE RELATIONSHIP BETWEEN PERSONALITY AND ESSENCE

We have a personality and we are essence.

While the discussion of the origins of the personality is beyond the scope of this book, understanding some basic principles about the relationship of the personality and essence is useful for coaches.

The following descriptions offer a brief glimpse into the development of the personality.[2] The caveat is that this experience cannot be replicated on two-dimensional visuals.

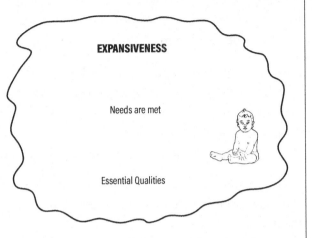

FIGURE 2.3 **UNIFIED FIELD**

EXPANSIVENESS

Needs are met

Essential Qualities

As we understand it now, we are all born sensitive to our environments. If we are fortunate to have a strong enough support system that provides emotional nurturance and guidance to us as babies, then we experience being part of an expansive, unified field. Consciousness has not developed yet, but there's no sense of separation. Babies are also sensitive (or attuned) to a particular aspect of essence.

Little ones grow up in imperfect environments. Parental figures cannot prevent the baby or young child from having emotionally difficult experiences, and even the best-intentioned ones may perpetuate these experiences unconsciously. These experiences, whether they take place regularly or occasionally, generally leave an emotional or energetic hurt within the child, who does not have the resources to process or release them. Thus, the original experience of expansiveness becomes more and more constricted.

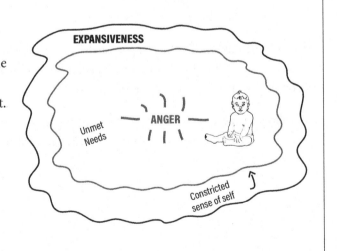

FIGURE 2.4 **ANGER**

EXPANSIVENESS

Unmet Needs

ANGER

Constricted sense of self

For example, little ones become angry and even enraged when they do not get what they want. (We see this carrying on into adulthood, too.) If the anger is not soothed, the baby falls asleep with the emotion still locked into the developing neurological system.

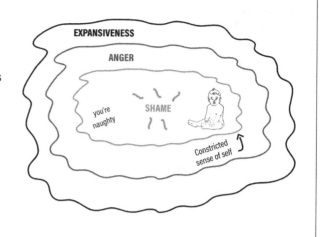

FIGURE 2.5   **SHAME**

Imagine that the little one is starting to interact with siblings or other children at a daycare and bites or hits another child. The child is scolded and may experience shame. This challenging emotion, too, can get locked into the child's neurology.

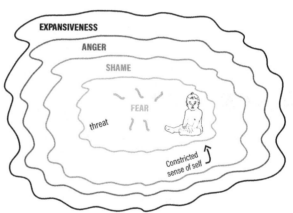

FIGURE 2.6   **FEAR**

And imagine that the child hears yelling or threatening sounds, or feels threatened by a large dog or unfriendly person. The child could naturally become scared, and the big emotion of fear arises.

Through all these experiences, additional layers of constriction are unconsciously developing. The child's filters are already shaping their reaction to what is interpreted as threatening or unpleasant.

FIGURE 2.7   **CONSTRICTION**

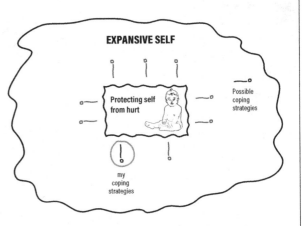

Inside the layers of constriction, the small lines extending out from the box like antennae reflect the filters provided by the Enneagram types.

Note that how children interpret their experiences will be affected by the perceptions associated with the filter of the child's temperament. A child who is most sensitive to Point Six will internalize the experience differently than one who is most sensitive to Point Four, for example.

FIGURE 2.8   **THIS IS ME**

As the child grows, becomes an adolescent, then young adult, and so on, the experience of constriction becomes a defining identity. Being inside of an emotional and energetic box is how the person knows themself. "This is me" inside this tiny little box. It's important to recognize that essence and spaciousness still exist but are not a part of the individual's usual awareness because they are hidden by the constrictions.

The stronger the levels of tension and constrictions are, the more the personality is in charge and the less conscious awareness and access there is to the always present spaciousness and essence of the person.

THE IMPORTANCE OF RELAXING IDENTIFICATION WITH THE TYPE

Identifying with our automatic way of living is the easiest and most natural thing in life. We are heavily conditioned to think that how we do life is life itself. Below are three examples of how different people could do life.

- If I am so used to thinking about other people and what they need, and wondering about how they will solve their problems, it wouldn't make sense to approach life in any other way. I have no idea what is meant by "take care of yourself."

- If I am so used to setting goals for myself and doing whatever I have to do to reach those goals in a way superior to anyone else's, the possibility of approaching life differently isn't even a matter of choice because no other options are visible to me.

- If I spend most of my efforts reserving my seemingly limited energy in order to think things through, to analyze all the ideas that I have about these things, and to plan for how I could use these ideas, it would not occur to me to use another approach.

When we identify with our personality—that is, how we do life—our usual set of strategies for getting our needs met, relying on our mask to protect ourselves, meeting challenges, and coping with stressors take up the vast majority of our life. This leaves little room for a fresh or creative response. Thus, identifying with our automatic selves may be easy; however, it is limiting and often detrimental to ourselves, to others, and to our environment.

Noticing and learning ways to relax and release our grasp from these usual patterns provide a powerful key to becoming free from unnecessary constraints. This also opens the door to becoming free to choose new possibilities from an expanded sense of self.

Seldom are we able to unhook ourselves from our long-held and heavily practiced patterns by ourselves. A professional anchored in presence can see through various identifications, be with their clients through the sometimes painful experience of realizing the loss of contact with their authentic nature (which has been masked by patterns), and celebrate their clients' gifts. Just as the patterns most often are not in our awareness, neither are the qualities of our more expansive nature, which is held in deep reserve.

Deep coaching provides a natural and robust framework that allows us to meet clients in their familiar inner territory and then journey together to discover ways to let go of specific filters of past identity. Approaching the Enneagram with presence supports the movement into unfamiliar terrain that opens to a new experience of self. This new and more expansive experience of self becomes the basis for the client's capacity to reach outcomes that are aligned with their inherent strengths and true priorities. And working with the Enneagram helps clients to experience a greater sense of interconnectedness.

This approach to the Enneagram focuses on supporting clients in exploring, practicing, and experiencing what is beyond their usual way of knowing themselves, in effect, orienting clients back to their truer self. Specific ways of using the *Deep Coaching* approach include the following:

– Creating a nurturing and supportive environment for nonjudgmental inquiry, exploration, and capacity-building in being more aware and present

– Providing tools and practices for integrating transformative processes into the client's daily personal, interpersonal, and work lives

– Reflecting and acknowledging client decreases in mental or emotional struggle and shifts to expanding self-acceptance, sense of choice, and ease

– Developing the client's capacity for accessing their deeper sources of intelligence

– Enhancing client effectiveness in life and work relationships (such as in leadership, teamwork, teaching, consulting, and parenting)

– Encouraging clients to increase their compassion and acceptance of their human nature and unique life path

– Supporting clients in embodying alignment between their true inner guidance and outward expression of their true priorities

As coaches, we can work deeply with clients to support them in living from a more conscious and whole state of being while focusing on any number of possible topics, including life transitions, life balance, rehabilitation, career change, leadership development, business development, communications, spiritual companioning, relationships, and social and environmental justice, to name a few.

ADDITIONAL BENEFITS OF INTEGRATING THE ENNEAGRAM WITH COACHING

While most coaches realize that people see the world in different ways, it is a real challenge to decipher and create a coherent framework for what those different ways are. Below the level of the intellect, most people assume that others see and experience the world in basically the same way that they do. The Enneagram makes explicit what these wildly different views are, how they develop, and the impact those differences make.

Each of the nine blueprints forms a unique agenda and context that shapes the individual's life experience. The structure of the identity for each type has a pervasive influence on the individual with that type, at least until the system is exposed and new options become visible.

The Enneagram provides us an elegant way into understanding a client's particular interpretation of their world without getting stuck in the client's interpretation of the situation. Understanding the workings of a specific type helps us to quickly grasp the nature of the client's internal struggle and challenges to growth, such as typical ways that the client makes assessments of themselves and the world, the nature of the inner critic, and conditioned patterns of emotional and behavioral reactions. With the Enneagram in the background, we can listen deeply to the client.

Using these insights helps us to create rapport quickly as a coach. When clients feel deeply understood, they become more open and freer to make changes. When clients are met at this deep level, they may consciously or unconsciously sense that there is less for them to defend.

Common issues that clients bring to coaching focus on why others behave as they do, rather than in accordance with the client's wishes. Again, the internal assumption

> WHEN CLIENTS FEEL DEEPLY UNDERSTOOD, THEY BECOME MORE OPEN.

is that "Everyone thinks the way I do, and thus, should do what I would do under the same circumstances." Thus, the Enneagram offers significant value in helping people unlock their own worldview and begin to recognize that different worldviews provide very different responses to any given situation. It helps people to understand that each worldview comes with a different focus of attention.

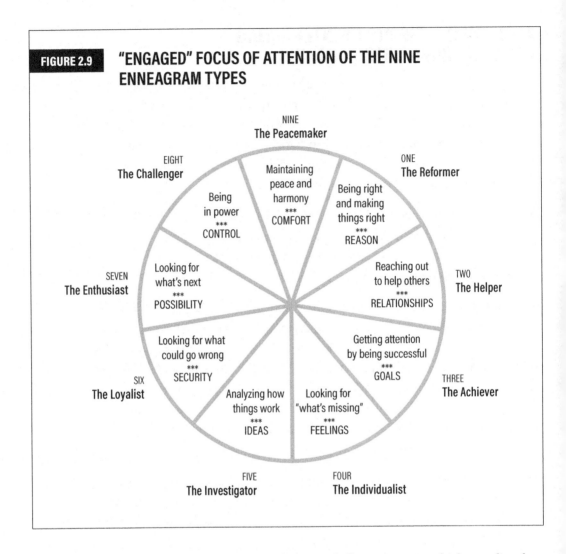

FIGURE 2.9 "ENGAGED" FOCUS OF ATTENTION OF THE NINE ENNEAGRAM TYPES

The engaged focus of attention figure identifies nine different ways in which people, when engaged with their personalities, focus their attention and organize their lives. If you read through these quickly, they may not seem to be that important. Take a few moments to sit with the potential ways of how each focus of attention could translate into thought, emotional, and behavioral patterns in every part of life. (See section 2 for more information on the focus of attention of each type.)

Every type's worldview also incorporates a fixed idea of who the individual is. That fixed idea leads us to feel justified in responding to the world as we do. We may feel justified in being angry, withdrawn, bold, aggressive, annoyed, and hurt, all because we take our fixed idea of ourselves so seriously.

The Enneagram provides information on the fixed idea of our type and how we can move beyond that limiting self-definition, leading to an expanded capacity for responding with more flexibility to situations as they arise. Ultimately, this results in reduced struggle and increased ease.

Many people have the innate sense that there is something wrong or missing in their lives. This sense can lead to thinking that they are inherently flawed and must mask their insufficiencies. If they live with that belief, it affects every thought, word, feeling, and action. No workshop, no amount of excellent coaching, no book that focuses on helping one be better can alleviate the pain and suffering of this belief.

> "THE FIXED IDEA THAT WE HAVE ABOUT OURSELVES AS SOLID AND SEPARATE FROM EACH OTHER IS PAINFULLY LIMITING. IT IS POSSIBLE TO MOVE THROUGH THE DRAMA OF OUR LIVES WITHOUT BELIEVING SO EARNESTLY IN THE CHARACTER THAT WE PLAY."
>
> — *Pema Chodron*[3]

A principle of the Enneagram is that we already have what we need; we don't need to fix ourselves. (Note: for some readers, this will be jarring, almost incomprehensible, information.) That is, we don't need to make something happen so that we can change. As we discover the underlying aspects of ourselves, we begin to recognize that we are not who we think we are, but so much more. The Enneagram gives us a powerful tool for finding what we thought was missing (and isn't) and for disidentifying with our old way of thinking about ourselves.

Most coaches know that the voice of the inner critic is a source of much human suffering. We only need to listen to our clients' stories about themselves for a short time to recognize how heartbreakingly unkind most people are to themselves. Riso and Hudson's work contributes significantly to our understanding of the specific message of the inner critic for each type. That is, the focus of the inner critic is type-related.

The voice of the inner critic has no redeeming value in adult life.[4] As coaches, we can support our clients in recognizing and disempowering this voice. Processes that are incorporated into this book help to further delineate how to work with these messages.

〰 Coaching Cue:

As you learn more about the Enneagram and the nine personality types, you will start to become attuned to personality-based cues that even a client who has not self-typed offers. A few examples of cues include volume, pace, and speed of speech; the posture, stance, and energy of the body; words or phrases that are used repeatedly; and the content of what the client says has brought them to coaching. These cues come across in virtual and in-person coaching.

Chapter 3

THE DYNAMICS OF CONSTRICTION AND EXPANSIVENESS
The Dynamic Nature of the Personality

In the closed personality system, it is easy to fall prey to the conditioned responses of the personality and lose oneself to the hypnotic effects of cultural conditioning. Both the activated personality and cultural messages reinforce the narrowing of the focus of attention. Around the same old circle we go, generally getting the same results. Yet it is in the present that we have more access to our more expansive nature, to our inner strength and inner authority. With a changing world that continuously presents new challenges, obstacles, opportunities, and gifts, the ability to respond effectively and authentically is essential.

When our clients can approach their growing awareness afforded by the Enneagram with curiosity, humility, truth, and acceptance of what is in their realm to attend to, they often experience unexpected changes—sometimes gradually, sometimes quickly. These shifts do not come from efforting, but from becoming less attached to habits that are no longer useful. Through addressing a habitual personality pattern in one part of life, clients often come to recognize that same pattern affects many parts of life. For example, a person who discovers she habitually overextends herself to others at work may come to notice that same pattern of overgiving to her friends. An internal shift might be reflected in her noticing the usual inclination to jump in to help when it is unnecessary for her to do so and instead checking in with herself to notice what is true for her in that moment. She might ask herself what she needs. With that shift in focus, she likely will experience a little more space and choice.

Another example is with a rehabilitation patient who is not used to taking direction from others and resists complying with the therapist's program for building physical strength. The patient has a pattern of directing others and taking charge. The resistance may continue until it is no longer working; his strength is not returning. He may come to see that though he habitually challenges the input from others, this therapy program is, in reality, an important resource. Resisting it makes no logical sense. He accepts his situation and becomes cooperative. He simply does what needs to be done. An important inner shift has occurred.

Recognizing that a situation that had previously activated a reaction is now met with more neutrality and objectivity is one piece of evidence that the personality exists along a continuum of health and flexibility.

When we are generative, open, responsive, alive, and present, we experience the higher end of our personality's health and flexibility and naturally express what is best within us. When we find ourselves stuck in nonproductive, defensive, and rigid reactions, we express the lower end of our personality's health and flexibility. As we learn to nonjudgmentally recognize our troublesome patterns and actually be with ourselves, we might notice an underlying feeling or sensation. Perhaps some sadness leaks through, or we recognize that a long-held resentment that is no longer relevant is still directing our behavior.

Understanding that we did not consciously choose these personality-driven patterns and that they are part of the human condition can help build the essential quality of compassion. This is not the same as offering an excuse for the patterns but can create openings to new ways of being.

Over time, we discover that our experiences are more neutral (as opposed to the energetic charge associated with certain situations that have pushed our buttons in the past), objective (that is, we see things for what they are, not interpreted through the layers of our own personal biases), and fluid. Our natural gifts and authentic generosity of spirit are available to us and to others.

Having the direct experience of our healthier nature does not mean that we give up our personality and that everything is "fine." That is neither possible nor useful. This is the distinction: When my personality is fully in charge, it has me and I will respond as I always have. When I have the experience of clarity and presence, I have my personality. When I am more present, I see and can use my personality to support me, but it is no longer the master.

Here's a metaphor to consider.

Imagine that you're swimming in a pool. The pool is all you know. It is life itself. The pool has sides that provide limits to where you can go. You don't know that there is anything but the pool.

Now, imagine that you've risen above the pool and see that it is contained within an expanse of water that is so vast that you cannot see any end to it. There are no edges.

The pool is like the personality. When you're in it, there's nothing more. The pool is all there is.

The vast expanse of water is like your higher, healthier nature. You're aware of the pool and can dip into it as you need. When it's time to take laps, the pool will do. But you recognize its limitations.

Like being in the pool, being caught in personality narrows and limits perspective. It is easy to get caught up in the drama of life and to get emotionally charged around various circumstances.

Living from presence gives you perspective, awareness, and choice. You have a broader viewpoint from which to observe the personality in action.

≋ Coaching Cue:

The Enneagram helps us to see what the personality is up to. At the same time, it gives us a template for moving out of total reliance on our personality and into a deeper relationship with our more expansive self. In that vein, it is useful to use language that connotes the notion of having a type rather than being a type. The language of being a type works to solidify one's identity with that type: "I am a Type ____." The language around having a type reflects that there is more to the person than the personality type. There's less attachment to the type. You might notice the difference between saying, "I have a Type ____ personality" and "I am a Type ____."

COACHING TOWARD EXPANSIVENESS WITH THE ENNEAGRAM

Transformation occurs as people recognize that their personality is only a part of their more expansive nature; it doesn't describe all of who they are. As clients gain greater access to the dimensions of their being that are beyond the personality structure, they begin to feel less separate. This expanded perspective provides a context for the coaching process.

Try this exercise, taking your time with it. Tense your hand into a hard fist. Hold it for ten seconds and notice how it affects you. What happens to your breath? Are other parts of your body tensing as well? Notice the sensations that you feel. Now, begin to release ever so gradually. Stay with your sensations as every tiny muscle, every cell, releases slowly, slowly . . . until your hand is fully open and relaxed.

When you tightened your hand, it became restricted in what it could do. It was more prepared for battle than for holding a gift. This is similar to what happens when our being tenses. We are more prepared for battle than for sharing our talents, recognizing opportunities, or receiving a gift.

Tension is a typical response to the daily stresses of life and is associated with the fight, flight, or freeze response. From an evolutionary perspective, this response was necessary for survival when our ancestors' physical safety was threatened. The fight, flight, or freeze response is still active in today's life, and most people live with an elevated stress response as part of normal daily life. If you are closely attuned to yourself, you may recognize tension physically, mentally, and emotionally. For example, even as you sit and read these words, you might notice tightness in certain parts of your body. It feels normal. Is this tension necessary in this moment? As you scan your body, what areas are ready to release the tension?

Stress is an internal response to both internal states and external circumstances. Sometimes we recognize that these circumstances are cause for alarm, as when a natural or human-made disaster strikes, when a high-speed car cuts in front of us unexpectedly on a busy highway, or when someone threatens us.

We might also recognize that the stress response is ignited under so-called ordinary circumstances—for example, seeing a person we're uncomfortable with at a party. Someone else who sees that same person may not experience a stress response. This reminds us that it is our personal history that automatically triggers a significant percentage of our stress-generating events.

> **CONTAINED WITHIN THE SYSTEM OF THE PERSONALITY IS A MECHANISM FOR GENERATING STRESS AND REINFORCING TENSION.**

What most people are less familiar with is that the personality itself operates at differing levels of constriction and tension. Contained within the system of the personality are mechanisms for generating stress and reinforcing tension. Anytime we resist reality, the stress response increases.

Consider times when you notice that you are tense for seemingly no reason at all. You might experience yourself as irritable, angry, jealous, anxious, resentful, suspicious, or controlling or have other emotional responses that do not particularly make sense to you in the moment. Or there might be a specific trigger, such as being unhappy with a friend, fear of being seen as weak, or feeling dismissed or unseen that appear to be the source of these same emotions.

Then there are the times when you might experience yourself as lighthearted, joyful, unfazed by other's behaviors, gentle, compassionate, and safe or experience other qualities that have a sense of ease and spaciousness. What is different? What explains the vast array of internal experiences and range of external behaviors that any one person can have?

Each person's experience can range from highly constricted and rigid to highly expansive and fluid. The personality often has been associated with how an individual shows up (or does not show up) in life. It seldom has been understood to be an expression of varying degrees of tension. Yet we can say that the personality is activated and/or magnified when the individual experiences an internal constriction. The patterns of the engaged or activated personality generate the greatest percentage of stress and constriction.

Appendix A lists a number of attributes that characterize the polar opposites of the personality along a continuum of constriction to expansion. I suggest taking a few minutes to review the characteristics of the highly expansive to highly constricted personality before moving on.

≋ Coaching Cue:

We all carry around unrecognized levels of physical, emotional, and mental tension and constriction that can be manifested in every dimension of life, that is, physically, emotionally, mentally, spiritually. Constrictions develop as a mostly unconscious strategy for self-protection.

One of the important values that you can bring to your clients is creating an environment that lends itself to the release of tightness and tension.

Examples of basic strategies:

- *Creating an atmosphere of absolute safety and trust.*

- *Being nonjudgmental toward your client. Clients intuitively know if coaches are judging them or their behaviors. Your unconditional acceptance of clients can be one of the most influential factors in creating safety.*

- *Starting session with attention to breath and regularly returning client's attention to the breath on a consistent basis.*

- *Including opportunities for physical release, such as stretches or movement, in sessions.*

Reflect back to clients what you notice that signals tension (e.g., tightness in voice, unusually rapid speech, holding shoulders tightly, sense of anxiety) and ask them to bring soft attention to the particular sensations associated with that area. Suggest directing breath and attention to that area to allow it to soften.

Notice what happens when you are paying attention to your own breath and request that the client does the same. What is the client's somatic or verbal response? What changes do you notice in the energy field that you and the client have co-created?

EXPLORING THE LEVELS OF HEALTH AND EFFECTIVENESS

While appendix A offers a general description of the polar opposites of personalities at their most expansive and most constricted levels, much work has been done to identify specific levels at which the personality exists. In 1977, Don Richard Riso began exploring the varying dimensions of personality, which resulted in what he discovered as the nine levels of functioning or effectiveness of each type. Together Riso and Russ Hudson refined the descriptions of behaviors, attitudes, fears, and desires that describe the nine levels of presence for each type. These nine levels are divided into three major categories: the three healthy levels, the three average levels, and the three unhealthy levels of type. To learn more about the levels of health (referred to as the levels of development in their early writing), read Riso and Hudson's *Understanding the Enneagram: The Practical Guide to Personality Types.*[1]

The discussion of the nine levels is beyond the parameters of this book; however, being aware that these levels exist is of value to coaches because:

- By learning about the paradoxical yet concise and predictable characteristics contained within each type, we are more able to accurately type ourselves and help others to land on their core type. These levels are intended to be used to build awareness for those who are interested in emotional, psychological, and spiritual growth. It is important not to use them to label or judge ourselves or others.

- As noted in chapter 2, the personality developed to serve as a coping mechanism to protect us from experiencing pain, though we eventually recognize that this is not possible. Paradoxically, the personality itself can be a source of suffering, especially as type patterns move people in the opposite direction of what would be most deeply satisfying to their inner being. It may be helpful to remember that what matters most is the direction we are facing—toward health and expansiveness or toward constriction.

- The levels explain the relationship of less healthy characteristics to more healthy qualities. They help us see what is best within a person of a particular type, even when that person is currently operating at a less than healthy level. The levels also draw our attention to the mystery that is beyond type. Of great value is the realization that there is not an us (the healthy people) and them (the unhealthy people). One's level of health is not static. That is, anyone (including growth-oriented professionals!) has the potential for experiencing different levels of psychological or emotional health in a day. It is both true and humbling that we are each working with our own point on the constriction-expansion continuum.

- The levels allow us to recognize that when we have continuing difficulty with another person, that likely both of us are functioning at a less than healthy level. This can be a window into compassion for others and ourselves.

Table 3.1 provides additional descriptors related to levels of health.

| TABLE 3.1 | AN INTERPRETATION OF THE RISO-HUDSON LEVELS MODEL FOR COACHES |

Healthy Levels of Type

Depending upon the depth of your own work and your professional focus, you likely will not be coaching clients who consistently are at this level of health. It is a small percentage of the population. However, you may well see glimpses of these qualities with some of your clients.

Levels 1-3 Characteristics
- Not attached to outcomes
- High level of ease and freedom
- Emotionally clear/neutral
- Curious, open, reflective
- Takes responsibility for one's own part of troublesome situation
- Makes a positive contribution to others
- Personality exists but is not driving the train
- Courageous in acknowledging difficult truths and engaging in healing
- Able to be with what arises, including pain, with presence and trust

Average Levels of Type

These levels are considered "normal" in most of Western society, so it is likely that most of your clients will be functioning at these levels of presence most of the time.

Levels 4-6 Characteristics
- Takes personality and self more seriously (the ego is more in charge but feels better about itself)
- Becomes emotionally charged around otherwise neutral situations
- Becomes more attached and identified with automatic patterns of personality
- Ego expansive (I'm important) or ego deflating (I'm worthless)
- Takes others' behaviors more personally
- Tries to change others
- Defense patterns such as blaming are activated
- Capacity to be with what arises, including pain, is more limited, but can develop with support and as the degree of presence increases

Unhealthy Levels of Type

Therapists and rehabilitation specialists tend to be working with clients that are at this level more of the time. People exhibiting these characteristics consistently are not appropriate candidates for coaching.

Levels 7-9 Characteristics
- There is nothing but one's personality (having a broader perspective is greatly compromised and not accessible)
- Deeply involved in destructive patterns directed toward self and/or others
- Highly defended
- Carries a heavy emotional charge
- Insufficient degree of presence to be with what arises until an inner stability develops
- In deep, unprocessed pain

This table is not theoretical. Each of the levels within the personality type relates to specific thinking, emotional, attitudinal, behavioral, and energetic patterns that can be observed and experienced. The more developed our capacity for observing our inner experience and the impact of our outer expression, the more we are able to identify but not be identified with specific patterns.

≈ Coaching Cue:

Note and reflect back when your clients appear to share their experience of a movement to a higher level of health during a session. This is more than just feeling better. A higher level of health is associated with some degree of release and opening, such as a longtime belief no longer holding truth, or an attachment to some aspect of one's identity falling away, or seeing through one's subjective ideas to recognize the objective reality of a situation, as examples.

When clients are ready, we can inquire with them into the conditions that supported this more expansive experience. These conditions might include having direct contact with body sensations, allowing their heart to open to themselves with compassion, or feeling completely accepted for who they are. The intent is to assist clients in realizing their own contribution to this process and, over time, decrease the dependence on the coach as a source of this experience.

Hearing clients report about their more expansive experiences between sessions is a cause for celebration.

One of the most profound ways of understanding the levels is "as a measure of our capacity to be present."[2] The more present we are, the less the patterns of personality have a grip on us and the less we react to external circumstances.

This metaphor may be useful: When we are at the highest level of our type, we are close to our most expansive nature. We experience a lightness in ourselves and live in an entirely different consciousness than when our personality is more engaged. It's as if there's a large, clear window and we experience the beauty, warmth, and embrace of the sun. Each time we get caught in fear and self-protectiveness, the constrictions in our personality create a veil. It is as if a translucent curtain falls between us and the sunshine. With each level we spiral down in our personality, another curtain drops, until eventually there are so many layers of curtains between us and the sunshine (our lighter nature) that it is difficult to see anything but a murkiness or darkness. Conversely, we can practice lifting the curtains, one at a time, to reveal more light.

This is akin to what is referred to as the veils of illusion that is the nature of the personality.

Section 2 of this book describes specific behaviors, attitudes, and patterns of people in each of the nine Enneagram types who are at the healthy and average levels of health.

If you are relatively new to coaching, you may be asking how to discern who you will accept as a coaching client. Of course, it is important to listen for and be attuned to certain qualities on the part of the individual seeking a coaching relationship. Is there curiosity about self-development? Is there a general orientation toward taking responsibility for oneself? Does the individual have certain goals or intentions in mind? Is the prospective client interested in making a positive impact on others? These are just a few examples of criteria that are foundational to a successful coaching relationship. A sign that coaching is not appropriate is when clients consistently place their attention on what is wrong with other people or external situations.

What are the cautions of working with this knowledge? First, it is important to reiterate that most people do not live full time at either end of the constriction-expansiveness continuum. Worst case, one could use table 3.1 as a scale for judging good/bad, right/wrong, better/worse. In other words, inappropriately used, it could be an instrument for comparison, evaluation, and judgment and creating adversarial relationships. Of course, that is not the intent.

SIGNIFICANCE OF THE CONSTRICTION-EXPANSIVENESS DYNAMIC

What is the significance for coaches working in the realm of constriction-expansiveness? What potential does it have for making a positive difference? Certainly, living in an unrecognized state of tension is a potential source for illness—including catastrophic disease, dissatisfaction and unhappiness, and ineffectiveness in all aspects of life. The more constriction we experience, the more we struggle.

Let's recall the brief narrative provided regarding the development of the personality in chapter 2. A major function of the personality was to protect the child from experiencing or reexperiencing pain that they could not process or tolerate at the time.

If not brought into awareness, that pain still likely exists. We can think of constrictions as building up around wounding experiences (even those that occur preconceptually and preverbally) that have not been acknowledged. Default patterns are associated with those tensions that keep one out of contact with one's innermost self. One way these constrictions show up is in the faulty beliefs that an individual carries.

Most people on the planet are walking around with these constrictions, and they are a source of both conscious and unconscious suffering.

As growth professionals, it is valuable to keep this awareness in mind. Your approach to working in this territory will be dependent on the nature of your professional practice and of your clients. Here are some approaches, with more found in section 3:

–   Bringing awareness to all the ways clients experience tension as a typical part of living will help shed light on it. Suggest mindfulness and meditation practices. Refer clients to body workers or movement practitioners who can support the release of certain levels of tension. As dynamic beings, it is valuable to look at what direction we are facing. Even when we experience one of our own troublesome behaviors, we can ask ourselves a basic question: Is this attitude, this thought, this action moving me toward more constriction or toward more ease? What supports or blocks the movement toward more ease?

–   Offer a more expansive perspective and reflect the higher qualities back to the client. Note when they are expressing a more spacious experience.

–   We can invite clients who wish to go deeper into more direct contact with current sensations, feelings, and images that may be related to the roots of a pattern. We do this through holding a strong container of presence to help them stay grounded. Chapter 11 provides guidance in using this process.

CONSTRICTING PATTERNS AS OBSTACLES TO INTENTIONS AND GOALS

The constriction-expansiveness continuum seems quite simple. And it is. On the other hand, the experience of being constricted is so normal in daily life that we are unaware of its presence. It could be argued that constriction is the very nature of the personality.

We may not think of many behaviors and thoughts as being contracted. Here are just a few habitual examples of how humans do constriction at the average levels of personality. Many of these will be familiar to coaches as obstacles that inhibit their clients' realization of intentions.

–   Limiting beliefs: holding on to illusions about one's possibilities, abilities, worth

–   Being on automatic: not stopping to reflect, not being curious about options

–   Grasping at something: continually striving to obtain

–   Resisting what is: focusing on wanting another person or situation to be different

–   Keeping busy: not allowing in moments of inner quiet or reflection

–   Holding one's breath: forgetting to consciously breathe

- Denial: refusing to acknowledge a troubling situation
- Worrying: continual mental activity over worst-case, future scenarios
- Not telling the truth to oneself or to others: holding back on what needs to be acknowledged and/or communicated
- Judging: a focus on what is perceived as flaws
- Avoiding hard situations: moving away from situations requiring attention
- Trying to control others and situations: demanding compliance to their way
- Trying to change others: putting relentless effort into causing another person to think or do as they think or do
- Overobligating oneself: scattering and depleting one's energies
- Trying too hard: keeping in the mode of struggle
- Having an overly busy mind: overthinking, analyzing, projecting, overanticipating
- "See me": putting energy into having others see one in a certain way
- Becoming aggressive: raising the voice, demanding attention
- Withdrawing: leaving a situation physically, mentally, or energetically

Each personality type has predictable patterns of constriction.

Some specific patterns may be known mentally by the client (e.g., "I always have to keep busy. I just don't know how to stop myself."). In fact, these behaviors are often a reason an individual gives for seeking coaching. Patterns may be a source of frustration and self-judgment.

EMOTIONAL HOOKS AS CONSTRICTIONS

Emotional hooks are the recurring physical and emotional reactions experienced when one of our proverbial buttons has been pushed. All of us have situations that habitually elicit specific emotional charges. Not surprisingly, these situations often involve other people. The number of situations that result in an emotional charge are far too numerous to cover. However, you may notice a reaction just by reading from a short list of potential buttons below. Note that any of these situations will be neutral for some people and will create an emotional hook for others.

-   Being asked (or told) to do something you don't want to do
-   Feeling unseen or unheard
-   Feeling rushed by another person
-   Feeling blocked in getting what you want
-   Feeling taken advantage of
-   Being lied to
-   Someone else taking credit for your idea or efforts
-   Communication that is blunt
-   Communication that is vague
-   Someone doing a job below your standards
-   Feeling ignored
-   Someone who is overly positive
-   Someone who continually looks for problems or reasons something won't work
-   Not having your efforts sufficiently appreciated or recognized
-   Being in a situation where another person can't make up their mind
-   Not having choices or feeling trapped
-   Having someone unexpectedly put the spotlight on you
-   Someone disagreeing with an idea that you've thought long and hard about
-   Someone else's anger

There are many cues that tell us that we are emotionally hooked.

One cue is a physical sensation that can be experienced as a tightening or perhaps change in temperature in some part of the body. This sensation may be felt in the belly, the solar plexus, the chest, the neck/vocal cord area, or the head. Because it is experienced as uncomfortable, the sensation may be overridden by an automatic behavior. Thus this somatic cue may become hidden and not easily recognized.

Another cue that signals the existence of a hook is the instant arising of a powerful and familiar emotion, such as anger, shame, fear, rejection, or frustration, among others. When we are caught in the grasp of the emotion, a habitual behavioral pattern, such as one of those listed in the previous section, typically follows.

The cycle of an emotional hook—the physical sensation, the experience of the powerful emotion, and the resulting behavior—can happen so quickly and automatically that people often say, "I don't know what hit me." In his book *Emotional Intelligence*, Daniel Goleman describes this experience as an "emotional hijacking."[3]

Clearly, the emotional hook is a reactive and constricting experience that all clients have and that impacts the client's movement toward their desired outcomes. Deep coaching adds value by helping the client bring awareness and presence to the cycle, along with tools and practices for sensing into its origins, healing, and allowing it to relax.

THE PARADOX OF CONSTRICTION-EXPANSIVENESS

Interrupting a default pattern is one of the most challenging things we can ask a client to do. It is the nature of the personality to convince the individual (at an invisible level, of course) that the habitual pattern is, in fact, the best way to live. It is not surprising that when a pattern is brought to a client's attention or when clients recognize the pattern for themselves, a sense of pride or discomfort, embarrassment, grief, or resistance can arise. After all, these patterns have served the person as a survival mechanism and have played an important role up to now in how the person thinks of themselves. Thus, these historic patterns are not bad or wrong; they simply lose their effectiveness and at some point are no longer needed as protection.

The pattern no doubt plays a pivotal part in keeping the client stuck (constricted). For example, a person who identifies with the Type Three Achiever personality may have had great success and recognition for her efficiency and accomplishments in culturally valued roles. She has an underlying urge to engage in pursuits that are more personally meaningful but feels caught in the pressure to constantly produce. That leaves little room for being in touch with her heart. A person who identifies with the Type Five Investigator personality may want to pursue having a significant relationship. He may have little idea that his pattern's preoccupation with ideas, creating plans, or being secretive would leave a potential partner questioning his true availability for a relationship.

Table 3.2 gives more examples of type-based patterns that are obstacles to realizing goals and intentions. Please note that the examples of client goals are relevant to people with any type and thus are not limited just to people with the type noted in the examples.

TABLE 3.2	**EXAMPLES OF CLIENT COACHING INTENTIONS AND TYPE-BASED OBSTACLES**	
Enneagram Type	**Example of Client Coaching Intention**	**Type-Based Patterns That Create Obstacles to Realizing Intentions**
ONE	To feel calmer and at peace	Feeling responsible for fixing things
TWO	To get clear on personal priorities	Singular focus on what other people need
THREE	To create life balance	Feeling the drive to be competitive in every part of life
FOUR	To find the ideal job	Feeling they are above certain tasks that are a part of any job
FIVE	To find the right person to have a significant relationship with	Withdrawing from intimate conversations
SIX	To find personal fulfillment through the next career move	Looking for a position that guarantees security and stability
SEVEN	To become proficient at time management	Having so many interests and trying to do it all
EIGHT	To be a more effective boss	Being intense in telling employees what to do without listening
NINE	To be an effective collaborator	Avoiding conflict and direct communication

From this table, you can see that the personality pattern works in opposition to achieving the intention. Thus, personality patterns play a profound, if often challenging, role in the coaching process. People unconsciously sense that their patterns are the foundation upon which to make changes, not the basis for changes themselves.

> PEOPLE UNCONSCIOUSLY SENSE THAT THEIR PATTERNS ARE THE FOUNDATION UPON WHICH TO MAKE CHANGES, NOT THE BASIS FOR CHANGES THEMSELVES.

By supporting a client in surfacing and bringing compassion to the roots of the pattern, we help create a healing threshold that allows for a transformative experience.

〰 Coaching Cue:

Sometimes clients can become self-judgmental when they forget to act on the new information and experiences they are learning. It helps to remind them that historic patterns are insistent; they can be expected to surface as the default mode. That's why helping clients to build the capacity for presence is so vital. It is both courageous and healing to support a client's inward journey to expose the beliefs and wounds that the constrictions have protected.

Chapter 4

ORIENTING TO YOUR CLIENT'S HIGHEST NATURE

We need a conscious context that has parameters to help guide our work with clients. This context needs to be large enough to allow for enormous client growth, shifts toward desired outcomes, and responsiveness to individual differences. It also needs to be sensitive to the quiet explorations of the inner voice, allow for experimentation in what may feel like foreign territory for the client, honor the unknown, and recognize subtle movements toward or away from the client's greatest joy and realness. Powerful coaching revolves around the movement of clients toward their own highest nature.

ANCHORING THE PROFESSIONAL-CLIENT "FIELD" OF PRESENCE

You are sitting with a client, or a team, or a circle of people who have come together with a shared intention of doing "deeper" work, perhaps without even knowing what "deeper" means. You might be working in person or virtually. Now what?

Using deep coaching, we come to understand that we are not doing anything to our clients.

We do provide the space and the conditions, along with inquiry, perspectives, feedback, and practices, that allow clients to experience themselves in new ways. Anchored in the power of presence, this robust approach is grounded in the sacred body of wisdom available through the Enneagram, self-knowledge, and a counterintuitive orientation to change that guides a client to turn toward self. Approaching the change process in this way supports clients in coming into contact with their in-the-moment inner experience, which often yields profound insights and release of previously unrecognized sources of long-held emotions, beliefs, or other constrictions and is often followed by a newly experienced spaciousness. Coaches and facilitators are attuned to their own in-the-moment experience while staying attuned to the client's experience.

None of what happens during this process is (or could be) planned by the coach or the client. Having engaged in this process, clients often report experiencing an inherent okayness.

GUIDING PRINCIPLES FOR SUPPORTING THE EXPERIENCE OF PRESENCE

What qualities support clients in developing greater contact with their own experience, with becoming more intimate with themselves? The following are some of the guiding principles that have been used for many years in the deep work to nourish a kind relationship with oneself and to develop a foundation for coming into direct contact with one's more authentic nature.

As professionals, we continue to develop our personal capacity for experiencing and expressing these qualities in our own lives, do our best to express these qualities with our clients, and support the development of our clients' capacities for experiencing these qualities for themselves.

Developing the Capacity for Self-Observation and Noticing

To take the next step in developing a more intimate relationship and connection to oneself requires being able to see oneself clearly.

Self-observation and the capacity to notice what we are experiencing and what we are up to are powerful allies in awareness and growth. An abundance of neuroscientific research has shown that self-observation is vital in moving beyond familiar patterns and identifications formed through the personality. The observer state of consciousness exists outside of default habits of the ego. Rather, it is a presence-based state that allows us to witness whatever is occurring at the moment with neutrality and nonattachment.

From the deep coaching perspective, noticing, which will be further addressed in section 3, refers to directing attention to our inner sensations, feelings, thoughts, urges to act, and internal movement.

Developing these capacities is fundamental to supporting positive, sustainable change and transformation for clients.

Self-observation and noticing must be approached with nonjudgment. Releasing the messages of criticism is challenging because judgment is deeply ingrained within the psyche. Yet judgment is a mechanism of the ego and not rooted in presence.

Five Vital Qualities to Support Clients' Healthier Relationships with Themselves

1. Bringing Curiosity

Bringing true curiosity to one's experience in the moment supports the capacity of noticing. Curiosity, which stems from an open-mindedness and willingness to not know in advance, brings forth awareness that something is stirring within. For example, we may notice that our client's face reddens and bring curiosity to that, perhaps to learn that an internal shift has occurred. We can encourage our client's curiosity about somatic sensations that arise when confronted with an uncomfortable truth or when a surprising insight occurs. We can be curious when tears unexpectedly arise or when a new feeling shows up.

From this perspective, curiosity is not focused on answering "why" questions, trying to explain a situation, but is simply noticing the existence of something at work within us. This attitude toward curiosity contributes to the experience of spaciousness.

≈ Coaching Cue:

Coaches can support this quality through using the language of curiosity in the coaching process. For example, "Let's be curious about your experience and see what we can learn together," invites the client into a nonjudgmental inquiry that can lessen the threat that can come with having a part of the personality brought into aware- ness. "I'm wondering what it would be like to . . ." Asking questions that take both you and the client into new unknown territory is a valuable skill.

Further, when clients are asked "Why?" they respond in a less than satisfying way to a situation; they are likely to come up with an answer that seems logical to them.

For example, people who identify with Type Seven personalities characteristically love starting things but find it difficult to stay focused to complete a project. They tend to get overwhelmed with the busyness of their lives. If asked why it is difficult to stay focused, a client may say "Don't you see? There are SO many wonderful things to do! And I want to try them all." The mind generates an answer that aligns with the inner logic of the personality.

What if you as the coach recognized that this client held a belief that their true source of satisfaction was somewhere out there— outside of themselves—and to stay focused on a project created a feeling of being trapped? This belief keeps the client in perpetual

BEING CURIOUS WITH A CLIENT ALSO DIMINISHES THE ERRONEOUS CONCEPT THAT THE COACH KNOWS WHAT THE CLIENT IS EXPERIENCING OR NEEDS TO FIX IT.

motion. You can recognize the power of such a hidden belief and now have a broader context within which to coach, bringing into focus the satisfaction that is possible right here in this moment.

The mind most often is not a source of an accurate assessment underlying the behavior. That is one reason that the "why" question in coaching is not useful unless posed with extreme care. Pay particular attention to the identified core beliefs underlying the client's personality patterns.

2. Practicing Radical Compassion

The experience of recognizing what is actually here is often very significant for clients. Insights and ahas become more powerful when accompanied by compassion and the willingness to allow the experience.

Too often, clients ignore, dismiss, or judge the experiences in their lives, as if they should not exist. Paradoxically, we unsuspectingly give energy to those areas of our lives that we do not want to acknowledge. Those aspects that are ignored do not disappear but create an internal struggle, lurking and growing even larger, popping out when least expected. The energy that is consumed by the struggle, whether or not it is conscious, deprives people of an acceptance of their full humanity and of their wholeness.

Compassion is central to the deep coaching approach as it honors and recognizes that each of us is on our own path back to ourselves. Every time we bring awareness to difficult places, to personality patterns that have created pain in our own lives or in others' lives, it matters.

> COMPASSION IS CENTRAL TO THE DEEP APPROACH AS IT HONORS AND RECOGNIZES THAT EACH OF US IS ON OUR OWN PATH BACK TO OURSELVES.

We and our clients are part of humanity becoming more conscious. Allowing for the breadth and depth of our own experience connects us to the whole of the human condition. We are not alone. We belong.

Compassion is no small matter. What if each of us infused our part of the world with compassion? This is a radical act.

〰 Coaching Cue:

Compassion is not something clients can simply add on to themselves. It must come from within. Many clients have not developed an affirming relationship with their hearts. Coaches can support that positive relationship by inviting clients to bring attention to their hearts, by checking in with what's happening in their hearts, by practicing kindness for themselves, and by becoming more attuned to this part of their being.

Human development professionals have an irrevocable responsibility to truly care for themselves, to embody kindness in their own lives. This quality is transmitted, however quietly, to our clients.

3. Embracing Honesty

Our personality structure filters how we see ourselves. Most of us have a distorted view of ourselves that we have unconsciously invested in and defended. It can be upsetting when others do not see us in the same way and do not share our personal agenda.

This will be true for our clients. Some may have an inflated view of themselves while others have a deflated view. As noted earlier, one of the great gifts of the Enneagram is to provide a mirror to see oneself clearly, perhaps for the first time. It can be shocking and freeing to realize that we are not our fixed idea of ourselves.

Acknowledging what is true can bring embarrassment, shame, understanding, and the uncanny experience of having the pieces of our personal puzzle put together. People who we have blamed for our circumstances may now be freed from our resentment. Real honesty allows for more compassion for ourselves.

Coming into alignment with our internal truth creates clarity around external situations, leading to the possibility of making different, life-affirming choices. Recognizing and embracing the significance of our blessings and gifts and honoring the deeper nature within comes with radical honesty.

Encourage clients to be with the range of their humanity, including their challenges, unique qualities, and gifts, with an open heart and nonjudgment to help them reach greater consciousness.

> HONESTY, FOUNDED ON CURIOSITY AND COMPASSION, IS A KEYSTONE FOR INNER FREEDOM.

≋ Coaching Cue:

Examples of questions that focus on helping clients discern their truth include: Check in with your heart. Does what you just said feel true? What's true for you now? How do you know when you are sitting with the truth? How do you experience it internally? What I just reflected back to you—did that ring true?

Most clients will need adequate time to check in with themselves to discern what lands as truth.

4. Summoning Courage

This is courageous work. It takes courage to look beyond the familiar world and into the unknown of new territory. The personality creates familiarity. Even when it creates difficulty for us, as it often does, the familiarity often wins out over exploring what is on the other side of the known.

What if I said no instead of my usual yes? What if I didn't have that drink tonight and let myself feel what I haven't wanted to feel? What if I opened my heart instead of closing it down in an intimate conversation? What if I expressed my anger instead of playing nice? What if I let you see my vulnerability instead of showing up as having it all together? What if I trusted my intuition instead of asking external experts? What if I tuned into my belly instead of being led by my thoughts in this situation? What if I took action on this priority now even if my feeling urges me to stay in bed?

"TO INVOKE COURAGE, IT IS BENEFICIAL TO FEEL PROPELLED BY SOMETHING MORE IMPORTANT THAN WHATEVER CHALLENGES MIGHT ARISE FROM BEING COURAGEOUS, SUCH AS FEELING DISCOMFORT, FEAR, OR SELF-DOUBT."

—ROXANNE HOWE-MURPHY [1]

Do any of these questions bring up a sense of dread?

We all have inner stories that shout out danger if we move beyond our familiar ways. Examples of stories might include trying to convince us that we will not be loved, or that we will be left alone, or that we will no longer be safe. And the stories sound so real. In fact, we all have collected data on how these stories are really true. These are the shadows in Plato's cave.

〜〜 Coaching Cue:

What is more important to your client than feeling stuck or lacking choice?

Clients sometimes downplay the significance of changes in behavior, thoughts, or heart that they have experienced. They might compare their changes to what they assume others have experienced. It's vital to affirm and celebrate any shift from the familiar to the new regardless of how it looks on the outside because we cannot know the magnitude of the client's internal leap.

5. Trusting the Process

For many of us, at least some of our professional training was based on theories of change that largely focused on the content of the client's life, assessing what was not working, and using our well-developed tools and techniques to remedy or fix what was wrong. It may feel like your responsibility is to provide answers and solutions for the client, relying on ideas to try to get somewhere. That somewhere may be out there.

These approaches to change have their own value. What they often lack is the coach's capacity to be with themselves and be with the client in the moment, witness what arises, and trust the many sources of intelligence that become available when given space and acceptance. Thus, the process is based on being present to what is showing up—what is unfolding at every moment.

It is completely counterintuitive for professionals with credentials and degrees to let go of knowing the client's answers in advance. Yet, if we allow it, from the first moment we begin work with our clients, we enter the unknown when we ask: What would you like to focus on today? What is here for you? What is showing up within you?

It takes courage (and practice) to trust that previously unforeseen and generally more robust outcomes will be realized when we release our need to control and know the answers in advance.

Section 3 will address the multiple sources of intelligence that we call upon, both within ourselves and within the client.

≋ Coaching Cue:

Just being alive means that we live in the unknown. Bringing that honesty to coaching takes courage and acknowledges that we are opening to all the sources of guidance that are available to us when we bring ourselves back to presence.

IN ADDITION TO TRUSTING THE PROCESS, WE ARE ALSO CALLED UPON TO TRUST THE CLIENT'S INNATE INTELLIGENCE, AS WELL AS OUR OWN.

The Power of Qualities Anchored in Presence

All of these qualities invite us to first be with ourselves so that we may meet our clients at a profound level. These qualities provide a way to hold our clients, their experiences, and their movement toward their higher intentions. Individually, each quality offers a powerful space for positive change. Integrated together, they enlarge the space for clients to come into an authentic relationship with themselves that is anchored in presence. While clients may not see themselves as whole beings whose presence is needed, we perceive them in just that way, even with the challenges they are confronting. These qualities help us provide guidance, support, and nurturance. It is a rare privilege to see through the veneers and into the brilliance and hearts of our clients.

More perspectives on these qualities can be found in chapter 4 of *Deep Living with the Enneagram: Recovering Your True Nature.*

THE ROLE OF INNER PAIN

Moving toward one's highest nature requires experiencing and moving through some degree of inner pain.

Constriction coincides with living on automatic, lacking sufficient self-reflection and curiosity. This results in avoiding a real relationship with ourselves. We lose contact with ourselves when we ignore our inner experience and get lost in the surface content of life. In less healthy states, we are more reactionary, defended, confident in our historical beliefs, and attached to a guarded and constricted self-image. We confuse our masks and defenses with our more authentic selves.

Positive development toward expansiveness comes with being willing to see ourselves and our circumstances more clearly; discovering the falsehoods that we've taken as our truths; relaxing and releasing concepts and somatic tensions; and allowing our hearts to take us in.

At the core of this inner movement is how coaches understand the role of pain. First, the process of discovering the underlying Enneagram type dynamics that have shaped our lives, our choices, our personal and work relationships, and our very relationship to the world brings us in touch with long-held and often unconscious wounds.

We can return to the section in chapter 2 on the relationship between essence and personality to note the layers of constriction that develop as part of being born into this world. We again are reminded that the personality structure developed to protect us from experiencing more pain when we were very young, so coming to discover this part of ourselves will, of course, involve bumping into painful places. Coming into contact with pain is a necessary part of the healing and awakening process.

〰〰 Coaching Cue:

Gently meet internal pain for what it is: a place of constriction that served as a buffer against experiencing further pain when the client lacked the capacity or resources to handle it. The pain will almost always show up as an uncomfortable sensation in the body. Your client likely has more resources now to move through the pain, such as the ability to breathe into it, to be curious and notice, to allow the experience with compassion and perhaps some degree of trust that the sensations will shift into something different. Emotions also accompany pain when it is met with kindness: grief, sometimes shame, regret, guilt. Along with these, a client may experience relief, clarity, or a sense of lightness, which can become a doorway for new possibilities that the client did not previously imagine. Pain, held in presence, is most often trans-formative. Meeting it in presence often leads to a release of some belief or emotion, creating an opening to more spaciousness.

Here are two factors that support coaches in meeting their clients in this tender space.

First, without having entered into your own tender territory, exploring the deep veins of your inner life as illuminated by the Enneagram, you likely will not be adequately prepared to be present with deeper levels of emotional and spiritual pain that are arising for clients.

Second, we can recognize that pain, as difficult as it can feel in the moment, can be held in spaciousness. There is more to the client than pain. The spaciousness that accompanies presence is healing.

Chapter 5

THE ENNEAGRAM AND YOUR CLIENT

THREE ENTRY POINTS FOR USING THE ENNEAGRAM WITH CLIENTS

The primary focus of your work will largely determine the kind of clients you engage. In some settings, self-awareness through the Enneagram is not the top priority, though it may be introduced at a later point in your sessions. Even in these circumstances, the Enneagram can provide value to you as a coach. Here are three ways you can think about using the Enneagram. They represent three different stages or entry points in which a client knows about or wants to engage with the Enneagram:

ENTRY POINT 1

The client is unaware of the Enneagram. Through listening deeply to the client's questions, comments, stated struggles and challenges, and desires, you may hear information that provides hints to the client's type. Paying attention to the client's tone of voice and verbal pacing and rhythm (e.g., fast/slow, hesitant/assertive, soft/loud) may provide further hints.

You cannot be certain of type, of course, but you might have a silent (unshared) hypothesis. Your hypothesis can lead you to ask questions relevant to the client's concerns that also connect with the client's type structure. If your hypothesis is accurate, the client will likely feel seen.

For example, in an introductory call with a potential client, I heard comments that reflected the concerns of someone whose core type was Six. She was contemplating a courageous move in leaving her longtime association with a solid, stable organization to start her own practice in the same field. She shared her training background, experience, and successes in delivering her services. Beyond her concerns about enacting the logistics needed for running the business, I also heard an underlying doubt about whether she really knew enough about the services she would be providing. When I asked what she could trust about herself, she stopped. That question tapped into tender territory.

While you might not need to know the Enneagram to have a similar experience with a client, it does provide a useful framework for meeting clients where they are.

ENTRY POINT 2

The client knows of the Enneagram and perhaps has read about it or even names their core type, but this knowledge has not made a significant difference.

For example, a client's interest in coaching may revolve around struggles in the workplace, feeling misunderstood and frustrated by the behaviors of others, and wanting to know if the Enneagram can be helpful in improving the environment.

It is not uncommon to find that clients have been erroneously typed by themselves or someone else. We also may find that some people have a limited knowledge of the Enneagram framework and use the type itself as a reason or excuse for their behavior, which does not lead to growth and development. You can co-discover with clients the specifics of the identified type(s) that resonate and if the identified type is accurate or needs to be reassessed. When you integrate the Enneagram into the coaching process, clients begin to learn more about what drives their behaviors and perspectives, use practices that support becoming more present, and discover new ways to respond.

Working at this level with the Enneagram generally involves shorter-term coaching relationships but could be part of a longer engagement.

ENTRY POINT 3

Clients at this level have a commitment to deeper work and often consider themselves on a spiritual journey. They are taking more responsibility for how they meet life, want more internal freedom, and have intentions to be more conscious. They find great value in coming into contact with their inner world, recognizing how it impacts every part of their life. The Enneagram may be the primary framework used, but it is often supported through practices from other wisdom traditions.

Working at this level with the Enneagram generally involves a long-term individual coaching or facilitated group commitment.

These entry points are not mutually exclusive; you may find yourself bringing in the Enneagram on more than one level with some clients.

DEVELOPING TRUST AND RAPPORT WITH CLIENTS

One of the first tasks of a coach is to develop trust with the client. The Enneagram is a powerful tool for creating a safe environment that builds rapport and trust as it helps us become more attuned to the client's core motivation, inner environment, and basic operating principles. By working with the Enneagram in depth, we can refine our capacity to listen and tune into the client quickly. Trust is more quickly established when clients hear questions that tap into their inner experience. A client who feels seen and heard is more likely to relax into the coaching relationship and be more honest. Thus, used carefully and with presence, the Enneagram is a robust tool that will be beneficial in a wide variety of settings.

For example, a client who had some knowledge of the Enneagram and who had already self-typed herself mentioned at the end of our first conversation that the Enneagram had given us a shared language and knowledge base. She revealed, "I felt like you got me in the first ten minutes of our conversation. I didn't have to give you my whole history or tell you about my challenges or strengths right up front because you were already tuned into me. That saved us a lot of time, and I felt comfortable with you immediately."

INTRODUCING YOUR CLIENT TO THE ENNEAGRAM

For clients who are new to the Enneagram or skeptical of it, you will need to find your way of presenting it to them.

One way is to assess why clients come to you. What are the major themes underlying their interests, their dreams, and their intentions? Depending upon your answers to these questions, you can provide a context for introducing the Enneagram. For example, here are several reasons why a client may choose coaching:

–   The client is dissatisfied with their life. They want to realize more fulfilling and positive results—whether in work, relationships, finances, or lifestyle balance, for example.

–   The client is a mid-level leader who has received low ratings for their lack of effectiveness, especially in the area of relationships, in the workplace. This client aspires to being chosen for higher levels of leadership.

–   The client wants to begin their own business but is filled with self-criticism. They give themselves pep talks that may offer limited momentum but are overtaken by subsequent doubts. Their intentions are to develop a strong foundation for the business and get out of their own way.

– The client is in the midst of an important life transition—for example, in work, in a primary relationship, or in a move. Or perhaps the person is experiencing the normal changes associated with midlife change. Transition is a time for reflection and deeper self-understanding in order to make healthy choices for the next phase in life.

– The client, a longtime community organizer, is frustrated and angry that the efforts of their organization to create meaningful social justice initiatives have fallen far short of the goals set. The client is burned out and is questioning their next steps.

Here are suggestions for how you might introduce the Enneagram, with awareness of the client's intentions:

– The Enneagram provides a system for identifying your primary type or worldview. First, by going through the process of identifying your primary type, you can begin to recognize the default automatic patterns that guide how you see the world and yourself, as well as how you live your life, make decisions, cope with stress, and interact with others. You'll probably be surprised to discover that some of the repetitive habits are actually patterns associated with a particular Enneagram type that are shared with a substantial percentage of the population.

– When you operate from a specific range of behaviors that make perfect sense to you, your results are likely to be far more limited than what you want and your impact is likely to be more limited than what you want or are capable of.

– The Enneagram gives us important information on how we beat up on ourselves. You'll learn how to notice what the inner critic is doing and develop strategies for lessening its impact on you.

– The Enneagram sheds light on the motivations underlying the choices you've made in the past and can provide insights on a much broader range of choices that are available to you. It can be quite a relief to realize that those habits that no longer serve you can be relaxed over time and that other creative responses will become available to you.

– As a person who is interested in self-development, you'll appreciate the depth of insight that you'll gain through the Enneagram. You'll also have the opportunity to practice accessing more sources of your natural intelligence.

– By gaining information on other Enneagram types, you begin to see how others who are important to you respond or react to their life situations.

- When used in an intentional way, the Enneagram helps you create more possibilities for desired results, to be more aware of your impact on others, and, by understanding yourself better, learn to be more self-accepting and compassionate with yourself (and others).

- Working with the Enneagram can support you in meeting and healing the pain in your life, staying grounded and centered even when circumstances are difficult, and discerning how to most effectively focus your energy.

- Working with the Enneagram helps you develop self-knowledge as a basis for psychological and spiritual well-being.

In addition, any of the benefits discussed in chapter 2 could be used to introduce your clients to the use of the Enneagram.

UNDERSTANDING THE VALUE OF SELF-TYPING

Mostly, clients lack in-depth insight of the Enneagram when they come to coaching. Clients may want you, the professional, to tell them what their type is. This is not encouraged for several reasons:

- The actual behaviors of different types can look similar and thus be difficult to determine. What distinguishes one type from another are the underlying motivations. So, while it is useful for the coach to be able to suspect what a client's type is, it is somewhat presumptuous to claim certainty.

- The Enneagram is a dynamic system. While the vast majority of people have a predominant home type, people can shuttle to the behaviors of other types under certain circumstances. For example, if a client comes to you after having been highly stressed for an extended period of time, they may actually rely on the behaviors of another type. Under those circumstances, the coach would likely mistype the client.

- Even professionals with extensive Enneagram experience have been known to mistype their students or clients, sometimes with negative impact on the individual. Only the client can truly know their own type.

- Typing another person short-circuits the learning process and often backfires, creating defensiveness.

The power of the Enneagram is activated when people are able to identify their own type. The process of recognizing their own patterns and gifts helps clients come to terms with their life script and creates ownership of the transformative process.

STRATEGIES AND STEPS FOR SELF-TYPING

You and your clients can use a number of approaches in discovering their core Enneagram type.

Reading

– Read descriptions of each of the types in section 2 of this book.

– Read expanded descriptions of types in my companion book *Deep Living with the Enneagram: Recovering Your True Nature* or other sources listed in the For Further Reading section.

– Read online descriptions of types at www.enneagraminstitute.com. This website has extensive descriptions of each of the types.

Reading can be used as part of the client's action plan between sessions, and they can bring insights into subsequent sessions for exploration.

Typing Interviews

Participating in a typing interview with a qualified teacher or coach is a powerful approach to discerning what type a client most resonates with.

The Enneagram Interview Process (EIP) is included in appendix B with the creators' permission.[1] It includes descriptions of each type that you can read to the client, along with key themes to help in the discernment process.

Panels

A number of teachers, especially those trained in the Narrative Tradition, offer what are called type panels. These panels bring several people who share the same core type together to discuss specific characteristics that helped them to recognize their type and share some of their reactions or responses to various situations. It can be very helpful to hear how the experiences of others align with your own experience.

Panels are also included in some Enneagram educational programs offered by other teachers.

Online Assessments

Several online tools can help users identify their top Enneagram core types. Two of the most scientifically validated are the RHETI, available through www.enneagraminstitute.com, and the IEQ9, available through www.integrative9.com.

Note of caution: It's natural to take the results of assessments, even highly validated measures, as the final answer when trying to find one's place on the Enneagram map. However, it is wise to consider online assessments as a starting point. Rather than solely relying on assessment results, clients should continue the exploration through additional processes listed here.

Landing on their actual core type can take considerable time for some people. If that is true for any of your clients, you can affirm that the adventure of discovering more about themselves is a significant aspect of self-typing. It cannot be rushed.

A key indicator that the discovery process has found gold is the experience of having one's hidden inner world described in considerable detail. A typical response to that discovery is, "I thought that was just me."

THE PATTERNS OF MOVEMENT TO OTHER TYPES: ARROWS OR ACCESS LINES

As discussed in chapter 3 on constriction and expansion, most people will vary in their degree of presence, perhaps several times in one day. That means that the person may be more reactive when less present and more open and effective when more present. As coaches, we will likely see this vertical movement with our clients, as well as in ourselves.

Beyond the vertical shifts within the dominant personality type, each Enneagram type has patterns of movement that incorporate the patterns, challenges, and gifts of two other specific types. These movements are shown by the inner lines that connect the points around the Enneagram. (See figure 5.1.) They are generally referred to as arrows or lines of access, indicating that the person has a direct line to these types.

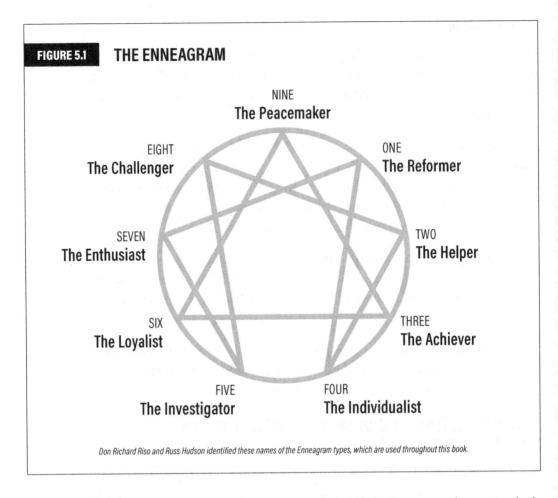

FIGURE 5.1 **THE ENNEAGRAM**

NINE
The Peacemaker

EIGHT
The Challenger

ONE
The Reformer

SEVEN
The Enthusiast

TWO
The Helper

SIX
The Loyalist

THREE
The Achiever

FIVE
The Investigator

FOUR
The Individualist

Don Richard Riso and Russ Hudson identified these names of the Enneagram types, which are used throughout this book.

These lines reveal the dynamic nature of the personality and the Enneagram's amazing brilliance in capturing predictable movement that people will experience, along with the possibility for profound transformation. Coaches can use their awareness of these dynamics as a context for increased understanding of the client to support the typing process, to coach more powerfully toward positive outcomes, and ultimately, to help increase the value given to the client.

≋ Coaching Cue:

We meet each client where they are. Period. The insights provided by the Enneagram help us recognize patterns, possible motivating factors, the movement to access points, and the more elevated nature of the person, but those insights do not override being present to our client. Eventually the Enneagram acts as an inner resource you can call upon.

You will see that Types Three, Six, and Nine are connected by an inner triangle. A person who identifies with the Type Three personality, for example, sometimes will experience the inner states and demonstrate the outer behaviors associated with Types Six and Nine. You will also note that Types One, Four, Two, Eight, Five, Seven, and returning to One are connected by an inner set of lines. As with the types on the triangle, specific circumstances will lead a person identified with a Type One personality, for example, to experience the inner states and demonstrate some of the outer behaviors associated with Types Four and Seven.

See table 5.1 for a quick reference on the movement that people will experience between types. When reading the chart, start with column 2, which states the core type. From there, you can quickly see what other types the person will most likely experience. (For a more in-depth look at lines of access, see appendix C.)

The combination of the core type's characteristic patterns, combined with the characteristics of both points connected by lines of access, are part of a person's personality configuration. The points in both directions not only reflect a natural movement but are needed for growth and the realization of wholeness.

TABLE 5.1	**IDENTIFICATION OF TYPES ASSOCIATED WITH THE LINES OF ACCESS FOR CORE ENNEAGRAM TYPES**	
Access Line *(The Stress Point)*	Core Type	Access Line *(The Integration Point)*
FOUR	ONE | The Reformer	SEVEN
EIGHT	TWO | The Helper	FOUR
NINE	THREE | The Achiever	SIX
TWO	FOUR | The Individualist	ONE
SEVEN	FIVE | The Investigator	EIGHT
THREE	SIX | The Loyalist	NINE
ONE	SEVEN | The Enthusiast	FIVE
FIVE	EIGHT | The Challenger	TWO
SIX	NINE | The Peacemaker	THREE

ACCESS LINE: Stress Point

Sometimes when people see the word "stress," they automatically think that this is something bad and to be avoided. This thought is associated with distress in which the demands seem to surpass the level of one's resources. Eustress is the positive version of stress that accompanies new opportunities, challenges, and growth points. It, too, can create an inner strain.

In other words, stress IS a part of life—especially whenever one feels overly stretched. A relief valve is sometimes needed to provide additional resources, information, balance, or stability. What has been traditionally called the "stress point" serves that function.

In the past, this point has been misinterpreted to indicate that the person is losing presence or spiraling downward. This inaccuracy has again led to the thinking that experiencing this point is a negative experience. Consider the following.

Clients sometimes come to us when they have been living in a period of considerable distress, and their behaviors may present themselves in the direction of the stress point. With awareness, this direction can be recognized as providing a place of information and balance. I will use myself as an example. As someone who identifies with Type Nine, here are just three of many ways that I have experienced the underlying emotions and behaviors of the Six as messages:

- I get caught up in the mental activity of worry (with the Nine's rumination) that generally saps my energy and leads to anxiety. When I'm aware of this happening, it helps me to stop, take some breaths, and return to my belly, where I feel more balanced. From a more grounded state, I can assess if the act of worrying is useful and determine if action on my part is needed.

- In my Nineness, I notice that I'm tending toward behaving in solo mode over an extended period of time and not reaching out to either provide or accept support. This awareness allows me to pause, check within, and assess what sources of support are available to me or what opportunities for engagement and contribution are available. At Point Six, I'm more engaged and experience being part of a community.

- When I get scared, I can breathe and call upon the quality of courage that is such a powerful quality at Point Six. This process helps me become more aligned in body, heart, and mind.

≋ Coaching Cue:

You can help bring awareness to this direction (point) by asking the client to contact the behavior or emotions and by asking what message this experience might carry. You can also inquire about how this experience is supporting your client.

ACCESS LINE: Integration Point

The direction or access line to the integration point also carries necessary growth experiences. It has been misinterpreted as only moving toward a higher state of oneself. One might look at the gifts and highest levels of this point and want to jump into them immediately.

In psychological terms, integration means to fully accept and embrace those parts of oneself, both those seen as positive and those interpreted as negative, that have been hidden from consciousness, that is, in the territory of the shadow. So this point includes both the qualities and behaviors of what might be considered highly desirable and those that we reject.

In fact, many of those behaviors and attitudes that we most want to deny in ourselves are located in the average levels of health of this point, which I call the hidden dimension of self. A cue that this hidden dimension exists within is when we are triggered by the less-conscious behavior exhibited by a person whose core type is our integration point. A typical response to that person might be, "I would NEVER act like that!"

These qualities, attitudes, and behaviors must be addressed, acknowledged, and compassionately owned in order for the person to have a sustained experience of the higher levels of the type. This is tender territory. Allowing ourselves to embrace both the rejected side and brilliant gifts of our integration point leads to a sense of emotional maturity and wholeness.

The discussion of each type in section 2 will include brief indicators of this point.

Keep in mind the access line/integrating point for your clients. Ask questions that reflect the embodiment of the qualities of this type. Below are examples of integrating-oriented questions.

| TABLE 5.2 | EXAMPLES OF QUESTIONS REFLECTING FOCUS ON INTEGRATION ACCESS POINT |

Core Type	Question Reflecting Movement toward Integrating Type
ONE	What brings you joy? *(toward Type Seven)*
TWO	How are you expressing your own creativity? *(toward Type Four)*
THREE	How could you contribute as a member to support this group in realizing its goals? *(toward Type Six)*
FOUR	What specific steps can you take to contribute to this cause that is important to you? *(toward Type One)*
FIVE	What conscious action steps could you take to make a significant difference in the outcome of this project? *(toward Type Eight)*
SIX	What happens when you drop down into and experience your body? *(toward Type Nine)*
SEVEN	What helps you stay deeply engaged in a priority project and take it to its highest level of development? *(toward Type Five)*
EIGHT	How could you tell your children what they mean to you? *(toward Type Two)*
NINE	What will it take on your part to achieve this important outcome? *(toward Type Three)*

Illuminating Nine Paths of Coaching through the Enneagram

Chapter 6

UNDERSTANDING THE HUMAN CONDITION:
The Architecture and Dynamics
of the Personality

Section 2 of this book focuses on the descriptions and characteristics of each of the nine Enneagram types. This material can be used to:

– Learn basic information about each of the nine variations of the human condition

– Develop rapport with the client more quickly, even if the client does not undertake the self-typing process, by understanding the different world-views of the nine types

– Guide clients through the self-typing process as an important step in advancing their self-understanding

– Help clients use the Enneagram to gain clarity on their experiences and to have access to more real choice

– Discover the unique gifts and expansive qualities of clients

– Learn how understanding the personality structure can support you as a human development professional in best serving your clients

As noted previously, the environment in which you work, the reasons that clients seek you out, and your own experience and preferences will determine how you use this deep coaching material.

It is vital to understand that excavating the personality structure is not in service of making the personality "bad" or "wrong." The personality exists and will until our final breath. It is a necessary dimension of the human experience living on this earth, and we can celebrate its gifts. But we and our clients can change our relationship to the personality, putting it in its proper place.

By understanding the architecture and dynamics of the personality, we can create avenues for awareness, build the capacity for compassion for self and others, support our clients' wholeness, and assist clients in being more deeply connected to their truer nature, more present to objective reality and to the realization that they are not alone but are inherently connected with all of life.

WE AND OUR CLIENTS CAN CHANGE OUR RELATIONSHIP TO THE PERSONALITY, PUTTING IT IN ITS PROPER PLACE.

We also remember that while our core Enneagram type has far-reaching impact on our interpretations of all of life, each of us has been affected by our own life circumstances: early parenting, the environment and access to positive role models, the quality of education and other resources available in our childhood and youth, and the social or cultural dynamics that supported or hindered our development. Thus, when we say yes to working with a client, we are saying yes to acknowledging the whole person, not merely a type.

THE ICEBERG MODEL: THE ARCHITECTURE OF THE PERSONALITY

We have come to see the personality as an interrelated configuration of elements that together form a cohesive framework. Each element of the personality complex reinforces and builds on the others. When the complex is allowed to operate within itself, it exists as a closed or uninterrupted system.

Carl Jung provides insight on the use of the iceberg visual as a metaphor for the human experience.[1] What is visible above the water are those aspects of ourselves that are available to the conscious. And the part of us above the waterline is what others see in us. But the vast majority of an iceberg lies below the waterline. So it is with the human personality.

Thus, in 2003, colleague Wendy Appel and I created the original version of the Enneagram iceberg model to help make sense of the different elements that make up the architecture of the personality's structure.[2] What lies above is what is visible, such as behaviors and the energetic style of the person; what lies below are the elements that shape and inform the personality. To create sustainable shifts with our clients, we must work above and below the waterline.

FOR COACHES TO CREATE SUSTAINABLE SHIFTS, THEY MUST WORK ABOVE AND BELOW THE WATERLINE.

The iceberg model included in this second edition is a result of several revisions and additions that have been made over the years as the deep coaching work has evolved. Keep in mind that the descriptions of the Enneagram nine types focus on various levels of the personality. These descriptions represent the internal perspectives and subsequent outer expressions of people with the particular core type under consideration. While external variations in human expression can be easier to identify, it is the internal world that can be challenging for the individual to recognize, and that is central to the functioning of that personality.

You will find more detailed descriptions for each personality type in *Deep Living with the Enneagram: Recovering Your True Nature*. This section of *Deep Coaching* offers a solid introduction to the nine Enneagram types, with emphasis on how understanding the nine variations of the human condition and the relaxing of personality patterns will affect the coaching and facilitation process. Many coaching cues are included.

As a reminder, the coaching cues included in sections 1 and 3 are mostly appropriate for coaching clients across the nine types.

The Iceberg Model Explained

A visual template of the iceberg model is shown in figure 6.1. Here you will see a depiction of an iceberg, with descriptors located above and motivators located below the wavy waterline. Refer to the visual as you read the description of each of the sections of the model. This generic framework will be used to present the specific information on each of the nine personality types addressed in chapters 7, 8, and 9.

Note: The coaching cues that are included in this chapter are not reiterated in the descriptions of each type in chapters 7, 8, and 9. I recommend that you return to this chapter to review descriptions of each of the personality elements and refresh your recollection of the coaching cues as you work with your clients.

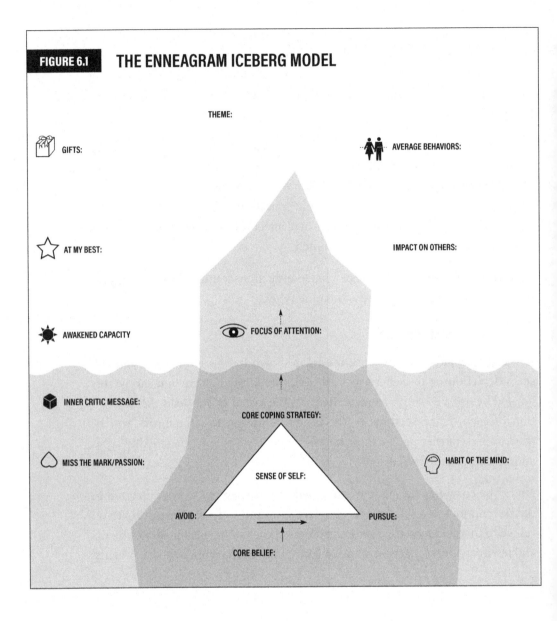

FIGURE 6.1 THE ENNEAGRAM ICEBERG MODEL

THEME:

GIFTS:

AVERAGE BEHAVIORS:

AT MY BEST:

IMPACT ON OTHERS:

AWAKENED CAPACITY

FOCUS OF ATTENTION:

INNER CRITIC MESSAGE:

CORE COPING STRATEGY:

MISS THE MARK/PASSION:

HABIT OF THE MIND:

SENSE OF SELF:

AVOID:

PURSUE:

CORE BELIEF:

THEME

This is a descriptive thread that helps to capture the personality of a particular type. The theme is a metaphor for the type.

ABOVE THE WATERLINE

 When I'm Expansive and at My Healthiest Levels (Gifts and At My Best)

This section includes behavioral and attitudinal descriptors that characterize an individual who has a higher degree of presence and functions at a healthy level of the particular type. Refer to table 3.1 to review the short list of descriptors of the healthy levels.

As a coach, keep in your mind and heart the awakened nature, healthiest qualities, behaviors, and attitudes of a person who identifies with a specific type. This information will help you hold the client's magnificence, even when the client is not expressing these qualities. This expands your capacity for holding a vision of what is possible for your client at the client's healthiest level. You can also share this information with the client at an appropriate time to provide feedback and recognition of the gifts that are available from within. Being aware of the highest qualities of a client's type helps you coach a client to their aspirations and inherent strengths.

☀ Awakened Capacity

Each person has a particular awakened heart capacity based on their core type. This capacity is freed to be expressed as a person heals and relaxes protective layers of their heart. The quality of this capacity is beyond the ego's control and cannot be made to happen—it can only be experienced in the depth of presence. The heart's natural expansiveness is experienced, resonating with deeper aspects of oneself.

Coaching Cue:

With clients who are consistently this present, you are more likely to experience their:

- *Vulnerability, transparency, and curiosity around their explorations*

- *Capacity to recognize an expanded perspective and display a sense of cosmic humor*

- *Delight in the ease with which life is flowing*

- *Willingness to explore a topic that has previously been kept at bay*

It is a rare privilege to witness clients at this level of health. If they seek coaching at all, these clients will be attracted to coaches who actively practice presence.

You also may notice that some clients will pop into an in-the-moment experience of this greater degree of presence, even though that is not their usual state of consciousness.

Distinguishing Characteristics When the Personality Has Its Grip on Me

There is tremendous variation within the expression of the type depending upon one's degree of attachment to the personality structure. This section describes a person living in the average levels of health in the type. We remember that the personality is more pronounced as a way to cope with inner discomfort and external difficulties. (Refer to table 3.1 for review of the average levels of health across types.)

Where I Put My Attention When Identified with the Personality (Focus of Attention)

Energy follows attention. This section indicates where people put their attention. We can consider this as a point from which behavioral, emotional, and attitudinal patterns emerge.

For example, imagine that Type One is your core type. The focus of attention is on doing good and being right. If you have a Type One personality, or at least an active Type One dynamic in your life, you will probably recognize this focus of attention quite easily. If not, it may be more challenging to have an inner experience of how this narrowing of attention plays out in daily life. It entails monitoring verbal and written communications to make sure you are in alignment with what is good and right, as well as scanning for cues from the environment to determine if you need to make a change or fix something. It may mean always being on the alert, ready to defend what you are doing, or offering rationales for your behavior. Being criticized for not doing things right can feel like a major threat to your sense of self, and thus, well-being.

The arrows pointing toward the tip of the iceberg indicate a core cognitive-emotional dynamic of the types.

Impact on Others (+ Positive and – Negative)

Our behaviors, attitudes, and general energetic orientation have consequences in relationships with others. This section briefly distinguishes between the positive impact a person has when functioning at higher levels of effectiveness and presence, and the negative impact, which is typically related to less healthy levels of effectiveness and presence. When we operate from less healthy levels of awareness and presence, we typically are unaware of our impact on others and are surprised to learn that our impact does not reflect our intention.

Although most clients want to have a positive impact, they typically overestimate or underestimate their impact on others, especially in the beginning stages of coaching. Clients can gain perspective and distance from their internal story by taking an honest, objective look at their impact on others. Each Enneagram type has a particular impact on others, which can either be positive or negative.

≋ **Coaching Cue:**

The discernment between intention and actual behavior and its impact is often an important topic in coaching. At the core of this strategy is guiding clients to practice stepping into the perspectives of others and gaining an awareness that their own actions, words, attitudes, and energy do make a difference.

BELOW THE WATERLINE

The Ego Code's Inner Logic

Here we meet the mechanisms of the personality structure that work to create an internal coherency within the human experience. The dynamics of the personality structure are vital to understand because it helps us recognize why our clients (and I include all of us, too) often experience the insistent pull of our habitual patterns. These dynamics are powerful because each contributes to an inner logic that reinforces the ego's internal coherence that feels completely right to the person. The inner logic provides a code to keep the person from straying from this coherency and breaking its rules. That is why I initially introduced the term "ego code's inner logic" in the second edition of *Deep Living*.[3] Each type has its own version of this logic.

The ego code is based on and reinforces a core belief that we are separate from the creative source, the divine, the absolute, from life itself. (Note: use whatever language is relevant to you or your client). In chapter 2, the impact of the unexamined core belief is discussed (refer to "The Personality as an Energetic System: "I Believe""). Each Enneagram type comes equipped with a particular core belief. That core belief leads the person to want certain experiences repeated over and over that are unconsciously expected to bring happiness and fulfillment, such as safety, control, or a particular self-image. This supposedly satisfying experience is what the person pursues and will go to great lengths to create.

What a person pursues is one of the personality's driving mechanisms found in what I call the Triangle of Identity. The Triangle of Identity, directly connected to a person's core belief, also includes the avoidance of specific experiences ("what I avoid" on the iceberg model), the primary coping strategy, and the sense of self—all default mechanisms that reinforce a person's sense of separateness. The Triangle of Identity provides a shorthand visual of the ego code's inner logic for each Enneagram type.

The ego code's inner logic—which starts with the core belief—is how we do life and becomes the basis for our small self stories and interpretations of events. It is another reflection of the closed system of the unexamined personality. No wonder clients may question if sustained positive change is really possible.

〰 Coaching Cue:

"How we do life" is embedded in every part of the human experience, including in neurological pathways, in the body's constrictions and posture, in the emotional patterns that hold inner tension, in our mental and emotion-based stories. As coaches, we do not set out to fix how a client does life because there's nothing to fix—and it's not under our control as coaches. What we can offer is an environment of nonjudgment, curiosity, skillful inquiry, reflection, kindness, and spaciousness to allow the client's deeper sources of guidance to become engaged.

The power of the personality requires us to practice presence and support our clients in developing an ever-deepening sense of presence, because it, too, is powerful.

Section 3 of this book will focus more on building capacity for presence.

Note: this section starts at the bottom of the iceberg graphic and works up.

Core Belief

Each type carries with it a core belief about itself in relationship to others and to life. It is based on a deeply held sense of separation.

This core belief was most likely formed in the earliest stages of childhood and reinforced during our development. It is precognitive and exists at an unconscious level. Pervading the person's sense of what is obvious and true, it is a cornerstone of the ego identity and seems to be beyond questioning. (Recall the role of belief in creating obstructions as discussed in "The Personality as an Energetic System" in chapter 2.)

When we listen carefully to a client, we can hear reflections of this core belief in the client's decisions and reasons for the choices they made. For each of the types, a few examples will be provided of what the client may say and do or not do.

Triangle of Identity

The Triangle of Identity is a key feature of the personality structure for coaches because it highlights a source of repeating patterns, internal struggle, procrastination, limiting beliefs, and strategies.

The triangle highlights the particular way the inner struggle shows up for the client. The uninterrupted cycle of pursuing a particular experience that is believed to bring one happiness, combined with avoiding a particular experience (which is often nearly opposite of what is pursued), is reflected in the person's primary default coping strategy. These contribute to the sense of identity, which limits the person's perceptions of options. The Triangle of Identity captures the conscious or unconscious belief that "this is the way life is," and how, when uninterrupted, real choice seems elusive, at best, or even nonexistent.

Appendix E provides a reference chart highlighting the Triangle of Identity for each of the nine types.

What I Pursue

Look on the lower right corner of the Triangle of Identity. The ego structure is designed to pursue what it assumes will bring the client the greatest satisfaction. The ego tries to recapture a deeper quality (essential nature) that was lost in earlier years but is no longer in the person's conscious awareness. The ego can never satisfy what it is trying to achieve, but since it doesn't know that, it can go to greater and greater lengths to try to recreate that quality. The best it can do is replicate what is truly desired by using the ego's unsatisfactory version of that state. Failing to achieve lasting satisfaction, the ego tries harder and harder, only to create more dissatisfaction and pain for the individual.[4]

≋ Coaching Cue:

Most likely, this form of seeking will show up clearly in a coaching relationship over time. You may notice that the client repeats the same underlying pattern, though it may occur in very different circumstances. Be aware that clients often want to magnify this inclination as an initial coaching goal.

What I Avoid

This is depicted in the lower left corner of the triangle. Each specific Enneagram personality type reveals what the person will try to avoid at all costs. This experience is diametrically opposite of what the ego is pursuing. To move in the direction of avoidance makes no sense to the ego and, in fact, can feel terrifying. Clients may carry long-held stories that have convinced them that going into this territory will result in disaster. In truth, what is avoided is of central importance to the client's sense of wholeness.[5]

≋ Coaching Cue:

You will likely notice a specific area of avoidance, as it may be skirted in coaching sessions. As clients become aware of this avoidance, some may want to prove to themselves or even to you that they have no fear and want to jump headfirst into big action steps toward what they would typically avoid. For most clients, even acknowledging this area requires smaller steps. Your careful discernment will be important in assessing when (or if) your client is ready to inquire into how this area of avoidance is affecting them.

My Core Coping Strategy

Each Enneagram type is a specialist in certain behavioral and attitudinal strategies. These coping strategies, depicted at the top of the triangle, keep the personality intact and congruent. They are a practical interpretation of what is avoided and what is pursued by the personality and appear to be exactly what is needed. However, the coping strategies primarily operate on automatic whether or not they are effective and appropriate for the situation. These default strategies typically orient the person toward constriction, away from what would lead them to a higher level of health and flexibility.

Sense of Self ("I Am...")

Each type is particularly invested in a way of seeing itself, leaving little room for us to see ourselves as we actually are. Most of us have a distorted and either overinflated or overdeflated view of ourselves that probably does not match what is real. These fixed ideas are reaffirmed by the narrowing of our focus and collecting data that supports our self-view. Experiences that would provide contradictory data are easy to dismiss. The particular sense of self that is included here is based on the Riso-Hudson description of each type at a high level of health. In other words, many people see themselves at a high level of health for their own type whether or not they are actually operating at that level of health.

Paradoxically, what the ego is set up to pursue and avoid—which is reflected in the core coping strategy and sense of self associated with the type—is what leads to increased suffering, dissatisfaction, unrest, and inner and outer struggle.

≋ Coaching Cue:

How might you address the Triangle of Identity when you notice reflections of it during your work with clients? First, this is tender territory. For some clients, "what I pursue" and "what I avoid" may seem to be beyond questioning, and if so, we respect that.

If and when it is appropriate, you can share the Triangle of Identity symbol, inquiring with the client about how it relates to their experience. This exploration requires a capacity for self-observation, along with an attitude of curiosity and nonjudgment. For example, you could ask: "How has this inner logic served you in the past? How has it limited your sense of real choice?" or "Might it relate to your current dissatisfaction?" Working with the Triangle of Identity often provides an accessible entry point for your client's developing awareness and naturally leads to a deeper exploration.

Having this awareness brought to the surface can be challenging. Recognizing that how we have approached our lives has been based on some faulty premises, ideas, and interpretations is likely to bring forth a range of emotions, including astonishment, anger, shame, grief, or relief. It is important that coaches who are working at this level have engaged personally with this material and have the capacity to be with their clients with tenderness, compassion, and strong support.

 ## Fixation of the Personality (Habit of the Mind)

Each type has a particular habitual pattern of the mind that is called the fixation of the type. This mental habit is the ego's automatic, limited, unquestioned way of interpreting one's life and solving the problems that come with living. This pattern, developed in early childhood to compensate for the loss of connection with one's true essence, permeates the whole personality. But relying on this particular habit of the mind to deal with life limits people from growing. Recognizing how pervasive the fixation is and how it shows up in one's life is important in transformational work.

 ## Where I Miss the Mark (Passion)

This powerful element of the personality structure creates an obstacle to one's connection to the heart's depths and to the sense of wholeness and fulfillment. In Enneagram language, this is called the passion of the type. In lay language, "where I miss the mark" refers to a habitual driving and reactive emotional pattern that plays a significant role in self-identity. It has an energy that moves a person in the opposite direction from their more expansive and openhearted nature. As an innate element of the internal type structure, it acts like psychic wallpaper and feels like the truth. Thus, it cannot be easily seen from the inside. Naming the passion often feels very personal, and perhaps, somewhat intrusive.

Upon learning about this personality element, sometimes people remark that they've been found out.

One way of understanding this element is that it covers up a wound deep within one's heart, resulting in layers of protection.[6]

≋ Coaching Cue:

As with each of the other personality elements discussed, you can engage in compassionate and curious inquiry with your client with both the passion and the fixation. We are in tender territory. Ask questions such as: Do you recognize anything about this experience in your own life? What is happening for you as we explore this? What sensations are you experiencing? Additional inquiry could address the impact of this element on the quality of the client's experience. There is nothing to fix. Being present with this inquiry is essential and often healing. We are simply inviting the client to become more conscious and perhaps less constrained about these various elements in their life over time.

What the Inner Critic Insists Upon

The inner critic, or the superego, is the function of the personality that has internalized the voices of authority—the rules, standards, and dictates—from childhood. Riso and Hudson identified a specific rule associated with each Enneagram type that is included in the type descriptions in chapters 7, 8, and 9.[7]

Note that the inner critic symbol is located just under the waterline. It is a potent force in keeping the rest of the personality in check. When we are in its grip, the inner critic tells us what we can and cannot do, feel, experience or express, and can give harsh feedback if its dictates are not followed.

Note: the remaining sections are listed as additional information and are not referred to on the iceberg model.

What Causes Me Stress

Each type experiences particular sources of stress that can be nonissues for people who are of a different Enneagram type. Thus, it is often when the individual's personality is more activated that particular events or situations are perceived as threatening. The source of stress is seen as the cause for discomfort and ignites a predictable reaction. When the personality relaxes, the particular source of stress (unless it is an objectively dangerous or life-threatening situation) is seen in more neutral terms.

When I'm Most Constricted and Inflexible

These behavioral, emotional, and mental patterns are evident when the person is controlled by the closed personality system and believes there are no options.

Most people experience times when they drop into these unhealthy patterns. If a client is unwilling or unable at this time to develop new insights and awareness, therapy is more appropriate than coaching.

Lines of Access

Remember that the Enneagram is a dynamic system. Each type description includes reference to two other Enneagram types that share an internal line with the core type. See chapter 5 on arrows or access lines for further explanation. Brief characteristics of the two types are included in this section. They may help clients in self-typing.

Additional Notes

– There are additional descriptors and elements of the architecture of the personality that are not included in this description.

– As complex, dynamic human beings, we all have access to the strengths, challenges, and internal dynamics of every type.

– It's important to note that the descriptions of the types need to be read or presented with sensitivity and self-care. To see for the first time the nature of one's inner psychological structure can be quite unsettling. It is not unusual to feel that one's conscious or unconscious secrets have been exposed and feel some embarrassment.

– It bears repeating that we are not making the personality "wrong." Learning about the personality structure allows us to develop a healthier relationship to it so that we have a personality rather than we are a personality. The implications of this shift are enormous.

THE SOCIAL STYLE GROUPINGS

One way to get a handle on the nine wildly different Enneagram types is to cluster them into groups of three. While there are several approaches to clustering the types, the following is a way I have found to be useful in the typing process. Karen Horney was a psychotherapist who studied the strategies people use to get what they want and to manage the stress or anxiety triggered by the demands of interpersonal relationships. Horney noted that these strategies are developed in childhood and can continue to be used unconsciously through adulthood to help people deal with this interpersonal discomfort and create a stronger sense of safety.

Exercise

Take a moment to consider this scenario:

You are about to walk into a professional meeting comprised of some people who are acquaintances and others you do not know at all.

What do you notice about your body's responses? What are your thoughts? What is your emotional state?

What do you notice about your behavior? How much does your outer behavior reflect your inner experience?

For example, do you feel a sense of discomfort but mask that with friendly chatter? Do you quietly say hello and look for a place to sit? Do you confidently approach the facilitator of the group and introduce yourself? Do you look toward the floor and go immediately to your seat?

Your honest reflection about this scenario may give you a window into your customary approach to dealing with the stress of interpersonal relationships.

If you pay close attention, you may notice that you have a heightened level of stress or anxiety. This is not uncommon. Settings that involve interpersonal communication often are accompanied by some underlying, if hidden, discomfort.

Thank you to Wendy Appel, MA, and Pam Fox, MBA, for their early collaboration on this exercise.

Riso and Hudson recognized the connection of Horney's work to the Enneagram and identified three Enneagram types that corresponded to each of Horney's interpersonal coping solutions.[8]

- Horney's resigned solution in which the individual moves away from or withdraws from others: Riso and Hudson identified Enneagram Types Nine, Four, and Five as withdrawn types corresponding to this solution. They rely on private, introspective strategies. See chapter 7 for an expanded description of this social style and the three Enneagram types most closely associated with this style, along with coaching implications.

- Horney's expansive or aggressive solution in which the individual moves against others. Riso and Hudson identified Enneagram Types Three, Seven, and Eight as assertive types corresponding to this solution. They rely on assured, confident strategies. See chapter 8 for an expanded description of this social style and the three Enneagram types most closely associated with this style, along with coaching implications.

- Horney's compliant solution in which the individual moves toward others: Riso and Hudson identified Enneagram Types One, Two, and Six as dutiful types corresponding to this solution. They rely on service-oriented, responsible strategies. See chapter 9 for an expanded description of this social style and the three Enneagram types most closely associated with this style, along with coaching implications.

People in the average range of their Enneagram type tend to rely on their dominant social style (interpersonal coping) strategy.

≋ Coaching Cue:

What is particularly interesting for coaches is that each of these interpersonal strategies has a particular energetic quality that may be quite obvious in some clients. The energetic quality that a client displays may provide useful information and feedback to help the client to self-type. Further, as a client becomes more attuned to the often unconscious nature of their usual interpersonal coping style, they can evaluate whether this pattern helps them achieve their desired outcomes. If the pattern isn't effective, the client can practice new choices and begin making shifts. As Horney noted, humans are naturally oriented to health and growth. Appendix D includes a somatic coaching exercise that invites clients into a direct experience of the energy associated with each strategy.

YOUR RELATIONSHIP WITH ENNEAGRAM TYPES

It's important to remember that we all exist along a continuum of constriction and expansion with a greater or lesser degree of identification with the personality. This is a reminder to meet our clients where they are with kindness and acceptance.

We all have type biases. Chapter 12 offers specific examples. For now, as you move through the following type chapters, I recommend noting what might push a button, what seems so obvious to you as a "right" way to approach your work, or what experience surprises you that it is a type pattern rather than a characteristic that defines who you are? Develop your own list of possible biases that have the potential to interfere with your ability to show up for your client's coaching experience. Please be kind to yourself as you note biases. Noticing them rather than acting on them will support your presence.

In the process of diving deeper into the core beliefs and other dynamics that shape the outer behavior, you may also experience compassion and awe over the world that clients carry within. Your heart may break open as you discover that you cannot help but love your clients for the journey they are traveling.

Chapter 7

TYPES NINE, FOUR, AND FIVE:
The Private, Introspective Group

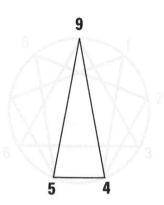

SHARED THEMES

Avoiding or withdrawing from active social, physical, emotional, spiritual, or intellectual engagement is one strategy for coping with the stress that accompanies interpersonal relationships.

At the average levels of health and effectiveness, three Enneagram types share the common personality structure of removing themselves from active engagement with external reality. Types Nine, Four, and Five each have an inner sanctuary or inner world that provides what feels like safe space in order to avoid external demands that may feel too overwhelming.

People who identify with any one of these types have their own way of disappearing. Each has difficulty staying present in their bodies and getting out of fantasy or mental abstractions and into sustained, purposeful action. They often secretly feel that they don't belong or fit in with other people. They may feel emotionally, spiritually, or mentally superior to others and simultaneously feel there is no place for them in a group. They tend to experience themselves as outside of the norm of society. Feeling left out, they lose the voting rights in their own life.

Being able to enjoy one's own company is a healthy attribute. However, when the private and introspective strategy is an automatic and habitual pattern, the result is that life is not lived in the objective, real world. Life goes on without their involvement.

Energetically, people with Type Nine, Four, and Five personalities often appear pulled back and away from the action. Their energy may sit on the sidelines, occasionally experimenting with the edges of participation, only to pull back if it feels like too much is being asked of them. Others may get a feeling of energetically being pulled into their inner world. They can convey a sense of mental or emotional vacancy or being detached from their bodies. They may be physically awkward.

Those relying on these strategies are not necessarily quiet. In their own realm of comfort, they can be expressive and talkative. However, there is some element within these individuals that can seem untouchable, unreachable.

TYPE NINE

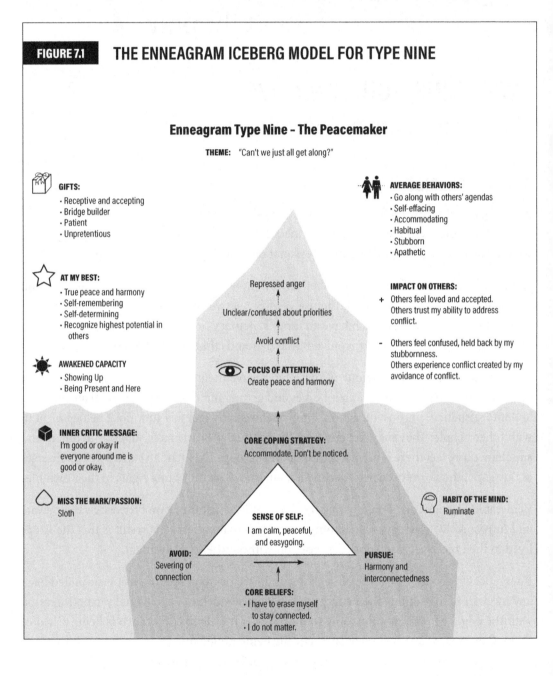

FIGURE 7.1   ## THE ENNEAGRAM ICEBERG MODEL FOR TYPE NINE

Enneagram Type Nine – The Peacemaker

THEME: "Can't we just all get along?"

GIFTS:
- Receptive and accepting
- Bridge builder
- Patient
- Unpretentious

AT MY BEST:
- True peace and harmony
- Self-remembering
- Self-determining
- Recognize highest potential in others

AWAKENED CAPACITY
- Showing Up
- Being Present and Here

INNER CRITIC MESSAGE:
I'm good or okay if everyone around me is good or okay.

MISS THE MARK/PASSION:
Sloth

AVERAGE BEHAVIORS:
- Go along with others' agendas
- Self-effacing
- Accommodating
- Habitual
- Stubborn
- Apathetic

IMPACT ON OTHERS:
+ Others feel loved and accepted.
  Others trust my ability to address conflict.

− Others feel confused, held back by my stubbornness.
  Others experience conflict created by my avoidance of conflict.

Repressed anger

Unclear/confused about priorities

Avoid conflict

FOCUS OF ATTENTION:
Create peace and harmony

CORE COPING STRATEGY:
Accommodate. Don't be noticed.

HABIT OF THE MIND:
Ruminate

SENSE OF SELF:
I am calm, peaceful, and easygoing.

AVOID:
Severing of connection

PURSUE:
Harmony and interconnectedness

CORE BELIEFS:
- I have to erase myself to stay connected.
- I do not matter.

TYPE NINE: THE PEACEMAKER
THEME: "Can't we all just get along?"

ABOVE THE WATERLINE

 ### When I'm Expansive and at My Healthiest Levels (Gifts and at My Best)

I am receptive and open to others. I am able to accept others as they are and where they are.

I am a bridge builder. I am good at listening to and understanding the differences in viewpoints and finding elements of commonality to bring people together.

I am patient. I recognize and trust the natural rhythm inherent in achieving certain outcomes and tend not to push to reach a goal before its time.

I am unpretentious. What you see is what you get. I am genuine.

I bring a sense of peace and harmony to wherever I am. Others can be at ease with me.

I am self-remembering. I consider my own priorities and include those in my day-to-day life without being overly focused on myself.

I am self-determining. I take the initiative on those actions that reflect what has the deepest meaning and purpose for me and I follow through.

I recognize the potential in others. I can see what is possible for others and see the commonalities among and between people.

 ### Awakened Capacity: Showing Up, Being Present and Here

Being in contact with the substance of my body and its dimensionality and experiencing a deep, grounded relationship to the earth provides the foundation for engaging, interacting with, and embracing life, regardless of what's going on. My heart is opened through showing up.

Distinguishing Characteristics When the Personality Has Its Grip on Me

I go along with others and their agendas so that I don't create a scene. It's just easier to do it that way.

I am self-effacing, downplaying my value and removing myself from the focus of attention.

I am accommodating to the wishes of others, thereby avoiding the potential for emotional discomfort.

My life is based on unthinking habit. I operate on autopilot, staying busy with whatever is getting my attention in the moment and often not accomplishing what is important to me.

I am stubborn. I appear to agree with others but do not follow up with action. I have a semi-sweet exterior disposition but do not allow others to get to me.

I am apathetic, indifferent, and numb. Basically, I am missing in action.

Where I Put My Attention When Identified with the Personality (Focus of Attention)

I focus on creating peace and harmony, even if only at the surface level. I look for the positives in the situation in order to downplay and ignore conflict or other difficulties. I try to make sure that everyone around me feels comfortable. I easily forget about my priorities and become confused. In this process, I repress my anger and lose touch with my energy and vitality.

Impact on Others

+ Positive

Others feel loved, accepted, valued.

Others experience the Nine's groundedness and sense of presence.

– Negative

Others feel confused and held back by the Nine's outward niceness and inner resistance/stubbornness.

Others experience a lot of conflict.

BELOW THE WATERLINE

The Ego Code's Inner Logic

Core Belief

I believe that I have to forget myself in order to stay connected to others. I believe that if I do voice my perspective, I will lose my psychic and emotional connections to other people, which feels deathly. Therefore, I need to forget myself, my agenda, and my ideas.

I believe that I'm no one special and that my presence is unimportant. Therefore, my perspective or my active engagement does not matter.

 Coaching Cue::

Examples of what you might hear your clients say or do/not do:

- *I just didn't get around to it. I forgot.*
- *It's not that important. I'm not that important.*
- *I didn't want to make a scene.*
- *My spouse wanted to do this, so I went along.*
- *I didn't want to upset or disturb anyone.*

△ Triangle of Identity

What I Pursue: Harmony, Connectedness, Comfort

I don't want to make others uncomfortable. That feels untenable to me.

I can find comfort in watching TV, procrastinating or not pursuing some activity that I would like to try, not speaking up, and all forms of numbing out (narcotization).

What I Avoid: Taking Action That I Perceive as Possibly Severing Connection or Creating Discomfort

I don't speak up and share my perspective. I avoid arguments and expressing anger. I remove myself from uncomfortable situations, such as disagreements and arguments. I believe that I'm above engaging in that kind of behavior.

My Core Coping Strategy: Accommodating Others

I withdraw, especially in meetings or in settings in which there is conflict. I am careful not to rock the boat, so I look for points of agreement. I go along with the agendas of others.

Basically, I avoid inserting myself and my energy into my life, and this reflects my feeling of being unseen. I erase myself.

Sense of Self ("I Am . . .")

I see myself as being calm, peaceful, and easygoing. I see myself as being a nice person. I want others to see me as peaceful and nice, which I feel helps me stay connected to them.

 ## Fixation of the Personality (Habit of the Mind)

Rumination is the process of soothing oneself through repetitive reviewing of an idea of thought. Ruminating leaves me feeling a blurry version of peace, as it replaces the need for acting on matters of priority.

 ## Where I Miss the Mark (Passion)

I don't fully engage in the matters that shape my life. I tend to stay on the edge of activities, groups, and events rather than getting fully involved. I live along the frame rather than being inside the picture. I take pride in being detached from situations that involve conflict and opinions. I may be very busy in relatively unimportant activities but lazy when it comes to taking a stand, making a decision, and moving into action. This passion is called sloth.

 ## What the Inner Critic Insists Upon

That other people must feel good in order for me to be okay.[1] That it is not okay for me to feel good, happy, and comfortable if others are upset, in pain, or uncomfortable. As long as I am caught in the web of my inner critic, I will try to maintain the impossible task of making things good for everyone else at the expense of my own life's priorities.

What Causes Me Stress

Conflict causes me to feel stressed. I just don't feel like I know how to handle conflict, so I want to avoid it at all costs.

Making decisions causes stress. When I don't know what I want and need to make a choice, I can see all sides of the issue. I prefer others to make the decision, though I'm not often happy with their decision.

When I'm Most Constricted and Inflexible

I tune out and deny anything that might cause discomfort.

I become immovable. I will not budge.

I am confused and disoriented.

I feel powerless and unimportant.

I disappear.

Lines of Access

Type Nine shares a line with both Types Six and Three. Below are just a few ways that the characteristics of either of these types might show up or the reactions I might have to these characteristics in others. Refer to the discussion of these two types for further insight.

At Type Six: I can become anxious and worried. A gift from the Six is moving into action, which brings alertness to the Nine's vague, foggy mind.

At Type Three: It's really hard to admit, but I want to be seen. I can be jealous and critical of the successes of those whose core type is Three. I deny my narcissism. With awareness and presence, I begin to recognize my self-worth.

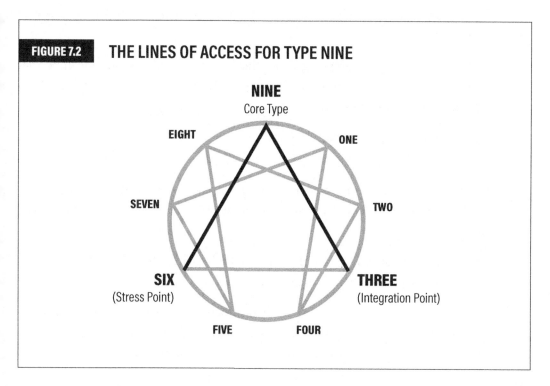

FIGURE 7.2   **THE LINES OF ACCESS FOR TYPE NINE**

Type Nine Case Study

Robert came to coaching providing the following information about himself:

I am recently married and am bored with my work. I struggle with the lack of meaning with my current job and want to find something that will fulfill me. I feel like I have something to offer strategically in the right work setting. I need a good income and a good benefit structure. I feel somewhat paralyzed and just have no idea how to move forward. Besides, change is really difficult for me. It requires energy that I'm not sure I have.

I also have had a strong relationship to God but seem to have lost that.

Robert was a bright, young man who came to coaching with considerable self-awareness and a strong spiritual yearning. He appeared quite laid-back, belying the position of authority he already held in his company.

His intentions for coaching included:

- Discovering his heart's work

- Developing a five- to ten-year plan

- Creating more of a presence of the spiritual in his daily life

- Discovering God's purpose for him

As Robert explored his Type Nine personality, he reported recognizing the following longtime patterns:

- I realize that I constantly go along with others in an effort to accommodate to their interests, viewpoints, and needs. I want others to be okay, so my tendency is to shrink back and disappear in public settings.

- I didn't realize how much I avoid conflict. That shows up in my family relationships, my marriage, and my work.

- I question if I have anything to offer as, more often than not, I just feel overwhelmed. I can cover it up at work, but I've seen myself as not being anyone special and being a fake.

- I tend to think about things a lot. I tend to not take action, at least on the important things. Yet I'm always so busy doing something.

One major theme of Robert's coaching fieldwork focused on gaining connection to his body. He found that he barely recognized any sensations at all, and that walking or moving in any way with a felt sense of being in his body was absolutely foreign. With committed practice, he started developing a whole new relationship to his body, which gave him ground to stand on.

While in coaching, Robert was offered several new opportunities, requiring him to reflect on what his priorities and areas of greatest interest were. As he gained clarity on what his preferred work option was, for the first time he engaged in negotiations around the financial structure and responsibilities of the position, rather than simply going along with what was initially offered.

With a stronger relationship to his body, he also reconnected with his spirituality. Again, rather than waiting for the perfect time to be spiritual, he integrated his practices into his current experience.

Robert's goal of a five- to ten-year plan no longer seemed useful. Although he had an eye toward the future, he began living with more of his values and priorities in place. Today.

SUGGESTIONS FOR COACHES WORKING WITH INDIVIDUALS WHO IDENTIFY WITH TYPE NINE

Acknowledge Their Inner Experience

I believe and subsequently rationalize that I don't count, that it doesn't matter whether or not I show up. My presence doesn't matter.

I can look very busy, giving a lot of attention to many different tasks. This keeps me from focusing on what is personally important. I am not fully engaged, or I disappear altogether from situations that may entail serious conversation, decision-making, and action. I may see myself as living along the frame rather than being inside the picture. I may secretly take pride in feeling superior to those who are involved in merely human endeavors.

I forget what I commit myself to. I just don't remember to remember.

Offer Counterintuitive Questions/Comments

What is important to you? What is your most important priority? Why is this important to you? How does it reflect your purpose or values?

Check in with your heart. Is your heart in this?

What will it take on your part to achieve this important outcome?

What is the next best step to take? What does this step specifically look like? When will you take this step?

What will you complete today?

What do you risk by not being focused on your priorities? Is there something you are protecting?
    Co-create structures with these clients to help them remember and stay focused on completing what is important to them.

Your presence matters. You are important to this (family, company, meeting).

What would you do differently if you recognized that your presence is important?

Let's identify the ways that your presence matters now.
    Consider the various environments and settings in which the client is involved.

What are you experiencing in your body right now?
    Support them in becoming more familiar with being in their body.

What makes you angry? How do you express your anger so that you are heard? Practice saying what you want, even if a significant other wants something else.
    Encourage them to voice ideas and feelings that are different from what others express and to recognize that conflict is part of being alive.

Invite into awareness how choices are made.

Issues That May Arise in the Coaching Relationship

- Remember that clients who identify with Type Nine tend toward wanting to keep the waters smooth. They may agree to fieldwork that they do not really want to do, or they may follow through on certain tasks not because it's their priority but because they perceive it as being important to the coach. Be curious about the motivation underlying decisions: "Who are you doing this for?"

- The average Type Nine communication style tends to be slow, indecisive, vague, and filled with long pauses. Ask the client to become more specific and detailed in their thinking and decision-making.

- Invite these clients to experience sensations in their bodies and come back to their breathing. This may be helpful in creating clarity. It also may create discomfort for the client. Be respectful, encouraging, and consistent.

OBSERVATIONS AND WORKING WITH YOUR PREDOMINANT PATTERNS

Below are some of the patterns that are associated with the Type Nine personality constellation. The process of working with these patterns in order to gain more emotional health and an increased sense of inner peace includes the steps outlined below.

1. Become a detective and recognize when the pattern shows up.

2. Create a little distance between yourself and the pattern as you normalize it.

3. Be with the experience of the pattern and its associated sensations.

4. Allow the experience with compassion and nonjudgment.

5. Acknowledge and accept what is showing up.

Refer to appendix F for an expanded version of this process.

Discounting Yourself

Notice the tendency to discount yourself.

The act of discounting can take on a number of different behaviors.

- For example, have you noticed instances in which you go along with others? Not wanting to disappoint others, you find it easier to acquiesce rather than voice a different opinion. You may think that you don't have an opinion, and if you do, you should be above having one. More likely, you really don't know what you want for yourself.

- You forget your own agenda. After a meeting with another person, you realize that they did most of the talking. You listened. You learned something about them. They learned very little about you. What value did you receive from the conversation? You may notice that it feels rude to be the first to initiate your side of the conversation rather than waiting to be asked.

- You have something to say in a group but feel awkward in speaking up. That would focus a lot of attention on you, and you think to yourself that what you have to say may not really be very important. You feel upset when someone says what you were thinking and their comments are positively received.

- You simply forget what is important to you and what your priorities are. They get shoved to the side. And you numb out.

Withdrawing from Real-Time Engagement

Notice the tendency to withdraw from engagement and participation.

If this is a predominant pattern for you, you may also notice your tendency to avoid conflict or situations that have the chance to produce conflicting ideas, strong emotions, or even mild dissent among people. Has disengaging resulted in ignoring actual problems that need to be resolved?

What Anger?

Become familiar with your experience of anger.

You might ask yourself, "What anger?" Notice your evaluation of what it means to be angry. Those who identify with Type Nine typically think that anger is a negative expression and one to be avoided at all costs—either in themselves or hearing it from others.

Notice your ego's attempt to make anger wrong in some way. Can you notice how much of your emotional and physical energy you use to repress your anger?

Notice your tendency to make nice on the outside but put the brakes on when interacting with others. Notice the resistance that is in your body. When you get curious about the resistance, you may find anger lurking not far below the surface.

FIELDWORK PRACTICES

1. Ask yourself what you need and want.

It may take time to discover what is really important to you. Your priorities have taken a back seat to making certain that those around you are okay first. Try making a list of things you really loved doing as a child. Be conscious about paying attention to things that speak to your heart.

2. Develop a relationship with your body.

Because it can be so challenging to remain in touch with your physicality or your place in space, it is important to incorporate useful, body-oriented strategies to keep reminding yourself to pay attention to your body. Here are some possibilities:

- If you like walking, practice being very aware of your body's movement and feeling your feet touch the ground while you are in movement. Be present to your belly as you walk.
- Practice belly breathing several times throughout the day.
- Get frequent massages.
- Find a form of yoga that quickens your energy.
- Study aikido.

3. Take intentional, focused action on your priorities. Notice the choices you are making.

Take strong, purposeful action. Perhaps that means structuring your time so that you can enroll in classes or workshops that focus on your interests, needs, or work-related goals. Notice the temptation to back down at the first inkling of resistance on the part of a significant person in your life. Remember, this is for you.

At the beginning of each day, ask yourself what your most important priority is to focus on. Focus on completing some aspect of your priority daily.

4. Learn about your anger.

Anger can feel very threatening, so it may be useful to work with someone who can create a safe space for you to practice experiencing your anger.

Having anger doesn't mean that you go around yelling at people. But it does mean that you allow yourself to feel the energy of anger moving through your body. And it does mean that you get in touch with an instinctual energy that can fuel your movement and expression toward greater health and liberation.

5. Speak up.

Practice saying what's on your mind.

Movement to Highest Levels of Health

To move toward highest levels of health, people who identify with Type Nine must eventually:

- "Let go of the belief that their participation in the world is unimportant or unwanted; thus, they can truly connect with themselves and with others."[2]

- Fully embrace their physical, human experience. They must reconnect with their physical existence and consciously be in their body as they move through the world.

- Allow themselves to feel their anger and integrate it into their larger sense of being alive.

- Be fully and openheartedly present in the here and now.

- Recognize that great inner peace arises from being engaged and present.

TYPE FOUR

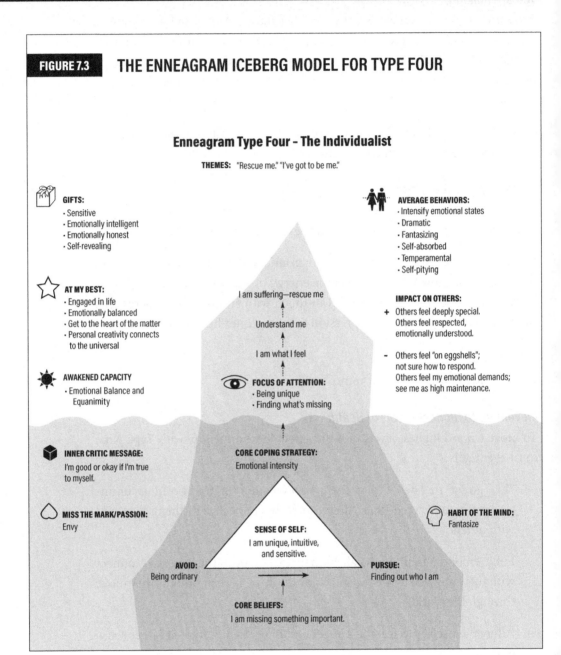

FIGURE 7.3   **THE ENNEAGRAM ICEBERG MODEL FOR TYPE FOUR**

Enneagram Type Four - The Individualist

THEMES: "Rescue me." "I've got to be me."

GIFTS:
- Sensitive
- Emotionally intelligent
- Emotionally honest
- Self-revealing

AT MY BEST:
- Engaged in life
- Emotionally balanced
- Get to the heart of the matter
- Personal creativity connects to the universal

AWAKENED CAPACITY
- Emotional Balance and Equanimity

AVERAGE BEHAVIORS:
- Intensify emotional states
- Dramatic
- Fantasizing
- Self-absorbed
- Temperamental
- Self-pitying

IMPACT ON OTHERS:

+ Others feel deeply special. Others feel respected, emotionally understood.

− Others feel "on eggshells"; not sure how to respond. Others feel my emotional demands; see me as high maintenance.

I am suffering—rescue me

Understand me

I am what I feel

FOCUS OF ATTENTION:
- Being unique
- Finding what's missing

INNER CRITIC MESSAGE:
I'm good or okay if I'm true to myself.

CORE COPING STRATEGY:
Emotional intensity

MISS THE MARK/PASSION:
Envy

HABIT OF THE MIND:
Fantasize

SENSE OF SELF:
I am unique, intuitive, and sensitive.

AVOID:
Being ordinary

PURSUE:
Finding out who I am

CORE BELIEFS:
I am missing something important.

TYPE FOUR: THE INDIVIDUALIST
THEME: "Rescue me." "I've got to be me."

ABOVE THE WATERLINE

 When I'm Expansive and at My Healthiest Levels (Gifts and at My Best)

I am sensitive to the emotional environment and experiences of others.

I am emotionally intelligent. I am aware of my emotions and those of others and work with the emotional experiences and interactions to further understanding.

I am emotionally honest. I take time to understand the motivations behind my emotions and neither deny nor magnify them. I look for the insights that I gain from understanding my emotions.

I can reveal my emotional depths in original, creative ways.

I am engaged in life and feel connected to others in deeply emotional ways.

My emotions are even and balanced. I recognize and appreciate the changes in my emotional state but do not get overly attached to any of these emotions.

I can dive into the heart of the matter, getting to the underlying emotional thoughts and reactions of a situation. I can ask emotionally difficult questions.

My personal creativity taps into universal themes. This can help others learn more about the depths of life for themselves.

 Awakened Capacity: Emotional Balance and Equanimity

I recognize my authenticity when I'm in direct contact with my heart. I revel in it. Emotions come and go, but the sensations that I experience from a deep sense of groundedness in the present moment open my heart to the always available depth, beauty, magnificence, and mystery of life.

Distinguishing Characteristics When the Personality Has Its Grip on Me

I generate intense feelings through my imagination.

I am dramatic, experiencing and expressing overly charged emotions related to even the most mundane event.

I have an expansive fantasy life, which feels more interesting than day-to-day life. Ordinary life can feel beneath me and too superficial.

I am absorbed in my emotions and myself. I don't distinguish between life and emotions. They are one and the same. My emotions are me.

I can be temperamental with dramatic mood swings. People never quite know what to expect from me. My highs are high, and my lows are low (and there are more lows than highs).

In self-pitying, I feel sorry for myself and am looking for the sympathy of others.

Where I Put My Attention When Identified with the Personality (Focus of Attention)

My attention is on feeling special and feeling like I have a unique life. My emotions, especially painful emotions from the past, play out powerfully in my life, and I use them to reexperience my past and to define who I am now. I desperately want others to see my pain but suspect that they'll never really understand me. I long for someone to rescue me from my suffering.

I also focus my attention on what's missing in different parts of my life, whether in work, in my relationships, with my friends, or in the experience I'm having right now. I often think, "If only___, then this situation would be so much better."

Impact on Others

+ Positive

Others feel deeply understood and respected.

Others are inspired by the depth of authentic expression and originality of the healthy Four.

– Negative

Others walk on eggshells, unsure of what mood the person with a Type Four personality will be in.

Others may be exhausted by the Four's emotional demands and need for attention.

BELOW THE WATERLINE

The Ego Code's Inner Logic

Core Belief

I believe that I am missing something important that would make me whole. I am convinced that because I am missing an important something, I am so different that no one else can understand or help me. My uniqueness also exempts me from the expectations of others.

 ## Coaching Cue::

Examples of what you might hear your clients say or do/not do:

- *No one will ever understand me or be able to help me.*

- *Nobody sees me. I feel invisible.*

- *I didn't follow through with the phone call because that position sounded so boring.*

- *Why do other people get to have their wonderful lives?*

Clients may also want to go into great detail about their experiences, not allowing time for inquiry or reflection.

△ Triangle of Identity

What I Pursue: My Identity/Finding Out Who I Am

I want to know and express my uniqueness, and also have others recognize my distinct sensitivity. I use my feelings as my guide as they are what are most real.

What I Avoid: Being Ordinary

Being ordinary sounds like death. Nothing could be worse. I envy others for what they have but am repelled by what looks like their meaningless lives. Following conventional standards and norms is one of the hardest things to do.

My Core Coping Strategy: Relying on My Emotions for Truth/Being Emotionally Intense

My feelings are the basis of my truth.

I search for the ideal situation that will compensate for what I feel is missing in me. Because I can secretly feel superior to others who are less emotionally sensitive or less deep than I am, I emphasize my uniqueness, which creates distance and tension in relationships. When there's tension in a relationship, it feels like I'm being true to myself.

Sense of Self ("I Am . . .")

I see myself as being unique, intuitive, and sensitive. I want others to see my uniqueness and am frustrated when I think that they don't understand or appreciate me.

Fixation of the Personality (Habit of the Mind)

I fantasize about what could be and what could have been. My fantasies take on a life of their own and become more real than external reality. I spend a lot of time and energy on the way I want my life to look. My fantasies can easily become the focus of my life, with the result that I have a difficult time moving forward in my life and sustaining action.

Where I Miss the Mark (Passion)

I miss the mark when I become envious of others. I am constantly comparing my life to what I think the lives of others are like and determining that their lives are easier than mine. I believe that others fit in better than I do, and that I'm basically an outsider in life.

What the Inner Critic Insists Upon

In order for me to feel good or okay, I have to be true to myself.[3] That means that I have to follow my feelings, because to me, they are truth. If I'm feeling sad, then I must act sad, even dramatically sad, as that means I'm being true to myself, and I will get rewarded by my inner critic. As long as I'm caught in the web of my inner critic, I will continue to be trapped in emotional turmoil as a substitute for the equanimity of living fully in the world.

What Causes Me Stress

My stress level increases when I feel that others undervalue or misunderstand me. My stress is dramatically increased when others don't meet my emotional expectation and disappoint or even abandon me. Feelings of abandonment reinforce my innate sense that something important is missing within me.

When I'm Most Constricted and Inflexible

I become emotionally paralyzed and depressed.

I feel totally alienated from others and from myself.

I am self-loathing and tormented by delusions.

I feel hopeless and become self-destructive.

Lines of Access

Type Four shares a line with both Types Two and One. Below are just a few ways that the characteristics of either of these types might show up or the reactions I might have to these characteristics in others. Refer to the discussion of these two types for further insight.

At Type Two: I can become overinvolved in other people's lives, clingy and needy. A gift of the Two is relaxing my self-absorption and letting other people into my heart.

At Type One: I can be hard on others and self-righteous, but it's really hard to admit. I see myself as so sensitive and flawed and am judgmental of those who are critical and insensitive. I deny my judgmental side. With awareness and presence, I begin to experience my own goodness and inner alignment.

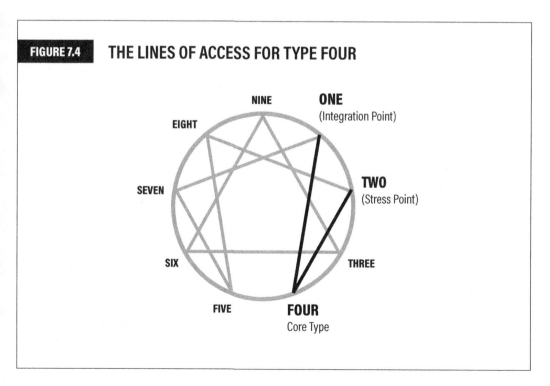

FIGURE 7.4 **THE LINES OF ACCESS FOR TYPE FOUR**

Type Four Case Study

Sarah came to coaching providing the following information about herself:

I am well known in my field for being a fierce advocate for a cause that I believe in, changing the education system. I have found myself working for this cause from the inside out because I thought that I could have more impact. The downside is that I feel isolated and alone in work. Even though people in the field call upon me as a thought leader, no one else really understands what my work is about enough to help me with it. I feel like I'm possessed by the negative, as I'm always in a crisis.

I've got to change my work life and my life. I guess I'm feeling sorry for myself, and I'm not thinking clearly.

Sarah came to coaching in what she described as a crisis mode. She felt that decisions had to be made right away, as she was under time pressure. She needed to decide whether she would stay with a prestigious organization where she felt alone or move to another organization.

Sarah was a statuesque woman who caught people's attention when she entered the room. She's clearly very bright yet spoke in somewhat muddled sentences when asked about herself. She didn't complete the preplanning questionnaire before the initial session but promised to do so.

Her intentions for coaching included:

- Getting clear about what was next in her work life

- Strengthening her relationships in her marriage, with her family, and with friends

- Developing a sense of self not so dependent on work

- Being energized, creative, and proactive about work

Initially, Sarah wasn't sure what the Enneagram could do for her. However, as she worked with various Type Four patterns:

- She spoke about her frequent fantasies and desires about how people would react to her work but often found herself alone and frustrated. She recognized that she was given feedback regularly that her ideas needed to be tested in real-life situations.

- She noticed her tendency to spiral into depression and to be negative about things and people around her.

- She noticed how often she found herself in crisis situations that seemingly demanded a lot of emotional energy.

– She recognized her need to receive a lot of reassurance and recognition for her unique contributions, as well as her self-absorption.

An initial focus of Sarah's work was to help her find her way back into her body.

As a woman used to living in a heady world, and a woman who could become intensely emotional, she found that her body was a source of some surprise. Having survived a life-threatening illness some years earlier, she realized that she hadn't really trusted her body. Her fieldwork included conscious walking and other forms of conscious exercise, along with becoming aware of inner bodily sensations. This seemed a bit mundane to her at the beginning, but as she stayed with it, she noticed that she didn't get as swept away by her moods.

When speaking about her work, Sarah would shine. Her creative approach to an academic subject matter could deeply touch and inspire the hearts of others, which was part of her true gift.

She eventually took a position in a progressive, non-high-profile setting where she could experiment with applying her theories. She surprised many of her colleagues by this apparent stepping down rather than to a more elevated position. Yet, after making this decision, her energy and creativity seemed to be naturally generated.

She decided to reach out more to her immediate family, and in doing so, challenged and eventually released the idea that she was on the outside of the family.

SUGGESTIONS FOR COACHES WORKING WITH INDIVIDUALS WHO IDENTIFY WITH TYPE FOUR

Acknowledge Their Inner Experience

I believe that my feelings are the truth. I believe my feelings, and my feelings are who I am. And I desperately want you or others to understand my feelings so that you will understand me. If you don't listen deeply to me, I will feel unseen, unheard, unacknowledged, and unimportant.

Because I am in touch with my feelings, I am especially sensitive and deep.

I resist changing who I am for fear of losing my individuality. Since I believe that my feelings are who I am, I will lose my sense of identity if I don't hold on to my feelings.

I sometimes feel unstable, like I must be missing something that everyone else seems to have. I don't measure up to others because I'm essentially flawed and sometimes hopeless.

I get caught in fantasizing about how a situation could be and find that I don't easily move into action. I'm not sure how to move into action. And if I take action, I might lose the intensity of my feelings, which would leave me feeling even less sure of myself.

Offer Counterintuitive Questions/Comments

What about this situation is working well right now?
> Encourage your clients to shift their attention from the past to what is working in the present.

What about you and your life is good right now? What is working well?

What are you experiencing in your body right now? What are you experiencing in the area around your heart right now?
> Help your clients shift their attention from their feelings to their physical being. This includes being in direct contact with sensations around the heart.

What would you like to create in your life now?

What next steps can you take today to move you toward your desired outcome?

What is the next best step for you to move toward your real priority?
> Support your client's movement into purposeful action, even when the action may feel mundane. These steps do not need to be big, but when realized, are ones that can create momentum. Co-create strategies that assist clients in becoming accountable to themselves.

Invite into awareness how choices are made.

Issues That May Arise in the Coaching Relationship

– Remember that clients who identify with Type Four carry a belief that no one else can really understand them or help them. They may believe that what works for others will not work for them. It is vital to recognize and appreciate their uniqueness as you listen deeply to their experiences. Also inquire if they are willing to be held to their commitments and how they would like to be held accountable, then follow through.

– The average Type Four communication style tends to be self-referencing, with emotional overtones. They may refer to experiences that are in the past with self-recrimination or longing. Ask the client to become focused on what actions or strategies they can use now in the physical world to move toward their desired outcomes. The physical world does not tend to be prominent on their radar screen. Invite clients to pay attention to their breath, develop a centering practice, and experience sensations in the body. This increased experience of physical substance and groundedness supports being able to take action.

- The client may put the coach on a pedestal and make you another object of comparison and, perhaps, envy. Let the client know that you are a real person with strengths and fallibility.

OBSERVATIONS AND WORKING WITH YOUR PREDOMINANT PATTERNS

Below are some of the patterns that are associated with the Type Four personality constellation. The process of working with these patterns in order to gain more emotional health and an increased sense of inner peace includes the steps outlined below.

1. Become a detective and recognize when the pattern shows up.

2. Create a little distance between yourself and the pattern as you normalize it.

3. Be with the experience of the pattern and its associated sensations.

4. Allow the experience with compassion and nonjudgment.

5. Acknowledge and accept what is showing up.

Refer to appendix F for an expanded version of this process.

Emotions Control Your Day-to-Day Experiences

Notice the tendency to let your emotional state color your entire experience of the moment or even the day. This tends to especially happen when you become absorbed with feeling down or depressed.

When you are feeling a particular way, do you express that emotion outwardly so that other people will know what you are feeling? This can be experienced as moodiness.

Notice when you exaggerate your emotional state. You might notice that this happens when you retell your story to others repeatedly or when you focus on reexperiencing the feeling. This may take the form of longing or yearning for things to be different.

Reliance on Environment to Reinforce Mood

Do you create environments that support or help you sustain your moods?

This might mean that you have to have just the right kind of day to tackle a task or that just the right chair in just the right color is necessary. You might be drawn to the exotic or unusual to reinforce your mood.

You might notice the tendency to overindulge yourself with too much of something—whether that be food, personal or home decor, or substances as a way to further reinforce your moods. Notice if you feel that you are somehow exempt from the so-called rules that apply to other people's behavior.

Lost in Fantasies

People who have Type Four personalities can spend a great deal of time fantasizing about their desired life, their desired partner, their ideal situation. For example, you might fantasize about having a more ideal body shape, having a more sensitive partner, having a better job, or being more talented in a particular skill. You might notice that you tend to reject anything that doesn't match your fantasized ideal. Do you sometimes think that what is available to you is beneath you?

Drama in Relationships

Notice the expectations you have of your relationships.

If you think other people have it better than you, you may tend to act with jealousy. Or you may tend to dump your miseries on your friends and expect them to rescue you from your unhappiness. Do you expect that others will take care of you and your problems?

Drama can be created by withdrawing or withholding information or affection from your partner. Those whose core type is Four often notice a tendency to create crises in a relationship, then having an emotional reconciliation.

Comparison and Envy

Notice the role of comparison and envy.

Do you think that other people have it easier than you or that your life just pales in comparison to others? Do you tend to either negatively or positively compare yourself to others—or both?

Do you hear yourself saying or thinking that there is just something wrong with you? Notice the tendency to feel that you are flawed in some way that no one else is. You might also notice that you think that no one else can ever really understand you because you are so flawed.

FIELDWORK PRACTICES

1. Develop a relationship with your body.

Because it can be so challenging to remain in contact with your physicality or your space and place, it is very useful to have a regular practice of mindful body movement, such as yoga or other forms of conscious physical activity.

Horseback riding, dance, aikido, and other interactive forms of conscious movement can support you in getting into your body and experiencing sensations, balance, and relationship to other living beings from a place of physicality.

2. Acknowledge your actual gifts and talents.

People who identify with Four are challenged with identifying and claiming their actual talents. Focus on relaxing the self-talk that diminishes what you have and taking meaningful action to use your talents in the world.

3. Find the extraordinary in the ordinary.

People who identify with Type Four tend to be attracted to the exotic, overlooking the amazing nature of what they may have thought of as ordinary. Appreciate the small things, the beauty surrounding you, and the gift of being here in this moment.

4. Become interested in and engaged with others.

Look for ways that you can help others and take meaningful action. This helps shift your attention from one of self-absorption to a balanced way of interacting.

5. Recognize feelings for what they are.

Feelings come and go unless we consciously or unconsciously hold on to them. While feelings offer us useful information, they do not define who we are, nor are they a reflection of reality. Remember that other people may respond to situations very differently than you do.

Movement to Highest Levels of Health

To move toward highest levels of health, people who identify with Type Four must eventually:

- "Let go of their belief that they are more flawed than others and are thus freed from their self-absorption."[4]

- Let go of emotional drama and recognize their capacity to cope with life's experiences. Recognize that they do not need to be rescued.

- Recognize that all human beings are unique and that they all have commonalities that are part of normal living.

- Claim their essential qualities of equanimity and forgiveness.

TYPE FIVE

FIGURE 7.5   ## THE ENNEAGRAM ICEBERG MODEL FOR TYPE FIVE

Enneagram Type Five- The Investigator

THEME: "I don't need much, but I need my space."

 GIFTS:
- Perceptive observer
- Curious
- Playful and whimsical
- Focused—able to concentrate

 AVERAGE BEHAVIORS:
- Retreat into my mind
- Private
- Detached
- Secretive
- Minimize needs
- Provocative

 AT MY BEST:
- Visionary and pioneering
- Profound insights and breakthroughs
- Clear-hearted
- In awe of life

Withdraw into dark world, provoke others

Minimize life force/feel small

Emotionally detached observation, self-sufficient

IMPACT ON OTHERS:

+ Others are inspired by my vision and original thinking.
  Others appreciate my innate playfulness.

− Others can feel demeaned by my intellectual arrogance.
  Others can feel pushed away and unloved by my demand for privacy.

AWAKENED CAPACITY
Unattachment to iceberg

 FOCUS OF ATTENTION:
Ideas—how things work

 INNER CRITIC MESSAGE:
I'm good or okay if I master something.

CORE COPING STRATEGY:
Mental intensity

 MISS THE MARK/PASSION:
Avarice

HABIT OF THE MIND:
Collect and retain

SENSE OF SELF:
I am smart, perceptive, and observant.

AVOID:
Being ignorant

PURSUE:
- Knowledge and understanding
- Making a contribution

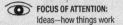

CORE BELIEFS:
- There's no room for me.
- I'm the cause of the problem.
- I'm on my own.

TYPE FIVE: THE INVESTIGATOR
THEME: "I don't need much, but I need my space."

ABOVE THE WATERLINE

 When I'm Expansive and at My Healthiest Levels (Gifts and at My Best)

I am a perceptive observer with a clear, objective mind.

I am curious about many things. Learning new information and understanding how life works is fascinating to me.

I am playful and whimsical. I can be slightly mischievous and bring humor to otherwise difficult or threatening ideas.

I can stay focused and see a project through to the end.

I'm visionary and pioneering. New ways of understanding and new ideas arise spontaneously.

My observations can lead to revolutionary breakthroughs and changes in people's understanding and in solving practical problems.

I am unsentimental. I see life objectively, without an emotional reaction.

I am in awe of life—its mysteries, its majesty, its workings.

 Awakened Capacity: Unattachment

When in real contact with my grounded body and sweet heart, my mind is clear. I trust that insights and my particular way of knowing are available as needed. I enjoy the freedom that comes with releasing my attachment to stored knowledge and am freer to respond and live as a participant in the world.

 Distinguishing Characteristics When the Personality Has Its Grip on Me

I live in my mind and analyze the situation.

I am private. I like to work alone, behind closed doors. I don't like others to bother me.

I am detached. I distance myself from external activities and from my feelings. I'm preoccupied with my ideas and am mentally intense.

I minimize my physical and emotional needs. I ask for little from others. For example, I may not spend time on my appearance or physical care.

I am secretive and actively keep my private thoughts and ideas to myself.

I can be provocative, seeing the dark side of life and pushing other people to face it as well. I don't mind making others feel uncomfortable.

👁 Where I Put My Attention When Identified with the Personality (Focus of Attention)

I put my attention on the inner world of ideas. I like to figure out how things work. I want to know as much as possible about a particular subject matter so I can master it. Really, I want to know more than anyone else about the topic. The world of ideas and analysis is safer than having to deal with other people's emotions and life situations, which could overwhelm me. My mind is the basis of my reality and is my escape.

Impact on Others

+ Positive

Others are inspired by the Five's vision and ability to think originally, creating new possibilities.

Others appreciate the Five's innate playfulness and generosity of spirit.

– Negative

Others can feel demeaned and even contemptible by the intellectual arrogance of the average Five.

Others can feel pushed away and unloved by the Five's demand for privacy.

BELOW THE WATERLINE

The Ego Code's Inner Logic

Core Belief

I believe that there is no room for me in the external world. It seems to me that all the seats are taken at the table. I also believe that there is no support available to me and that I am on my own. My life is based on scarcity of resources. I believe that I'm the cause of problems, so others are better off if I stay out of the picture.

 Coaching Cue::

Examples of what you might hear your clients say or do/not do:

- *I've got to work out solutions on my own.*
- *People are difficult for me. They expect too much from me. I often feel like an alien.*
- *Don't expect me to let you in. That would be far too invasive.*
- *I need more time to figure out the solution (or to get this project done).*
- *Why would I want to focus on my breath or body sensations?*
  That won't get us anywhere.

△ Triangle of Identity

What I Pursue: Knowledge and Understanding, Making a Contribution

I need to be knowledgeable, often in rarefied topics that escape the attention of most people. Gaining in-depth knowledge is a way to feel competent and masterful. This becomes my contribution to others.

What I Avoid: Being or Appearing Ignorant

Why would I participate in activities or interactions that make no sense to me? They will only deplete my energy and leave me feeling small and shaky.

My Core Coping Strategy: Being Mentally Intense/Analyzing

I cope by instructing others on what I know about a topic.

I am self-sufficient, minimizing my physical and emotional needs, and withdrawing into intellectual pursuits. I don't ask others for anything because they may want something back from me. I would become depleted if I used my energy that way.

Sense of Self ("I Am . . .")

I see myself as smart, perceptive, and objective. I think of myself as having something unique and insightful to offer, and I'll stay in my head to get the insight or to prepare as long as I think I need. I need to be mentally well prepared before moving into action, so I don't like to be rushed into what I consider premature activity.

Fixation of the Personality (Habit of the Mind)

I live in my mind and retain its activity.[5]

I observe rather than participate in life. I think that thinking about what is going on in the world and in my life is the same as participating in the world and in my life. My mind seems like the safest place for me, and I don't perceive that there is anything external in life to support me.

Where I Miss the Mark (Passion)

I need to hold on to what I have, which might be material goods or my knowledge. Since I rely on my mind for creating a safe structure for me, I hang onto whatever I think will support me. I may refuse to let others know what my feelings are; I'm not even sure myself. Thus, I withhold myself emotionally and energetically from others. This passion is called avarice.

What the Inner Critic Insists Upon

My inner critic insists that I must master something—ideas, information, understanding a particular subject matter—in order for me to be okay.[6] It insists that my mastery is based upon my mind and that I must know more than others about a given topic. As long as I am caught in the web of my inner critic, I will continue substituting what's in my head for real life, which is grounded in my body.

What Causes Me Stress

My stress is greatly increased when others make emotional demands on me or want more of my time and energy. I believe that I only have so much energy available, and if I give too much to others, I will be depleted.

When I'm Most Constricted and Inflexible

Everything is meaningless to me.

I cut myself off from all.

I focus on the dark side of life and provoke others to do the same.

Lines of Access

Type Five shares lines with both Type Seven and Eight. Below are just a few ways that the characteristics of either of these types might show up or the reactions I might have to these characteristics in others. Refer to the discussion of these two types for further insight.

At Type Seven: I can become hyperactive and scattered. The gift of the Seven is letting go of isolating myself and now experiencing joy in the moment.

At Type Eight: I can be bossy, demanding, and even domineering, though it's hard to admit. This is at odds with my self-image of being intellectual and withdrawing. I deny my desire to control and can be critical of others who are bossy. With awareness, I begin to experience my inner vitality and ability to be decisive.

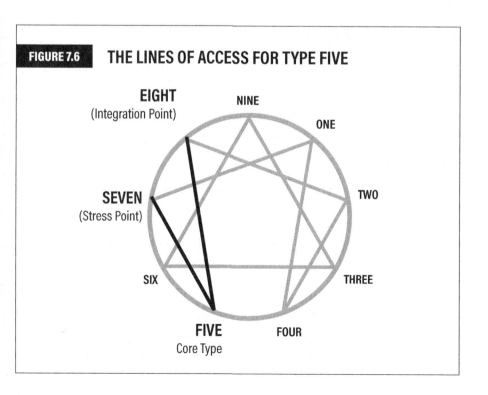

FIGURE 7.6 **THE LINES OF ACCESS FOR TYPE FIVE**

Type Five Case Study

Tom came to coaching providing the following information about himself:

My girlfriend and I have been trying to decide what to do about our relationship. We really care for each other, but she thinks I withdraw from her too much. I often feel like she wants too much from me. It's hard for me to be in a constant conversation about anything, let alone our relationship. We're in couples counseling, but hard as it is for me to do this, I've decided to focus on learning more about myself. There must be something I don't understand. I just want to make a smart decision about our relationship, and I need more information on all fronts.

Tom was a sweet guy with a strong commitment to figuring things out and was clearly focused on gaining more information about himself. He wanted reading material and any other information that might help him increase his understanding. It seemed he wasn't energetically connected to his body.

His intentions for coaching included:

- Developing more self-knowledge based on the Enneagram

- Discerning between his unresolved "stuff" (inner struggles) and what was really true for him about the relationship

- Gaining insight on how his personality type may have impacted his unsatisfactory work situations in the past

The following are among the Type Five patterns that Tom recognized:

- It is hard for me to stay in a conversation. Once I'm done, I'm done. I typically physically withdraw from the situation and find some privacy.

- Not only do I physically withdraw, but my routine is to analyze all the information I can get my hands on. I want to feel prepared for the next conversation. And that always happens in my head.

- It's hard for me to move into action. I've come to see that I spend an inordinate amount of time planning before anything ever gets done.

- I don't really feel safe in the external environment. It doesn't feel very friendly to me out there, and I get irritated if someone interrupts my privacy.

As Tom developed his self-observational skills, he began to see all the ways he stayed removed from situations requiring emotional and social contact. At work, he would seek out the most private office, and in the past, he didn't accept a job where he had to be in an open cubicle. He recognized how awkward and anxious he felt in social environments. In response to social demands, he focused on ensuring that he would be able to talk at length about a topic in which he had extensive knowledge.

One major theme of coaching centered on supporting Tom in reconnecting with his body. He was initially wary of this, as he seldom exercised and simply had little awareness of where his body was in space. He found that massage helped him to experience his body in ways he couldn't ever remember. He also experimented with body-based meditation. He and his girlfriend practiced dancing at home before going to any clubs. Tom's task was to find what his body wanted to do and dance from there. In this way, he gained enhanced security from the most unlikely sources.

Tom recognized that he could never have enough mental information about his relationship in advance to be fully prepared for whatever might come. In time, he developed glimpses into a more intuitive way of knowing. He and his girlfriend decided not to continue their romantic relationship, but the decision was no longer based on just wanting to get away and into his own sanctuary.

SUGGESTIONS FOR COACHES WORKING WITH INDIVIDUALS WHO IDENTIFY WITH TYPE FIVE

Acknowledge Their Inner Experience

I believe that in order to understand how things in the world work, I need to be detached and disconnected. I believe that being detached allows me to be an impartial observer.

It's important for me to retreat to develop competence and expertise. I expect myself to be smarter on certain subjects than anyone if I am to matter.

I think that I lack sufficient inner resources and that if I interact too much with other people, they will want too much from me. Then I'll feel totally depleted and unable to function. Therefore, I tend to withdraw from interacting with others and am reluctant to share my resources with others.

I much prefer to maintain my privacy.

Offer Counterintuitive Questions/Comments

What would you like to create in your life now?

What sensations are you experiencing in your body right now? As you sense your connection to the ground, what are you experiencing? What are you noticing in your belly center? What is your body communicating to you in this moment? What is your experience of strength right now?

Help your clients appreciate a new form of information and intelligence available through being in contact with their bodies and with the ground.

Who or what do you most care about? Who and what are the sources of support that are available to you? How does interacting with others that you trust support you?

What is happening in your heart? What is this experience telling you right now? What gift is it offering to you now?

What part of yourself do you share with others? What happens for you when you share more about yourself? How is your heart affected?

Support clients in developing the capacity to be in contact with their hearts as they interact with others. Explore the impact that these interactions have on your client. For example, how do they affect your client's confidence in engaging in social relationships?

What is the next best step for you to move toward your real priority?

Invite into awareness how choices are made.

Issues That May Arise in the Coaching Relationship

– Remember that Type Five clients tend to rely on their mind for solving life's challenges. Being smart is important to them. They may tend to be emotionally disengaged and want to analyze their situation rather than move into engaged action. Be careful about falling for the Five's argument that more research is needed before action can be taken. A big stretch for this client is moving into action.

– The Type Five client will assess the expertise of the coach.

– The Type Five communication style can be detached, short, and authoritative, which can indirectly have an "I'm not all that interested" tone. This can be a mask for the social or emotional awkwardness the client may initially feel in the coaching relationship. Let clients off the hook by letting them know that coaching involves exploring and being curious. State that they do not need to be an expert in this relationship.

– It's a big step for this client to decide to work with a coach, and then follow through with contacting you. They might want to commit to only a few sessions, as it is hard to trust that another person may be able to provide coaching support. It is important for a coach to be able to engage mentally with this client initially. Encourage these clients to tap into other forms of intelligence, including the intelligence of the body and emotional intelligence. This may give them doorways into new ways of experiencing life, themselves, and relationships.

OBSERVATIONS AND WORKING WITH YOUR PREDOMINANT PATTERNS

Below are some of the patterns that are associated with the Type Five personality constellation. The process of working with these patterns in order to gain more emotional health and an increased sense of inner peace includes the steps outlined below.

1. Become a detective and recognize when the pattern shows up.

2. Create a little distance between yourself and the pattern as you normalize it.

3. Be with the experience of the pattern and its associated sensations.

4. Allow the experience with compassion and nonjudgment.

5. Acknowledge and accept what is showing up.

Refer to appendix F for an expanded version of this process.

The Inner World of Ideas

Notice your tendency to retreat to your intense mental activity, which limits your ability to experience the fullness of life.

Notice the tendency to withdraw into your mind.

At the average level of presence, you can be tempted to disengage from having a direct experience of external situations or of yourself, substituting analysis, comparison, evaluation, model-making, and mental commentary for participation and engagement in life. It's easy for you to mistake the model of a living world that you've constructed inside your mind for the real one outside your mind.

Notice if the inner world of ideas is taking more time and energy than is being given to engaging with the external world and living your life.

Getting Ready to Be Ready

You may notice that you have difficulty coming to the end of a project or task, as you're not sure that you've covered all of your bases. You may find yourself wanting to do more research or reading, even when others are asking (which may feel like pressuring to you) for a finished project or assignment.

You may find yourself wanting to practice, practice, practice, while being reluctant to give the final performance; perhaps you find yourself continuing to touch up a painting or reworking an article that you've written. People who identify with Type Five often find it hard to feel that they have prepared enough. A good question to ask yourself is, "When is enough enough?"

Minimal Is Best

Notice your tendency to minimize your needs.

Do you almost forget to eat? To sleep? To take care of daily living activities? You can get so engrossed in creating mental explanations for the workings of a particular topic that the external world is nearly forgotten. It's as if the body doesn't exist.

You may notice that the more energy is focused on your mind, the more intense and anxious you feel.

If this is a prominent pattern for you, you may also find yourself:

- Becoming more agitated with others, attempting to provoke them

- Being stingy with your time and energy—being unwilling to share with others

Just Observe

Notice your need to be in the role of the expert.

Being the expert on any given topic is one of the ways that people who identify with Type Five compensate for their feeling of awkwardness in social situations. The expert becomes a social identity and the basis for interaction.

Of course, people having other types can be experts as well. For a Five, it is valuable to notice when you feel compelled to know more than others and to let them know what you know. Showing your mastery of a topic may serve as a mask that protects your feeling of vulnerability.

A note on noticing: Noticing is not a mental exercise. It is a practice in increasing a neutral awareness of your physicality, emotional experiences, patterns related to the use of the mind, and human and physical surroundings. A caution to you is to not think about observing, but to give yourself a little distance from your mental processes so that you might observe them.

FIELDWORK PRACTICES

1. Use breathwork, meditation, or mindfulness to support the clarity of your mind.

It can be very useful to have a consistent meditation practice, and there are many resources available to support this.

2. Find your body! Awaken it with movement.

Because it can be so challenging to develop a relationship to your body and heart, finding a form of somatic practice that you can commit to is important. Yoga, aikido, chi gung, and other forms of conscious movement will help you focus on the inherent connection between mind, body, and heart.

This is one of the most profound practices you can adopt, as developing a strong relationship to your body and being aware of your own physicality is a keystone to your liberation.

3. Allow your "fair witness" to observe (nonjudgmentally) the tendency to buy the belief that you are separate from the rest of the world.

Be willing to stay with the neutral observer during this process, paying attention to the sensations that arise in your body and to the feelings that arise from your heart.

4. Notice what you ignore in life.

What areas of your life have you cut off? Friendships? Finances? Self-care? Taking care of your home environment? Identify one at a time and focus your energy on developing that aspect of yourself.

This may feel risky, so this will involve trusting that there are many more sources of support available to you than mental activities.

5. Begin to enjoy the experience of inner knowing in contrast with having mental knowledge.

As you become more grounded and centered in your body and experience your tender heart, you will have increased access to different forms of knowing that transcend mental constructs. You will strengthen the trust that you are part of all that is and the deep wisdom that comes from intuitive knowing.

Movement to Highest Levels of Health

To move toward highest levels of health, people who identify with Type Five must eventually:

- "Let go of the belief that they are separate from the environment—an outside observer—and are thus able to confidently engage in life."[7]

- Have direct experiences of life and not just observe it. Be in their body.

–   Become more present to the moment and realize that they don't have to figure things out. As they connect with their intuitive knowing, they strengthen their trust that they will know what they need to know.

–   Become more aware of the majesty and wonder of what is around them.

Chapter **8**

TYPES THREE, SEVEN, AND EIGHT:
The Assured, Confident Group

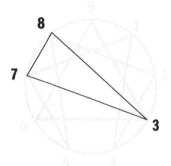

SHARED THEMES

Asserting or inserting one's power or influence into a relationship, conversation, conflict, or decision-making situation is one strategy for coping with the stress that accompanies interpersonal relationships.

At the average levels of health and effectiveness, three Enneagram types share the common personality structure of being externally oriented and having expansive energies. They are sometimes called the assertive types. People who identify with Types Three, Seven, and Eight communicate directly, and sometimes powerfully. They go after what they want and can demand that their wants get met. Other people typically know that an assertive type person is in the room: their voice and laughter are apt to be louder, they tend to move with assuredness and decisiveness, and they exude an air of personal power and confidence. They appear to be comfortable being at the center of attention, although people who identify with each of these types tend to keep other people at an emotional distance. They can come across as intense or demanding and have difficulty keeping their hearts open. Emotions may seem far too messy for them, and they may try to avoid the sense of vulnerability that comes with an open heart. They often secretly feel that important things happen when they are in the room. They also may feel responsible for making things happen.

Having the capacity to be direct and communicate clearly is a healthy attribute. However, when the assertive, confident strategy is an automatic and habitual pattern, the result is that these individuals may get what they want but at a high emotional cost. Not only does this strategy tend to distance others, but it distances these people from themselves. The externally oriented focus leaves little room for recognizing one's inner self.

Energetically, those in this group often are experienced as having big energy and being driven and even pushy. Horney called this strategy pushing against others. The intensity of their energy is used to protect themselves from being hurt and to be free to do what they want in the world.

TYPE THREE

FIGURE 8.1 ## THE ENNEAGRAM ICEBERG MODEL FOR TYPE THREE

Enneagram Type Three – The Achiever

THEME: "I can be anything I want."

GIFTS:
- Oriented to growth and learning
- Inspiring others to success
- Belief in self
- Ambitious

AT MY BEST:
- Tender
- Adaptable
- Authentic heart
- Inner-directed

AWAKENED CAPACITY
- Authentic and Truthful Heart

AVERAGE BEHAVIORS:
- Driven to be the best—compete
- Emphasize status
- Efficient
- Adapt/morph
- Emotionally detached
- Self-promoting

Be superficial

Avoid vulnerability

Adapt to every environment
Gauge feedback

IMPACT ON OTHERS:

+ Others feel uplifted and inspired. Others are motivated by my authentic nature.

− Others feel they "don't measure up." Others feel that they are inept and incompetent.

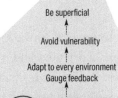

FOCUS OF ATTENTION:
Get attention by being successful

INNER CRITIC MESSAGE:
I'm good or okay if others think well of me and I'm successful.

CORE COPING STRATEGY:
Perform, adapt, push to be the best.

MISS THE MARK/PASSION:
Vanity

HABIT OF THE MIND:
Deceit toward myself and others

SENSE OF SELF:
I am accomplished, goal-oriented, with unlimited potential.

AVOID:
Being seen as a failure

PURSUE:
Being seen as having value

CORE BELIEFS:
- Life is a contest. I have to be the best.
- My worth and value come from my achievements.

TYPE THREE: THE ACHIEVER
THEME: "I can be anything I want."

ABOVE THE WATERLINE

 When I'm Expansive and at My Healthiest Levels (Gifts and at My Best)

I focus on developing myself and contributing my achievements to help the world.

I excel at motivating and inspiring others to do their best. I'm a good role model.

I believe in myself and in my abilities while remaining open and curious.

I am ambitious and focus on making a meaningful difference.

I am tender toward myself and others.

I am adaptable and can easily respond to changing circumstances while still remembering who I am.

I am authentic. I am in touch with my inner truth and make decisions based upon that.

I am inner-directed, paying attention to what has heart for me.

 Awakened Capacity: Authentic and Truthful Heart

Being in real contact with my heart allows me to experience the tenderness, sweetness, and preciousness of my own being. As I slow down and experience my truth and authenticity that is revealed through the heart, I discover my own inherent value and the inherent value of others.

 Distinguishing Characteristics When the Personality Has Its Grip on Me

I am efficient, focusing my attention on the goal at hand and minimizing my energy for non-priorities.

It's important to me to look and to be the best. I compete in every part of my life to come out on top.

I focus on the externals and on the world of appearances. I am aware of the status of what I achieve, what I do, and what I own.

I cover up any sense of vulnerability and do what is needed to come across as having it all together.

I constantly adapt myself to meet what I perceive to be the expectations of others. I can be chameleon-like and project an image of myself to others.

I am cut off from my feelings and emotionally detached. Feelings are too messy, and I'd rather emphasize getting ahead in life.

I overpromote myself to make myself look even better in the eyes of others, and especially to those who have prestige and high status.

👁 Where I Put My Attention When Identified with the Personality (Focus of Attention)

I look for attention and recognition. I get attention from others through being successful. I do whatever I can to look accomplished and to perform well in the eyes of important others. I gauge feedback from others and adapt if I think it will improve others' perceptions of me. Simultaneously, I lose my connection to my tender and vulnerable side.

Impact on Others

+ Positive

Others feel that they are uplifted and inspired to reach their higher potential.

Others are deeply touched by the authentic nature of the healthy Three.

– Negative

Others feel that they don't measure up to the Three's status or expectation.

Others feel undervalued and unimportant.

BELOW THE WATERLINE

The Ego Code's Inner Logic

Core Belief

I believe that my worth and value come from my achievements. I need to be outstanding. If I am loved, it is because of my success and excellent performance. I don't think I'll find satisfaction from just being myself, so I drive myself by being focused on external goals to achieve.

Life feels like a contest, and the person with the most rewards and awards wins, so I constantly strive to achieve one goal after another.

 ### Coaching Cue::

Examples of what you might hear your clients say or do/not do:

- *What's my next goal? Without a goal, I feel like a loser.*

- *Okay, now, just get it together. I can't let them see that I'm falling apart.*

- *I'll do whatever it takes to be the captain of the team or recognized as the best of my class.*

- *I'll collapse tonight, but tomorrow, I push on.*

- *Doesn't everyone have goals?*

Triangle of Identity

What I Pursue: Being Seen as a Success in the Eyes of Important Others

I take on goals that I perceive as having a high value in the eyes of those whom I value, whether that is a relative, a boss, or anyone with high status that I would like to positively impress.

What I Avoid: Being Seen as a Failure

If I perceive that I have not lived up to the values or standards of others, it reinforces a deep belief that I don't have real value for who I am. I avoid putting myself in situations where there's a good chance that I won't succeed.

My Core Coping Strategy: Adapting and Producing

I work hard, and I adapt or reinvent myself as I think is needed.

I compete to be the best in nearly every part of my life.

I abandon my true feelings and my heart in service of external goals.

Sense of Self ("I Am . . .")

I see myself as being outstanding, admired by others, and having unlimited potential. While these are positive qualities, they limit me when I don't allow myself to be vulnerable or even to be average in some things.

Fixation of the Personality (Habit of the Mind)

If I'm honest with myself right now, I realize that I am not honest with myself or others about who I am. I put on the mask of a certain persona, creating an identity that matches what I think others expect from me. Eventually, I begin to believe this false mask and forget about my authentic self. I can make myself be whatever I think others need me to be to receive their attention and recognition.

Where I Miss the Mark (Passion)

I (my personality) desperately want to be seen as the source of my accomplishments, my success, and whatever material wealth I have. I want to be recognized and given attention for rising to the top. I don't want to have to deal with my feelings or my spiritual being. This passion is called vanity.

What the Inner Critic Insists Upon

My only value lies in being successful and accomplished.[1] The rules of my inner critic insist that I must get attention from others for my successes; otherwise, I am a failure and have no inherent value in just being. For example, if I don't receive external recognition for a certain endeavor, that means I have no worth. As long as I am caught in the web of the inner critic, I will sacrifice my own heart's desires to the achievement of outer goals, which ultimately leads to inner emptiness.

What Causes Me Stress

I experience stress when others want me to be emotionally close and intimate. I experience stress when I expect myself to be accomplished in everything I do and when I feel compelled to have all the symbols of status and success. That results in keeping my guard up most of the time so that others won't see that I am feeling insecure or vulnerable.

When I'm Most Constricted and Inflexible

I do whatever it takes to look good. That means that I will lie to others about my accomplishments.

I will take the most expedient route, despite its impact on others.

I will use and exploit others to look successful.

I am totally out of touch with the desires of my heart.

Lines of Access

Type Three shares a line with both Types Nine and Six. Below are just a few ways that the characteristics of either of these types might show up or the reactions I might have to these characteristics in others. Refer to the discussion of these two types for further insight.

At Type Nine: I can become indecisive and disengaged. A gift of Nine is that I slow down and take in the value that is inherent in being human.

At Type Six: It's hard for me to admit, but I can become self-doubting and insecure. I can feel very shaky. I can be very critical of others who display these characteristics. But with increasing awareness and presence, I feel the support of the ground and experience courage.

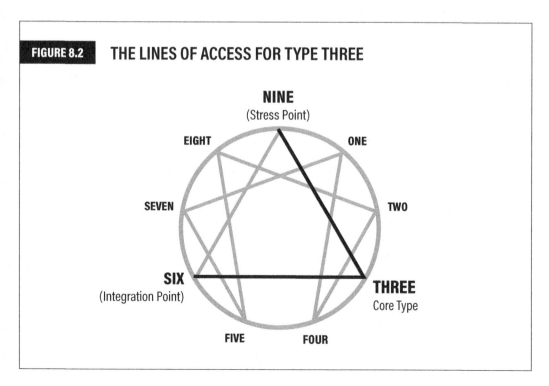

FIGURE 8.2 **THE LINES OF ACCESS FOR TYPE THREE**

Type Three Case Study

Janeese came to coaching providing the following information:

I feel like I am driving myself into the ground. I work extraordinarily hard to achieve top results, and for the most part, I've reached the goals I've set out for myself and that have been expected by my company.

I have needed my driving personality in order to prove myself as one of only a handful of Black women in this largely white and predominately male company. I have taken on a heavy moral responsibility to other women, especially women of color who want to be successful. But I'm so tired and just collapse once I'm at home.

I'm starting to experience some troubling health issues. Self-care? Ha! That's not built into the company culture and certainly isn't rewarded.

It's really hard to admit this, but since I've decided to pursue coaching, I will tell you: I'm losing confidence in my ability to stay on top of everything all the time.

Janeese is a talented, no-nonsense woman who likes results. She's at a new point in her life and admits that she hurts. She is aware of the pressure she is carrying and also senses that the image of herself that she meets the world with is a source of unease.

She identified these initial goals for coaching:

- Finding her way back to herself while continuing her work
- Identifying doable steps to address her health
- Exploring spiritual matters

The following are among the Type Three patterns that Janeese recognized:

- It's essential that I'm seen as successful and accomplished.
- I present myself in a way I think others value, which means that how I show up changes from situation to situation.
- I am really hard on myself—I never give myself a break. How can I?
- I'm not sure I have much of a heart.

The identification of her Threeness was also held in the context of the racial pressure she experienced in a high-profile work environment.

Janeese realized that the pressure of her professional environment mirrored the pressure she experienced internally from her core personality type, leading her to believe that she had little choice. She reflected on how her constant striving may have been connected to the health problems she was experiencing.

One major theme of coaching centered around listening to the quiet voice of her heart. This helped her open up, something she had not allowed herself to do in other situations. With further inquiry and self-reflection, she got in touch with deep levels of grief.

While this had not been an initial intention, she soon realized that she was lonely and desired more authentic relationships where she could also be real. She eventually joined a small group of spiritual practitioners where she reconnected with aspects of her faith in a supportive environment and began to connect with her heart.

SUGGESTIONS FOR COACHES WORKING WITH INDIVIDUALS WHO IDENTIFY WITH TYPE THREE

Acknowledge Their Inner Experience

I believe that my worth depends upon my success and being recognized for my achievements.

Much of my life energy is focused on working and doing. I'm very goal-oriented and I strive to achieve my goals.

I neglect and minimize the importance of my feelings and the feelings of others. Feelings are messy, and I don't have much time for them.

I work hard to develop myself and to be my personal best.

I place much of my attention on the external world and deny or ignore the existence of my spiritual and essential nature.

Offer Counterintuitive Questions/Comments

Tell me what your dream is. What do you love? What is your heart's desire?
> Help clients who identify with Type Three recognize deeper levels of feelings and desires. Encourage them to be in contact with their hearts.

What would it be like to accept that you are loved and accepted just for who you are?
> Invite clients to focus on their relationships and the inherent value of themselves rather than on their successes and prizes.

What are you willing to be just average at?

How does this question affect their heart? Remind this client that being average is completely acceptable. What is the impact of not needing to excel and be a star at everything?

Invite into awareness how choices are made.

Issues That May Arise in the Coaching Relationship

– Remember that clients who identify with Type Three will have the tendency to want you to see them as accomplished and successful, which they often are. The coach can certainly recognize these feats, while being careful not to equate the external signs of accomplishment with the client's inherent self-worth. A conversation on what success means can lead to fruitful insights. What aspects of life has the client put on the back burner?

– The average Type Three communication style tends to be direct, fast-paced, and action-oriented. These clients tend to focus on getting more visible signs of achievement, such as multiple degrees and certificates. They like bottom-line answers and tend to put doing and being into discrete categories.

– These clients may be attracted to a coach that they see as successful. The transformative work for these clients will come in finding their way into their own hearts. Focus on communication that comes from your own open heart and on questions that do not have obvious or immediate answers. Fieldwork can emphasize trying out activities that are done for their own sake and that have personal value.

OBSERVATIONS AND WORKING WITH YOUR PREDOMINANT PATTERNS

Below are some of the patterns that are associated with the Type Three personality constellation. The process of working with these patterns in order to gain more emotional health and an increased sense of inner peace includes the steps outlined below.

1. Become a detective and recognize when the pattern shows up.

2. Create a little distance between yourself and the pattern as you normalize it.

3. Be with the experience of the pattern and its associated sensations.

4. Allow the experience with compassion and nonjudgment.

5. Acknowledge and accept what is showing up.

Refer to appendix F for an expanded version of this process.

Living a Goal-Oriented Life

Notice the tendency to create goals in every part of your life.

Identify the consequences, both positive and negative, of living a goal-oriented life. What do you lose by focusing your energy on creating goals and striving to achieve them?

Notice that it can be challenging to even imagine another way of living. All that is required at this point is being willing to recognize and discern the difference between the compulsive quality of being goal-driven and keeping focused on what has heart and meaning for you.

Notice the tendency to feel that you need to be the best and to be outstanding. This can leave you experiencing the need to give yourself constant pep talks, like the little engine that repeated, "I think I can, I think I can . . ." and to get your act together so they never see you sweat.

Presenting a Successful Image

Notice that the focus on presenting a successful image is the source of great fatigue and stress.

If this is a core pattern for you, you may notice that:

- Even if you are successful, even extremely successful, you might occasionally get a glimpse of sadness and a sense that something is still missing.

- Regardless of your level of success, you may feel restless or the need to push yourself even further, especially if someone else is being acknowledged in your area of expertise.

- You may never feel authentically successful; that is, you may fear being found out by others, thus having the need to create more levels to the image you've created.

Seeking Attention

Notice your desire to seek attention.

The Type Three personality is the embodiment of the universal need for recognition and acknowledgment. You may want people to know who you are and how important you are. When that focus takes most of your energy, however, you can lose a sense of self.

To take this pattern to a deeper and more tender level, notice when the desire for attention is tied to feeling valued and worthwhile. Being both honest and compassionate with yourself is necessary to support you in moving to an experience of greater self-awareness and liberation.

People with Type Three personalities tend to have a great capacity for adapting to different circumstances.

- This quality can be an enormous asset when it reflects your ability to be flexible and responsive.

- It can be detrimental when you adapt in order to fit into an image that is perceived to be acceptable and look successful to others. It takes enormous energy to reshape your image and identity into what you anticipate will help you look good to others.

- Notice your capacity for identifying your own values, needs, and feelings. What is important to you? Notice if taking steps to identify your own feelings leaves you feeling vulnerable, even slightly naked. This may be a cue that your heart has not received much attention.

Stretching the Truth

Notice a tendency to stretch the truth.

Are there any places where you deceive others or where you deceive yourself?

You might notice the tendency to tell little white lies when it's convenient or to create false stories that will shine the best light on you. Sometimes deceit shows itself by putting on a different persona for different people. The tendency toward falseness is one of the unconscious Type Three strategies that takes you away from your authentic self.

FIELDWORK PRACTICES

1. Create time and space that is just for you—where you are not responding to any outside demands and there is no need to perform.

This time and space are for exploring you. For example, you might want to create a collage that reflects what brings you joy or create an altar or sacred space that speaks to your deeper self. You may want to take a process painting or writing class where the focus is on authentic expression, not product. You might want to engage in spiritual readings.

This will be part of your practice in turning your attention inward.

2. Practice sharing your real self with others.

You may want to begin by seeking out safe people with whom you can share your feelings, doubts, and needs. This practice of being real with others may create a sense of vulnerability, so be tender with yourself. You may be surprised to learn that others value your openness and more authentic nature.

3. Be curious about the urge to succeed—at any price.

Notice any motivations behind the desire to succeed. Who and what defines success for you?

4. Pay attention to your heart.

Stop and ask yourself what you are feeling.

Shift your attention from the outside to the inner world. Become more familiar with the sensations around your heart—begin to open your heart to yourself. Allow yourself to relax around your heart. Invite yourself into your heart. Breathe.

If this feels like foreign territory, identify people who can support you in the practice of being in your own heart. This may be a spiritual teacher, coach, mentor, or a group that focuses on developing qualities of the heart.

As you develop a stronger relationship with your heart, notice what changes in your life.

5. Practice asking yourself, "What is true about this situation?"

People with Type Three patterns can spin a situation to make it look good or acceptable. This can happen so quickly and automatically that you don't realize you are doing it. As you assess a situation that you are tempted to use to make you look good, ask yourself whose approval you are trying to get. Reflect on what deeper value there is for you in staying with what is true.

Movement to Highest Levels of Health

To move toward the highest levels of health, people who identify with Type Three must eventually:

- "Let go of their belief that their value is dependent upon the positive regard of others."[2]

- Allow themselves to experience the underlying hurt and grief that lies just underneath their mask of having it all together.

- Shift their center of gravity from outside to inside themselves.

- Begin to become more inner-directed and authentic.

TYPE SEVEN

FIGURE 8.3

THE ENNEAGRAM ICEBERG MODEL FOR TYPE SEVEN

Enneagram Type Seven – The Enthusiast

THEME: "I love life and want to experience it all!"

GIFTS:
- Playful and spontaneous
- Versatile
- Quick-minded
- Entertaining

AVERAGE BEHAVIORS:
- Keep moving to greener grass
- Keep options open
- Acquire things or experiences
- Scattered, distracted
- Uninhibited
- Excessive

 AT MY BEST:
- Accomplished
- Truly joyful in the moment
- Savor life
- Profound sense of gratitude

Frustration
↑
Anticipate the next thing
↑
Do many things/go many directions
Touch the surface of experience

IMPACT ON OTHERS:

\+ Others enjoy my adventurous spirit and planning.
Others are touched by my gratitude and awe.

\- Others feel the impact of my lack of follow-through.
Others feel left in the wake of my nonstop energy, activity, and restlessness.

 AWAKENED CAPACITY
- Wonderment through Sobriety and Presence

 FOCUS OF ATTENTION:
The world is full of possibilities.

 INNER CRITIC MESSAGE:
I'm good or okay if
I get what I need.

CORE COPING STRATEGY:
Don't miss out.

 MISS THE MARK/PASSION:
Gluttony

 HABIT OF THE MIND:
Planning

SENSE OF SELF:
I am free, spontaneous, and full of fun and life.

AVOID:
Being caged in

PURSUE:
Open-ended freedom to find happiness

CORE BELIEFS:
- My source of satisfaction is outside of me.
- I don't trust anyone else to be able to satisfy or nuture me. I have to take care of me.

TYPE SEVEN: THE ENTHUSIAST
THEME: "I love life and want to experience it all!"

ABOVE THE WATERLINE

 ### When I'm Expansive and at My Healthiest Levels (Gifts and at My Best)

I'm playful and spontaneous. I am energetic and can respond freely and in the moment.

I am versatile. I move with ease into a vast array of topics, tasks, and activities.

I am quick-minded and an avid learner. I have fun sparring with others and coming up with witty comments.

I am entertaining. My easy humor and sense of fun and happiness are enjoyed by others.

I am productive, practical, and prolific. I am accomplished.

I am truly joyful in the moment. I'm in love with life.

I savor life as it is now.

I have a profound sense of gratitude and awe about life.

 ### Awakened Capacity: Wonderment through Sobriety and Presence

When I'm in contact with my heart, the experience of wonder, gratitude, and an openhearted appreciation for the fullness of the present moment brings great joy. This experience is only available when I slow my pace and sink into the depths of life, allowing myself to experience what is here now.

 ### Distinguishing Characteristics When the Personality Has Its Grip on Me

I move to where the grass is greener, and it always seems to be greener someplace besides here.

I wait to the last minute to make plans in case something better comes along. I like to keep my options open—then I avoid feeling trapped.

I focus on acquiring and consuming experiences and things. I may never use what I get, but at the time, it feels like I have to have it.

My energy is scattered, distracted, and unfocused. I move haphazardly without a sense of direction and have difficulty staying with or completing projects.

I am uninhibited. I dismiss or override any need to limit myself.

I am excessive. I exceed what is needed, pursuing pleasure or acquiring far more than is necessary.

👁 Where I Put My Attention When Identified with the Personality (Focus of Attention)

I put my attention on all of the possibilities available to me and want to experience them all. While I do many things, I miss the experience because I am focused on anticipating what will come next. I miss the satisfaction that comes with being present, which reinforces an underlying sense of frustration.

Impact on Others

+ Positive

Others are invigorated and stimulated by enthusiasm.

Others feel engaged by my optimism and love of life.

– Negative

Others feel frustrated by my lack of commitment and follow-through.

Others are irritated by my restlessness and need for instant gratification.

BELOW THE WATERLINE

The Ego Code's Inner Logic

Core Belief

No one can be trusted to satisfy me. I am on my own.

I believe that my source of true satisfaction is somewhere out there, and it will be something even better than what I have now. I just need to keep searching for it, believing on one hand that it must lie just around the corner. On the other hand, I despair of ever finding it.

 Coaching Cue::

> *Examples of what you might hear your clients say or do/not do:*
>
> - *There are so many exciting opportunities. I want to try them all. What's next?*
>
> - *Don't ask me to deal with the details. That can get boring fast. And I came up with the idea. Time for someone else to step in and get it done.*
>
> - *I've always wanted to go to that destination (or try out that activity). I'm going to make plans for it right now.*
>
> - *I get so frustrated when my spouse wants me to stay home and take care of chores. I've made plans for something that I really want to do. Why can't he understand that?*

◁ Triangle of Identity

What I Pursue: Open-Ended Freedom

I want the freedom to do as I please. Even while I'm participating in one event, I'm planning for the next one. I'm proud of my spontaneity and flexibility, which allow me to respond in the moment to new opportunities. I'm on the go.

What I Avoid: Being Caged In

I avoid anything that could potentially cage me in an uncomfortable or painful situation. The sense of danger that comes with feeling trapped almost feels like death.

My Core Coping Strategy: Not Missing Out

I rely on being in the search for interesting new activities and experiences. I easily get excited about new opportunities, which seem to constantly come my way. I tend not to stay with anything (or sometimes anyone) for an extended length of time. And I have a backup plan.

Sense of Self ("I Am . . .")

I see myself as fun and enthusiastic. I am stimulating and stimulated. While these are positive qualities, they limit me when I don't allow myself to feel my sadness and to be in my heart.

 ## Fixation of the Personality (Habit of the Mind)

My mind is focused on anticipating that something better is out there.[3] And if it's not THIS, then it will be what comes next. The anticipation keeps me focused on planning what's next rather than what is right here in the moment. Thus, I miss what is available to me in the present.

 ## Where I Miss the Mark (Passion)

I miss the mark by trying to fill up my inner emptiness with things and experiences—now. By thinking that my satisfaction is going to come from finding it in the external world, I move farther and farther away from my heart. My insatiability ultimately leaves me feeling even more empty. I feel anxious that I may make the wrong choice and thus miss the one true source of happiness. Rather than selecting one choice, then, I will try to have as many experiences as possible. This passion is called gluttony.

 ## What the Inner Critic Insists Upon

My inner critic rewards me when I get what I need.[4] It rewards gluttony, my continual search for a new experience, or more material goods. It tries to convince me that being on the search will ultimately be fulfilling. As long as I'm caught in the inner critic's web, I remain focused on looking for the next thing without hope of real satisfaction.

What Causes Me Stress

My stress increases when I feel stuck with a commitment that keeps me from doing other things that I want. Conversely, my stress is increased when I feel overwhelmed by all the activities that I have gotten involved in. I have too many balls in the air.

When I'm Most Constricted and Inflexible

I escape from pain at all costs.

I'm impulsive and irresponsible.

I can be reckless and out of control.

I can become overwhelmed and paralyzed.

Lines of Access

Type Seven shares a line with both Types One and Five. Below are just a few ways that the characteristics of either of these types might show up or the reactions I might have to these characteristics in others. Refer to the discussion of these two types for further insight.

At Type One: I can become critical of myself and others, and even perfectionistic. A gift of One is that I am more conscientious of my responsibilities and begin to recognize the value in being of service.

At Type Five: It's hard for me to admit, but I retreat into my dark inner world where I feel isolated and overwhelmed. I can be very critical of others who display these characteristics. With increasing awareness and presence, I appreciate slowing down, being able to focus, and eventually gaining clarity.

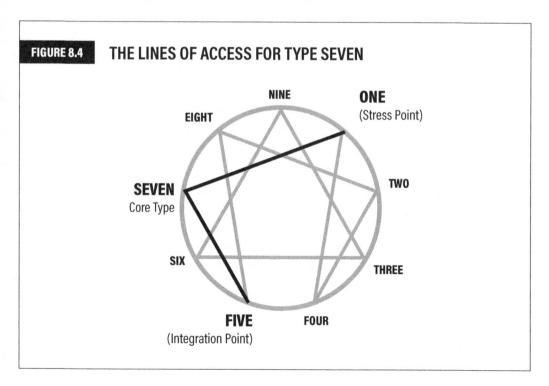

FIGURE 8.4 **THE LINES OF ACCESS FOR TYPE SEVEN**

Type Seven Case Study

Brandon came to coaching providing the following information about himself:

A few years ago I left a career in the entertainment industry, with the idea that I wanted to work independently on a career that would use my creative energies in an area that I have passion for. I get enthusiastic about new things and exciting places and interesting people, but I don't seem to have anything of substance to show for my enthusiasm. I feel like I'm going around in circles, and I'm frustrated.

I think I'm smart, so why don't I have tangible results? I guess I do have a lot of irons in the fire. I've made a lot of starts but haven't seen a lot of projects through. I'd also love to have a long-term relationship. That hasn't happened yet.

Brandon is a multitalented, witty, cause-oriented person who is outgoing, engaging, and fun. He's a guy on the move.

His initial intentions for coaching included:

- Creating a life and work that is fun, meaningful, and productive

- Learning how to be accountable for seeing projects through

- Producing tangible results and creating the groundwork for financial stability

When Brandon discovered that he had a Type Seven personality, he reported recognizing the following longtime patterns that were still active:

- I am always on the go, anticipating what will be next. It's hard for me to be still in mind and in body.

- I try a little of this and move on to a little of that. I haven't committed to anything. I've been fearful that I would miss out on something that would really be right.

- I get bored easily.

- While I enjoy being with friends, I realize that I haven't really opened my heart to let another person in. Maybe I haven't even let myself in yet.

One major theme of coaching for Brandon focused on slowing down and listening to his feelings. Feelings felt foreign unless they were just happy feelings. Brandon found sadness and other feelings he viewed as negative hard to tolerate initially. He eventually felt more at peace with himself when he allowed in whatever feelings he had. He also discovered that he massively underestimated the amount of time any task would take. As challenging as it was for him, his outer schedule slowly began to adjust to the realities based on the time required to fulfill a commitment, one at a time.

He was asked to cut the number of activities in his weekly schedule by half. This was a stretch, but as he did so, he realized that his schedule was still more than enough full. At the same time, he began to discern which activities filled not just his schedule but fulfilled him.

As Brandon worked with making more space for what he really wanted in his life, he realized that he was spending lots of time with people who weren't all that supportive. He took important steps in reassessing and reallocating his social schedule, spending more time with those with whom he could enjoy more heartful relationships.

He identified practices around gratitude, allowing himself into his own heart, more honest communications, and being aware of his higher intentions that support him in creating the life and work he has wanted.

SUGGESTIONS FOR COACHES WORKING WITH INDIVIDUALS WHO IDENTIFY WITH TYPE SEVEN

Acknowledge Their Inner Experience

I believe that I must stay up all the time, pushing my energy out into the world and keeping other people up.

Others expect me to be happy and positive all of the time.

I don't like to acknowledge anything negative. I have difficulty staying with negative or sad emotions for any length of time.

I have a lot of interests and am very curious, so I can become easily distracted and diverted from deeper purposes and commitments.

My energy can go in many different directions, so I notice that I have difficulty focusing and completing tasks that I eagerly start.

I often feel frustrated. Things just don't turn out the way I really want.

Others may not know this about me, but I am very hard on myself.

Offer Counterintuitive Questions/Comments

What are you feeling right now? Can you stay with that feeling for a little longer? Tell me about your sadness or disappointment.
> Encourage clients who identify with Type Seven to be with their pain, fear, and restlessness rather than trying to escape from these.

Let's look at the sources of support you have available to you. Who could you trust enough to ask for help? Who could you allow yourself to rely on?
> The issue of feeling that there is no one that they can rely on goes to the core for people who identify with Type Seven. Help them identify what support is available to them.

What is the impact on you when you complete a project?
> Support this client in focusing on a project and seeing it through.

I hear the voice of your inner critic right now. Does that feel accurate? What is the impact on you of believing the inner critic? In relationship to this topic we've been exploring, what do you truly appreciate and accept about yourself in this moment?

Invite into awareness how choices are made.

Issues That May Arise in the Coaching Relationship

–   Remember that clients who identify with Type Seven may show up in the relationship with a lot of energy and enthusiasm for coaching. After all, this is something new to explore. This client may be surprised by the amount of undiscovered feeling that surfaces as they are guided to experiment with allowing their energy to quiet. This may also cause some resistance, as sadness, disappointment, frustration, boredom, or related feelings are not considered acceptable. When asked, the client may stay with a feeling for only a moment, then decide "I've dealt with it, and it's time to move on." Support the client in recognizing and staying with feelings for incrementally longer periods of time until this is recognized as a normal part of life. As the capacity for tolerating their feelings increases, they find that they are more able to stay in the moment.

–   The average Type Seven communication pattern is generally fast-paced, action-filled, and outward-directed. Their energy can fill the room. Their sensitive, appreciative nature becomes more apparent as they slow their pace and take in what is good in their life right now.

–   People who identify with Type Seven will likely begin their relationship with a coach as friends. Because they have internalized the expectation that they need to be the life of the party, they may unconsciously try to entertain or be up for you. You can address this early on and gradually slow the pace of the coaching so that the client can relax this automatic pattern and the more authentic person can surface. You can also be instrumental in supporting clients in gradually reducing their long list of pleasurable activities to a realistic number. This process can be difficult but allows for a deepening of gratitude for each experience and greater levels of heart-based fulfillment.

OBSERVATIONS AND WORKING WITH YOUR PREDOMINANT PATTERNS

Below are some of the patterns that are associated with the Type Seven personality constellation. The process of working with these patterns in order to gain more emotional health and an increased sense of inner peace includes the steps outlined below.

1. Become a detective and recognize when the pattern shows up.

2. Create a little distance between yourself and the pattern as you normalize it.

3. Be with the experience of the pattern and its associated sensations.

4. Allow the experience with compassion and nonjudgment.

5. Acknowledge and accept what is showing up.

Refer to appendix F for an expanded version of this process.

Notice Your High Energy

The high energy of Type Seven can show up in different ways.

Notice your tendency to push your energy out into the world. This might show up as talking fast, sometimes forgetting to inhale.

It might show up as always being on the go, often overbooking yourself and trying to be in a lot of different places at almost the same time. One challenge you face is that there doesn't seem to be a limit to things to do and places to go. Notice when you put off making a decision to be with a particular friend to see if something even more interesting comes along.

Do you have a difficult time saying no to all the wonderful opportunities that come your way? Perhaps you notice that it feels that this is a once in a lifetime situation or that you'll miss out on something important if you pass.

Observe if you are trying to avoid something, such as a sense of boredom or another feeling that you have defined as negative.

This high, outward moving energy is fed by adrenaline and can be quite intoxicating. Living with an adrenal rush can feel quite normal for those who identify with this personality. While it may be fun to have this enthusiasm for all the possibilities in life, you might also notice that you're often exhausted or stressed. It can feel difficult to contain your energy.

Being the Entertainer and Being On

Those who identify with Type Seven often find themselves in the role of entertaining others and revving up the excitement. They sometimes find that they have trained others to expect them to be up and energized.

What does being up do for you? How does it impact your experience of yourself? Notice your own expectations of yourself as the center of an event. Notice how being up impacts the quality of your relationships.

Dealing with Pain and Grief

When you take a moment to slow down, what do you experience?

Notice if you have a sense of sadness or anxiety. Notice if it feels acceptable to experience something other than being up.

People who identify with Type Seven often try to avoid any sense of inner pain, as if once experienced, it will consume them. So there is a tendency to shortcut grief or other painful inner feelings and get on with it. Pain can feel useless.

Interrupting the grief process only serves to bury feelings that will surface at another, equally inconvenient time, but with perhaps more intensity. Notice what you tell yourself about having feelings other than those associated with being on.

Frustration and Impatience

Notice when you get impatient or frustrated. Stop and take a few deep breaths. What does impatience feel like? Notice what you tend to do to discharge the discomfort of impatience.

What does frustration feel like? What do you tend to do when you experience frustration? How does it impact your life? Notice how frequently you say that you are frustrated and how frequently you feel frustrated.

What's around the Corner?

You might notice that you tend to spend much of your attention on anticipating the next thing.

How do you experience anticipation? Notice when you are focusing on what's next rather than being fully attentive to what is happening now. Notice what the experience of anticipation feels like for you—where do you experience it? What are the consequences for you of living in the anticipation mode? What do you miss when your attention is enmeshed with anticipation?

FIELDWORK PRACTICES

1. Allow some spaciousness amid the mental activity.

With all the planning, anticipation, and mental chatter that is associated with this type, you may find yourself mentally fatigued. Commit to a meditation practice that supports you in coming back to your body and your physical sensations, which will help in creating mental spaciousness.

This practice requires patience. It is not meant to be figured out and completed in a few sittings. Quieting the internal mental messages is a lifelong commitment.

You may also discover that taking quiet walks in nature will support you in quieting yourself.

Somatic work can also be very supportive in developing a different relationship with your mind.

2. Practice a new way to schedule.

An automatic pattern includes being rushed and often late for appointments. You might notice that you have not given yourself enough buffer time between appointments or that you have allocated too little time for any one task or appointment.

Take a look at your calendar. Cut the number of appointments and activities by at least 25 percent each day for a week and see what happens. You may actually need to cut the number of activities you schedule by 50 percent to enjoy being where you are. Cutting your appointments by this percentage may feel impossible; however, give it time to work. Compassionately notice the internal pressure to fill every moment, and notice what is under this pressure.

3. Experience and stay with feelings.

At the average level, those identified with Type Seven tend to interrupt a complete processing of their feelings, both the positive and the painful ones. Allow yourself to have a direct experience of having your feelings. What happens when you simply stay with your feelings as they arise? What does THIS feeling that is arising NOW feel like in your body? In your heart?

You might notice that you need to slow down . . . way down . . . in order to have a fuller experience of your feelings, and ultimately, a deeper relationship with yourself.

4. Enjoy what is here now.

Take time to really be aware of the gifts you have in your life at this time and to take in the preciousness of life. Experiment with what it feels like to simply take in. You'll notice that this is a very different energy than pushing out.

What would support you in creating space to experience more of what is available to you in this moment? What is different for you when you do create space in which you can just be, rather than focus on doing?

5. Give yourself a chance.

People who identify with Type Seven tend to be both multitalented and impatient with slow-moving processes, so they tend to avoid staying with activities that require developmental knowledge or skill-building. By staying at the surface level, you shortchange yourself and often do not know what you are fully capable of. Take the time to bring your abilities to fruition.

You put pressure on yourself when you expect to be an instant expert. Of course, you're bright and can generally pull off new challenges with your charm. But there are other ways to share your talents. For example, experiment with slowing down your timeline between learning something new and delivering a workshop on it.

Stay focused on seeing tasks through to completion. Notice what you experience when you bring closure to a task. How does this feel?

Movement to Highest Levels of Health

To move toward the highest levels of health, people who identify with Type Seven must eventually:

- "Let go of the belief that they require specific objects and experiences to feel fulfilled so they are able to fully assimilate their experiences and be nourished by them."[5]

- Stop pursuing fulfillment outside of themselves and find it in the present moment.

- Let go of the conditions and rules they place on their own happiness.

- Allow the heart to open. Enjoy profound appreciation for the awe and beauty of life.

TYPE EIGHT

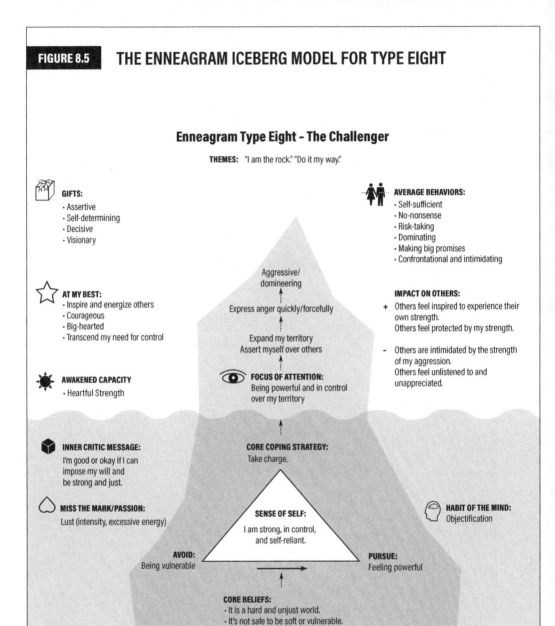

FIGURE 8.5   **THE ENNEAGRAM ICEBERG MODEL FOR TYPE EIGHT**

Enneagram Type Eight – The Challenger

THEMES: "I am the rock." "Do it my way."

GIFTS:
- Assertive
- Self-determining
- Decisive
- Visionary

AT MY BEST:
- Inspire and energize others
- Courageous
- Big-hearted
- Transcend my need for control

AWAKENED CAPACITY
- Heartful Strength

AVERAGE BEHAVIORS:
- Self-sufficient
- No-nonsense
- Risk-taking
- Dominating
- Making big promises
- Confrontational and intimidating

IMPACT ON OTHERS:

+ Others feel inspired to experience their own strength.
  Others feel protected by my strength.

− Others are intimidated by the strength of my aggression.
  Others feel unlistened to and unappreciated.

Aggressive/
domineering

Express anger quickly/forcefully

Expand my territory
Assert myself over others

FOCUS OF ATTENTION:
Being powerful and in control
over my territory

INNER CRITIC MESSAGE:
I'm good or okay if I can
impose my will and
be strong and just.

MISS THE MARK/PASSION:
Lust (intensity, excessive energy)

CORE COPING STRATEGY:
Take charge.

SENSE OF SELF:
I am strong, in control,
and self-reliant.

HABIT OF THE MIND:
Objectification

AVOID:
Being vulnerable

PURSUE:
Feeling powerful

CORE BELIEFS:
- It is a hard and unjust world.
- It's not safe to be soft or vulnerable.

TYPE EIGHT: THE CHALLENGER
THEME: "I am a rock." "Do it my way!"

ABOVE THE WATERLINE

 When I'm Expansive and at My Healthiest Levels (Gifts and at My Best)

I am assertive. I have the energy and confidence to meet and overcome obstacles.

I am self-determining. I make decisions for myself and follow through with action.

I am decisive. I quickly respond to problems by advancing appropriate solutions.

I am visionary, seeing new scenarios that others often do not see.

I inspire and energize others to act with confidence and courage.

I am courageous, protecting others who are in the underdog position. I can challenge those in positions of power when I think they are acting unjustly.

I am magnanimous, having a gentle and big heart.

With my focus on the well-being of others, I transcend my need to be in control.

 Awakened Capacity: Heartful Strength

With a deep capacity to care, I communicate directly and can mobilize action on behalf of others. When in contact with my grounded body and open heart, I am a force for good and kindness in the world.

 Distinguishing Characteristics When the Personality Has Its Grip on Me

I am self-sufficient. I think that I don't need anyone.

I am a no-nonsense person. I am direct, saying it like I see it.

I take risks, as I like the intensity of playing for high stakes.

I am dominating and refuse to compromise. I like to exert my influence on others and have them capitulate to doing it my way.

I make big promises. It gives me currency with others, increasing my stature, influence, and power.

I am confrontational and intimidating, overwhelming others with the force of my intense energy and anger.

👁 Where I Put My Attention When Identified with the Personality (Focus of Attention)

I put my attention on being in control to protect myself and others from the injustices of life. I place myself over others and expect them to fall in line. I continually expand my sphere of influence and ownership and make it clear that others should not impinge on my territory. I can be aggressive and not even aware that I overwhelm others with my intensity.

Impact on Others

+ Positive

Others feel my strength, support, and protection when it is needed.

Others feel inspired by the generosity of my spirit and my capacity to take a stand.

– Negative

Others can feel intimidated by my forcefulness.

Others feel unheard, unseen, and unappreciated.

BELOW THE WATERLINE

The Ego Code's Inner Logic

Core Belief

I believe that it's a hard and unjust world. I need to protect myself from the unfairness and injustice of others. I cannot show my vulnerability because others will take unfair advantage of me. Therefore, I must show my strength and power.

 Coaching Cue::

Examples of what you might hear your clients say or do/not do:

- *Hell yes, I take risks. I enjoy testing my mettle against the odds.*

- *I will take decisive action whether others like it or not. I will not let others push me or my family around.*

- *I'm not apologizing for saying it like it is. I get angry when others are mealy-mouthed or talk around the real issues.*

- *Who cares if I argue loudly and sometimes get forceful? Somebody here has to show others what it takes to get the job done.*

◁ Triangle of Identity

What I Pursue: Being Powerful and in Control
I need to be in charge of my own circumstances and of my future. I live life with gusto, putting out a lot of energy, and challenge those who would create obstacles.

What I Avoid: Showing Vulnerability
I avoid anything that I think makes me look weak, soft, or vulnerable. I will not allow myself to be taken advantage of, and any sign of weakness could be used against me. Being tender is very risky.

My Core Coping Strategy: Imposing My Will
I show my strength and power by imposing my will and my truth on others. I can easily dominate a situation. I expand my control over other people and over things. The more expansive my control, the more protected and less vulnerable I feel.

157

Sense of Self ("I Am . . .")

I see myself as a strong, assertive, and self-reliant person. I am strong-willed and get things done.

While these qualities are positive, overreliance on them results in having great difficulty difficulty in connecting to my inner experience and revealing my vulnerability, which is a source of authentic strength.

Fixation of the Personality (Habit of the Mind)

I objectify others so that they don't seem real or special to me. The other just becomes an object that could get in the way. This makes it easy to see the other person as a threat to my control, and I make the other person my enemy. This allows me to express my anger and rage.

Where I Miss the Mark (Passion)

I live life with intensity, sometimes excessive intensity. I use more energy than I need for most activities and interactions. The more I push outward and the more energy I expend, the more real I feel. My intense energy pushes other people away from me, which feels like it protects me. Ultimately, however, that creates the exact opposite of what I really want. This passion is called lust.

What the Inner Critic Insists Upon

I am strong and in control of a situation.[6] It doesn't allow me to discern between situations in which I could relax and those in which taking control would be appropriate. As long as I'm caught in the inner critic's web, I try to impose my control and truth over other people.

What Causes Me Stress

My overreliance on my bodily strength is a cause of stress. When I become overly self-sufficient, demanding, and controlling, my stress spirals up. It increases when I avoid revealing tenderness, especially to those I care about.

When I'm Most Constricted and Inflexible

I am dictatorial and can be violent.

I am filled with uncontrollable rage.

I am above the law.

Lines of Access

Type Eight shares a line with both Types Five and Two. Below are just a few ways that the characteristics of either of these types might show up or the reactions I might have to these characteristics in others. Refer to the discussion of these two types for further insight.

At Type Five: I can become withdrawn, secretive, and fearful. A gift of the Five is that I can step back and assess a situation rather than charging ahead impulsively.

At Type Two: It's hard for me to admit, but I can feel needy, rejected, and alone, the very experiences that make me feel weak. I can be very critical of others who display these characteristics. With greater awareness and presence, I begin to experience the powerful strength of my openheartedness.

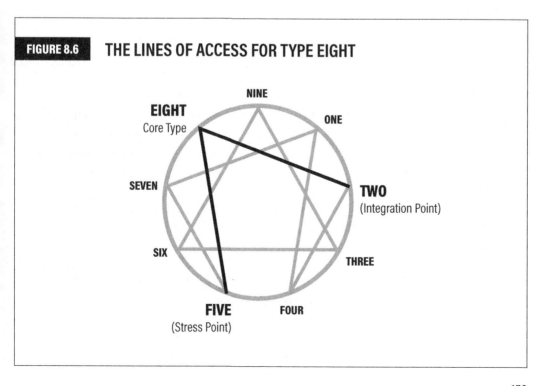

FIGURE 8.6   **THE LINES OF ACCESS FOR TYPE EIGHT**

Type Eight Case Study

Stella came to coaching providing the following information about herself:

This isn't working. I'm getting negative feedback at work from every direction.

Maybe I'm not supposed to tell people what I think, but it just seems to come out of my mouth. I'm not trying to fight people, but I keep hearing that I'm pushing too much.

I really don't understand what they are talking about. The people that work for me seem a little afraid of me, too. I just wish they'd stand up and tell me what they think.

I really want to do a good job and know that I have good ideas. But I'm tired of all this conflict, and it's having a spillover effect at home with my husband. I'm scared that he'll get tired of all of this and leave me.

Stella was a ball of energy. She exuded confidence (even if she's really not feeling confident) and strong energy. She had a hearty laugh but wanted to get to business quickly. Her impatience was evident.

Her goals for coaching included:

- Finding out how to reduce the negative feedback she was getting from work

- Finding ways of introducing her ideas in a more effective manner

- Getting along better with others, in general

Stella wasn't enthusiastic about exploring the Enneagram but had sufficient trust in the coaching relationship to give it a try. The following are among the Type Eight patterns that she recognized:

- She discovered her pattern of intensity. She never thought much about her big energy and just thought it was a sign of being confident and knowing where you are going. Now she was beginning to see how this could have a negative impact on others. Maybe other people did feel bulldozed?

- She knew she was quick to anger but thought that she had a right to it because it felt to her like people were against her. Instead, she started to recognize this as a pattern of her type.

- Her desire to control outcomes and to have control over others became clearer to her. She hadn't realized that this would distance her so much from others.

– She also knew that she had a special relationship with a few people who were really kind to her. She started to see that this would happen when she became more open and heartful.

It was clear that the coach needed to be confident, strong, and willing to meet Stella's energy with like energy initially. This gave Stella the experience of being met.

One major theme of Stella's coaching centered on ways she could begin opening to her heart. She identified special people that she cared for deeply and what she wanted for them. She experimented with new ways of showing them her affection. With her husband, it meant voicing her love. She had thought her actions showed her love but came to see that as an insufficient communication. Slowly, she practiced slowing down and communicating with friends, sometimes first in writing, then verbally.

She also began to recognize, with help from a few trusted allies, including her husband, that others were not against her. She practiced shifting her internal dialogue at work, and over time, her energy softened.

She also practiced making amends. The first person she was asked to do this for was with herself. Eventually, she had numerous individual conversations where she apologized. The (unexpected) outpouring she received from others reinforced the opening of her heart.

Stella remains a person of substance who is willing to take a stand on issues that particularly affect those with less power or who are the underdogs. She tends to have more heart mixed in with her boldness.

SUGGESTIONS FOR COACHES WORKING WITH INDIVIDUALS WHO IDENTIFY WITH TYPE EIGHT

Acknowledge Their Inner Experience

I believe that I must protect myself from being controlled by others. I'm not going to let anyone else tell me what to do!

I like to be in charge. I expect that others will look to me for direction. If not, I will give it anyway.

It's important to me to feel alive. (But I don't necessarily realize how intense I am).

I show the world that I feel strong and powerful. I don't let anyone get too close to me. And I don't want to show any part of myself where I might feel vulnerable.

Offer Counterintuitive Questions/Comments

How do you show others that you care about them? How do you know when a person needs you to listen to them? What do you do when you are really listening to another person?
>Support the person who identifies with Type Eight in being more emotionally available to others.

I'm on your side. I'm not against you.
>Diminish the need for people who identify with Type Eight to feel the need to constantly protect themselves. Coaches for these clients need to be firm and forthright. Speak the truth.

How do you show your more tender feelings?
>Provide absolute support for the expression of softer feelings and vulnerabilities.

What if you experimented with occasionally letting yourself off the hook of being the rock for so many people?

Invite into awareness how choices are made.

Issues That May Arise in the Coaching Relationship

- Remember that clients who identify with Type Eight want to be in control, to get to issues quickly, and to be action-oriented. Get clear from the beginning as to what outcomes the client wants to attain. These clients may have few trusted people that they can truly open up to, so the coaching relationship can be a source of immense relief and openness once trust has been established.

- The average Eight communication pattern is direct, bottom-line, no-nonsense, and passionate. These clients want a person who will meet their energy, so the coach's communication pattern also needs to be direct and confident. Clients want someone who they can push up against and have the experience that the coach is there with them.

- These clients often receive feedback that they are too strong, demanding, or intimidating. In short, their relationships with others are often strained. They may tend to dismiss this feedback, as they do not experience their own intensity in the way that others do. The last thing clients think they want is to feel and express their softer side. Be the model for being direct, strong, and openhearted. Being guided to notice and experience your fears can lead your clients to experience the strength that includes both their grounded capacity and their vulnerability.

OBSERVATIONS AND WORKING WITH YOUR PREDOMINANT PATTERNS

Below are some of the patterns that are associated with the Type Eight personality constellation. The process of working with these patterns in order to gain more emotional health and an increased sense of inner peace includes the steps outlined below.

1. Become a detective and recognize when the pattern shows up.

2. Create a little distance between yourself and the pattern as you normalize it.

3. Be with the experience of the pattern and its associated sensations.

4. Allow the experience with compassion and nonjudgment.

5. Acknowledge and accept what is showing up.

Refer to appendix F for an expanded version of this process.

Intensity of Energy

One of the challenges that clients who identify with Type Eight face is the intensity with which they live life.

Notice what your energy feels like to you. Can you sense it in your body?

Notice how you push your energy into others. You might experience that you are energetically pushing against others with the force of your energy. Notice the volume of your voice and how you physically push out your chest.

What are you looking for from the person you are interacting with when you're using your intensity? What happens inside you when the other person is also intense?

What happens when the other person backs away from you? What happens when you relax your energy, even just a little? What difference does that make in an interaction?

Notice how people interact with you. Do they tend to move toward you or away from you? Do others tend to keep a respectful distance from you?

You might notice that you feel more alive when your energy is big and is pushing against others. What are some of the consequences of your intensity on your mental, physical, and emotional health; on your relationships; and on other aspects of your life?

You might also notice that you want to own and control more things or people, scooping them under your sphere of influence. What urge is satisfied when you expand your territory of control? What motivation lies underneath this urge?

The Rock

Those who identify with Type Eight tend to feel that they need to be strong not only for themselves, but for others. And they define strength as not expressing their more tender feelings and not being vulnerable. Notice what being strong feels like for you. What physical sensations tell you that you are strong? What's underneath the compulsion to be strong? How does being the rock contribute to your sense of self?

Notice how it is for you to take a stand. How hard is it for you to have a change of heart or perspective? If you feel that once you've taken a stand, you can't change, what do you tell yourself about changing? What do you sense you are risking?

How satisfying are your relationships? Whose needs are being met when you take the stand of being the strong, in-control person in the relationship?

Where Is Your Tender Side?

People who identify with Type Eight think that they have to be tough, equating bold, big energy and directness with strength. Where is your heart when you associated this intense energy with strength?

Are there people with whom you can share your true feelings, your doubts, your sorrows? How do others get to know your more tender side? What requirements do you have for letting another person in?

When you allow yourself to experience more of your tenderness, what difference does it make for you? What difference does it appear to make in your relationships?

What Are You Against?

Notice a hidden sense that others are against you and will treat you unfairly or take advantage of you in some way. To protect themselves or others, you can put up a ready-made defense system that dares people to defy you. Others may feel that you are rejecting them from the outset and keep you at a distance.

If you have a sense that you or the territory that you control is being threatened, you might notice that you are quick to anger. Sometimes your anger explodes when you're not expecting it to, leading to aggressive behavior that you may later regret or have to explain away to others.

How do you discern a real threat from an automatic reaction? What if others were not really against you? What difference would that make in your interactions? In your anger level?

FIELDWORK PRACTICES

1. Become acquainted with a quieter dimension of your life.

It may be surprising to you to realize that anger does not necessarily always need to be expressed outwardly. Sometimes, it is more than sufficient to just allow yourself to feel the pulse of anger moving through you.

Get to know the circumstances under which you become most reactive, most angry. Are there certain things that are more apt to set you off? You might also notice if you are more reactive when you drink alcohol or use other drugs.

Once you begin to identify these circumstances, experiment with allowing yourself to simply have a direct experience of your anger. Wait and listen. Quietly observe how it rises up within you, then courses through your body without your having to do anything else. Notice what your anger wants you to do or say. Take long, deep breaths into your belly, and just observe the nature of this pattern without following through on your urges.

2. Experiment with your energy.

How do you know how much energy or force is required to complete a certain task or to have a successful negotiation? You may find that you tend to use the same amount of force, often an excessive amount, regardless of the amount that is required. You might experience this as an interpretation of your aliveness or willfulness.

Practice relaxing your energy, not holding on to something so tightly (both literally and figuratively). What does it feel like to let go?

What do you know about simply allowing rather than pushing? You have the capacity to use different amounts of energy in different circumstances. Practice discerning how much energy is needed.

3. Practice new ways of communicating.

Paying close attention: how would you describe the tone and volume of your voice? Without realizing it, you may come across louder and more insistent and challenging than you have realized. A practice in developing more effective ways to communicate is bringing your attention back to your body and heart, and truly listening to another person's perspective with an intention of understanding them more fully. You can also share your perspective, not from a place of having to get your way, but from an intention of mutual understanding and coming to a resolution that is satisfying to both parties.

4. Let yourself and others in.

People who identify with Type Eight are often surprised to experience their natural tenderness for others. You do have a big heart. Practice allowing your heart to be touched and the experience of your real feelings.

Giving yourself time and calming your energy helps you access the intelligence of your heartfulness. You may be surprised to discover that people are attracted to you.

What do you notice when you quiet and calm yourself? What is it like to let yourself into your own heart?

5. Enjoy without controlling.

What do you do to simply enjoy, without the need for owning or controlling?

Take time in nature just to be and experience your surroundings without a focus on outcomes. You may find it naturally restorative.

Learn to ground yourself in the moment. Explore coming into contact with your belly center.

Practice meditation and conscious breathing techniques to help you reduce your inner tension and stress. Walk more consciously, using a slower pace and taking in some of the neutral, external world.

Movement to Highest Levels of Health

To move toward higher levels of health, people who identify with Type Eight must eventually:

- "Let go of the belief that they must always be in control of their environment, which allows them to let down their guard and heal their hearts."[7]

- Find their innate strength in their vulnerability.

- Remember the simple joys of just being alive.

- Open their hearts to themselves and to others.

Chapter **9**

TYPES ONE, TWO, AND SIX:
The Service-Oriented, Responsible Group

SHARED THEMES

Figuring out the rules of engagement and what needs to be done is one strategy for coping with the stress that accompanies interpersonal relationships.

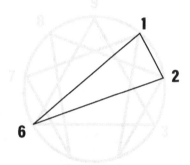

At the average levels of health and effectiveness, three Ennea-gram types share the common personality structure of having a strong inner sense of obligation. They are sometimes called the dutiful types. People who identify with Types One, Two, and Six have a premise that they have to take care of what they identify as their responsibilities before they can have what they want. They are vigilant, tuning into their surroundings to see what needs their attention. Following deeply embedded inner rules, they often feel it is incumbent on them to take action. Thus, their primary dutifulness is to their own mental rules and inner guideposts, which are subject to the mind's changing nature.

People who identify with each of these types have difficulty in quieting their minds. They may secretly feel that they are better than others because of the superior ways of taking care of others, remedying situations, or making things better.

Being of service to others is a healthy attribute. However, when the responsibility-based strategy is an automatic and habitual pattern, the result is that the person tends to feel burned out, stressed by the never-ending list of things that need to be fixed, and often unappreciated. Since the list of responsibilities continues to expand, there is never adequate time for them to take care for their own needs. Ultimately, they can sacrifice their own unlived lives in order to do what is right, to receive approval, or feel secure.

Energetically, these types often display what Horney called "moving toward others," as in surveying what they can do to help. They may convey a sense of urgency or the imperative to keep busy, becoming quite anxious when they don't know what to do next. They may seem overly ready to help out or to take on additional responsibilities, even at their own expense. They may also appear nervous and fidgety or tense and rigid.

TYPE ONE

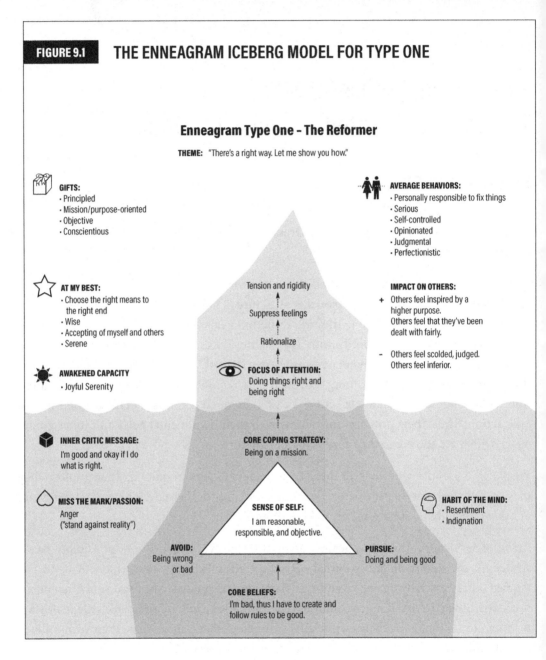

TYPE ONE: THE REFORMER

THEME: "There's a right way. Let me show you how."

ABOVE THE WATERLINE

 When I'm Expansive and at My Healthiest Levels (Gifts and at My Best)

I am principled, holding high ideals. My principles guide my daily living and decisions.

I am mission-oriented and have a higher purpose. I am involved in issues that have significance for the larger good.

I see things objectively, without emotional overtones or judgment.

I am conscientious. I have a strong inner compass of what is morally right or wrong.

The end is important. So are the means. I do not sacrifice one for the other.

I have wisdom that considers what is possible.

I am accepting of myself and others. I have come to recognize that to be human is to be imperfect, and that imperfection does not diminish my goodness.

I am serene and experience an inner quiet.

 Awakened Capacity: Joyful Serenity

I experience an ever-increasing capacity for accepting the fullness of the moment with a quiet joy and serenity. With a mind that's calm and accepting of what's here, I am filled with awe.

 Distinguishing Characteristics When the Personality Has Its Grip on Me

I feel personally responsible to make things right. This sense of obligation permeates my thinking.

I am serious and see life as weighty. There's no time for frivolous pursuits.

I am self-controlled and resist my inner impulses.

I have and often voice opinions on just about everything. I think and talk in terms of what should be done.

I am quick to judge others. I constantly judge myself and my every thought and action.

I spend a lot of energy in trying not to make mistakes. I seek perfection and am often disappointed in myself for not achieving it. So I try even harder.

👁 Where I Put My Attention When Identified with the Personality (Focus of Attention)

I put my attention on doing and being right. It feels deadly for me to be wrong, so I rationalize my decisions, having no room for questioning or uncertainty. I constantly monitor myself so that I will respond correctly to situations that arise, and I monitor my outer environment to assess what needs to be fixed. Emotions and impulses seem messy and irrational, so I suppress them. Thus, I often feel tense and rigid.

Impact on Others

+ Positive

Others can be inspired by the healthy One's integrity, conscientiousness, and willingness to take a stand for the higher good.

Others appreciate the One's concern and fairness.

– Negative

Others can feel judged, criticized, and inferior.

Others may feel the need to monitor or restrain themselves so they are not scolded.

BELOW THE WATERLINE

The Ego Code's Inner Logic

Core Belief

My core belief is that I have to guard against my own wrongdoing. I don't trust myself to be good, so I have my own rules and police myself before anyone else corrects me.

 ## Coaching Cue::

Examples of what you might hear your clients say or do/not do:

- *It's my responsibility for making and doing things right. It's easier to take on the responsibility than having to explain to others in detail what needs to be done right.*

- *If I'm not hard on myself and don't keep correcting myself, then something ugly could pop up.*

- *Yes, I have opinions. I can see very clearly what's right and what's wrong.*

- *What's wrong with these people that they can't figure this out?*

△ Triangle of Identity

What I Pursue: Being Right and Doing Good

I pursue doing things that I think are good and will result in me being a good person. When aspects of my environment are not dealt with correctly, I naturally take it on myself to remedy them.

What I Avoid: Being Wrong or Bad

I avoid being criticized, which magnifies my internal sense of being bad. I monitor and regulate myself to guard against the possibility that my emotions or instincts would overtake my logical mind. Dealing with imperfection is the hardest thing for me in life.

My Core Coping Strategy: Being on a Mission

I cope by turning tasks into a mission that will result in improvements. I have high standards and expectations, which help me focus on doing and being good.

Sense of Self ("I Am . . .")

I see myself as reasonable, objective, and responsible. I keep my emotions in check, as they only make things messy. As a rational person, I see things rightly and know the best course of action.

While these are positive qualities, when overused, they limit my ability to acknowledge and express my full human nature, including my emotional or spiritual dimensions. Any experience that is interpreted as being nonrational is suppressed, creating a buildup of explosive energy. This fixed construct obstructs my ability to recognize that my perspective is one of many possibilities.

 ## Fixation of the Personality (Habit of the Mind)

I experience a great deal of resentment, which is fueled by my judging mind.

I can have a strong sense of indignation and irritation when others don't act in accordance with what I think is best or when life doesn't unfold the way I think is right.

 ## Where I Miss the Mark (Passion)

I have a simmering anger toward many of the things that go on in the world. I generally don't express this anger directly because it could get out of control. But I certainly feel exasperated, and others can feel my great displeasure. In reality, I often resist what is.

 ## What the Inner Critic Insists Upon

My inner critic insists that I do what is right.[1] That is, I must follow my inner critic's assessment of what it deems to be right if I am to see myself as being okay. As long as I am caught in the web of my inner critic, I will be highly critical of myself and others.

My strong inner critic is quick to judge myself and others. It runs a constant commentary that is filled with shoulds and obligations. The judge is simply never satisfied and continuously compares, evaluates, and makes assessments, not only about the what and how, but ultimately, about the inherent worth of myself and others.

What Causes Me Stress

My stress increases when I try to control everything so that I do things perfectly. I become overwhelmed when I try to fix too many things at once. And I become fatigued by constantly adhering to high standards. My constant vigilance causes stress.

I become stressed when others don't understand how hard I am working to do things well. Not knowing what is expected of me also causes stress.

When I'm Most Constricted and Inflexible

I am constantly resentful.

I am unreasonable and closed to any compromise.

I am unethical and act in contradiction to stated principles.

I am brutal in my criticism and self-reproachment.

Lines of Access

Type One shares a line with both Types Four and Seven. Below are just a few ways that the characteristics of either of these types might show up or the reactions I might have to these characteristics in others. Refer to the discussion of these two types for further insight.

At Type Four: I can become envious, depressed, and irrational. A gift of the Four is that I experience feelings and become more able to relate to other people's feelings.

At Type Seven: It's hard for me to admit, but I couldn't care less about rules. I want to be free and indulgent and throw off my usual restrictions. I can be very critical of others who display these characteristics. With greater awareness and presence, I soften my critical voice and begin to experience the pleasures of life with gratitude.

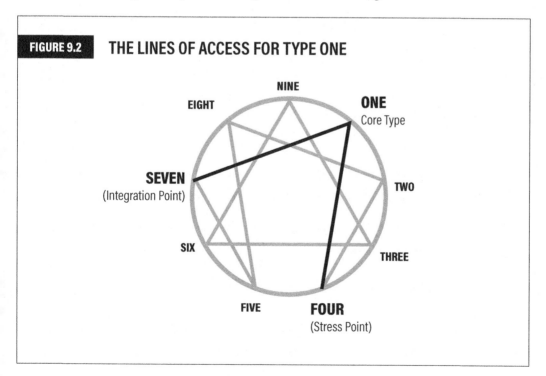

FIGURE 9.2   THE LINES OF ACCESS FOR TYPE ONE

Type One Case Study

Harris came to coaching providing the following information:

I've been promoted to an executive position within a statewide organization that focuses on creating housing alternatives for low-income and displaced families. I am well-positioned to be taking on this level of responsibility for this very important work. I have several direct reports and joined an executive cabinet that has been in place for several years. As its newest member, I can offer new ways of thinking to support our mission.

A few years ago, I received very painful feedback through a 360-degree assessment that I had come across as overly critical of staff and of the organization's operational strategies. I was close to getting fired, but I worked hard with a behavioral consultant, took classes, and focused on improving myself. Now, here I am.

What hasn't changed is that I'm very hard on myself and set exceedingly high standards for myself, and sometimes for others. I really want to do good work in this position. I'm looking for some additional resources to support me.

Harris's promotion reflected his competence and dedication to the mission, as well as his demonstrated willingness to gain new skills.

He initially identified these intentions for coaching:

– Learn how the Enneagram could help him be better

– Continue to strengthen his communication skills

– Explore the possibility of not being so hard on himself

After a reintroduction to the Enneagram, the following are among the Type One patterns that Harris recognized:

– How pervasive the focus on mission had been in his life; if he wasn't moving toward fulfilling a mission, his life did not have much meaning

– His tendencies to be rigid, inflexible, and certain; these qualities did not play as big a role as they had previously, but he was aware they were still present

– The right/wrong polarization dynamic; he was surprised that this was part of the type's patterns

– The centrality of the inner critic; to see the inner critic as a part of the personality that he could potentially have choice around was significant

In the coaching conversation, Harris was quite humble in reflecting on how his past type-related behaviors nearly led to his firing.

One major theme of coaching centered around changing his relationship to the inner critic, which included getting clear on the ways it showed up in his inner world, learning how to create some distance from it, and discerning between the voice of the inner critic and a more authentic source of truth. An important part of his journey focused on connecting more directly with his heart. As he began to experience more compassion for himself, his capacity to appreciate others increased. An ongoing practice is becoming less identified with the critic, which had been with him as long as he could remember.

SUGGESTIONS FOR COACHES WORKING WITH INDIVIDUALS WHO IDENTIFY WITH TYPE ONE

Acknowledge Their Inner Experience

I believe that I am flawed in some way and that listening to my internal critic is necessary to keep me from getting in trouble.

I worry about getting it right, which leads to procrastination or too much attention to detail.

I feel so responsible for making things work well. I sometimes feel like I'm the only adult in the room and must shoulder the responsibilities. Life is serious.

I work a lot. What is play?

Offer Counterintuitive Questions/Comments

What is perfect about this situation just the way it is?

What are other ways of looking at this situation?
> Offer the client the opportunity to identify other possible points of view. Consider ways to reframe the situation. Create spaciousness around this inquiry. This could include putting the situation in the middle of an Enneagram symbol and trying on the perspectives from several different type orientations.

What would it look like for you to be gentle with yourself? What would you have to give up?

What's happening in your heart at this moment?

What is good about you in this moment?

Invite into awareness how choices are made.

Issues That May Arise in the Coaching Relationship

– Remember that clients who identify with Type One are inclined to be very hard on themselves. They may have developed strategies to battle, negotiate with, or be resigned to the inner critic, none of which offer serenity.

– At the average level of health, the Type One communication style tends to be serious, rational, and reasonable. You'll likely hear a lot of shoulds and becauses or justifications for their decisions or behaviors stated in a voice of certainty. Bringing in a tone of curiosity and experimentation can help your clients open to new perspectives, lighten up, and soften the messages of the inner critic.

– Clients who identify with Type One may come into a coaching relationship believing that they need to be fixed. You may notice the client's tendency to focus on what's wrong with them or with the situation. Constructive feedback can be perceived as just another source of information confirming the client's sense of their inherent defectiveness. Remind the client that there is a distinction between using feedback as a process for learning and allowing the inner critic to hijack feedback as a mechanism that degrades their self-worth. It's very important to focus on successes and what brings joy into the client's life.

OBSERVATIONS AND WORKING WITH YOUR PREDOMINANT PATTERNS

Below are some of the patterns that are associated with the Type One personality constellation. The process of working with these patterns in order to gain more emotional health and an increased sense of inner peace includes the steps outlined below.

1. Become a detective and recognize when the pattern shows up.

2. Create a little distance between yourself and the pattern as you normalize it.

3. Be with the experience of the pattern and its associated sensations.

4. Allow the experience with compassion and nonjudgment.

5. Acknowledge and accept what is showing up.

Refer to appendix F for an expanded version of this process.

The Judge

The Type One personality structure places the inner critic front and center. You likely feel the heavy weight of an inner critic, also known as the judge, that is relentless in its negative commentary on others and on you. The critic has an endless number of rules and expectations for perfection.

The work of the judge is sometimes loud, and sometimes quiet, and is so persistent that it seems to have a life of its own. It also can feel like the voice of God.

What are the messages of your inner critic? Notice its persistence. What do you notice about the impact of the inner critic's messages to you? How does the inner critic affect how you relate to others? Detect the critic's expectations as you go through your day.

Notice how the standards or rules that the inner critic uses to evaluate your behavior change from situation to situation. Notice what you do to comply with the inner critic.

Resentment and Anger

Notice how often you are resentful or angry with yourself or others. Keep track of this for a few days. Is it okay for you to be angry, or do you try to suppress your anger? Notice how you express your anger. Even if it is unacceptable to be angry, how does it leak out? Listen to the sound and intonation of your voice.

What does your resentment feel like? How do you know when you are resentful? What do you tell yourself? What physical sensations do you experience?

How do you behave?

The Tense Body

You might realize that you tend to hold a significant amount of tension in your body. Tension is a way of suppressing unacceptable emotions and attempting to restrict unacceptable behaviors. Tension can be thought of as a physical manifestation of the inner critic.

Notice where you tend to hold your tension. Your shoulders? Your back? Your jaw? Where do you experience pain? Do you have frequent headaches or migraines?

How does bodily tension influence your ability to be flexible and to move with ease?

Shouldering Responsibility

Notice how you feel obligated to do the right thing and to fix whatever you deem needs fixing. Notice how you shoulder responsibility as a way to compensate for what you perceive others are not doing or are not doing well.

You may be quick to point out to others what needs to be done differently and take it on yourself to make sure it gets done in accordance with what is right. One of your challenges is to discern between your responsibility and the responsibility of others. You tend to constantly monitor the environment, and it may be hard for you to draw the line between what is and is not yours because it seems so obvious as to what needs to be done.

What responsibilities do you take on that truly are not yours? Notice what lies beneath the urge to take on additional responsibility. What is your inner critic's role in taking on responsibility that is not yours?

Talking Down to Others

Notice when you talk down to others so that they can see the errors of their ways. This is sometimes referred to as parent-to-child communication. Notice the tone of your voice. What is the underlying message that is being conveyed?

Notice what you do to try to convince others of the correctness of your perspective. Do you ever feel like you're scolding others?

How effective are you when you use this communication style? How influential are you?

Secret Behaviors

The inner critic is a tough taskmaster. It is impossible to demand that we control and restrict every aspect of our lives. Sometimes you might give yourself "escape hatches" as an outlet or release from these restrictions.[2] These indulgences might include overeating, gambling, or even illicit behaviors that you feel can be rationalized. These can become part of your secret life.

Do you recognize having any secret behaviors? If so, could they be a reaction to the heavy restrictions of your inner critic?

How have you explained these behaviors to yourself? How do you feel when you use them?

FIELDWORK PRACTICES

1. Get to know your inner critic.

The inner critic has cast itself as the central and most important figure of your inner psyche. It is important to learn as much about its workings as you can, without becoming attached to or identified with its messages. That is, create some distance between yourself and the critic and its messages.

You can become more familiar with the inner critic by writing down the messages that you have carried around in your head. Consider carrying around a pad of paper for jotting down all the messages that you hear. Up to now, these may have sounded akin to God's words. Now it is time to see them for what they are and their impact.

Remember that these messages keep you from your own knowing and your inner wisdom. In adulthood, the inner critic is not interested in your well-being or in helping you be better. It is only interested in its own survival. As you create distance between yourself and these messages, they will carry less weight and you will have greater access to your heart and to a quieter mind.

2. Look beyond the ego's perfection.

The ego will seldom, if ever, reach a sense of satisfaction with the way things are and the perfection that exists beyond our limited human way of seeing life.

Allowing yourself the gift of imperfection is humbling and freeing. Put down the burden of trying to make life perfect—it will always be imperfect from our human eyes, and after all, you (and we) are human.

3. People express themselves differently than you do. Consider this: what if they are not wrong or bad but simply see the situation from a different perspective than you do?

What would you need to let go of to allow for this possibility? To accept this as a valid alternative?

How might it support you to accept the viewpoints of others, even if those are different from yours?

What do you appreciate about others? Practice giving sincere compliments.

As for giving yourself a break, what brings joy to your life? What do you do for play? What brings laughter? What do you love?

If you don't know the answers to these questions, give yourself time to explore. Practice scheduling time every week just for you.

4. Take care of yourself (but not as a "should").

Here are some possibilities:

- Incorporate yoga or simple stretching exercises to focus your attention on taking care of your body. It will support your mental and emotional well-being, too.

- Develop a meditation practice. There are many meditation resources to support you.

- Drop your trying. Adopt enjoyment. Self-care can serve a higher purpose.

Perhaps the most important practice is to connect with your heart.

5. Accept tenderness and caring.

- Remember moments in which you were touched by others' kindnesses toward you. Spend time tapping into any experience of receiving this kindness you might have had.

- What would allow you to receive kindness, caring, generosity, and love from others now?

- Practice staying available and open to receiving.

Movement to Highest Levels of Health

To move to the highest levels of health, people who identify with Type One must eventually:

- "Let go of the belief that they are in a position to judge anything objectively and be able to approach life without emotionally reacting to it."[3]

- Embrace and become accepting of all of themselves.

- Let go of constantly monitoring themselves and their environments to determine what needs to be fixed.

- Accept the nature of the human experience with its strengths and its limitations.

TYPE TWO

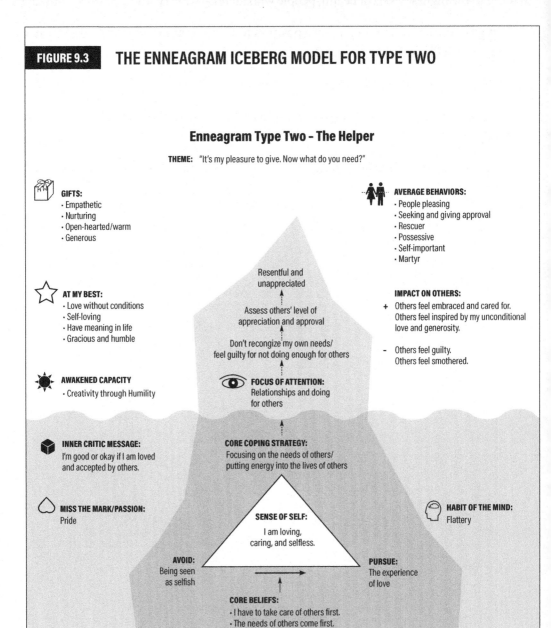

FIGURE 9.3 | **THE ENNEAGRAM ICEBERG MODEL FOR TYPE TWO**

Enneagram Type Two – The Helper

THEME: "It's my pleasure to give. Now what do you need?"

GIFTS:
- Empathetic
- Nurturing
- Open-hearted/warm
- Generous

AT MY BEST:
- Love without conditions
- Self-loving
- Have meaning in life
- Gracious and humble

AWAKENED CAPACITY
- Creativity through Humility

INNER CRITIC MESSAGE:
I'm good or okay if I am loved and accepted by others.

MISS THE MARK/PASSION:
Pride

AVERAGE BEHAVIORS:
- People pleasing
- Seeking and giving approval
- Rescuer
- Possessive
- Self-important
- Martyr

IMPACT ON OTHERS:
+ Others feel embraced and cared for. Others feel inspired by my unconditional love and generosity.

− Others feel guilty. Others feel smothered.

HABIT OF THE MIND:
Flattery

Resentful and unappreciated

Assess others' level of appreciation and approval

Don't recognize my own needs/ feel guilty for not doing enough for others

FOCUS OF ATTENTION: Relationships and doing for others

CORE COPING STRATEGY: Focusing on the needs of others/ putting energy into the lives of others

SENSE OF SELF: I am loving, caring, and selfless.

AVOID: Being seen as selfish

PURSUE: The experience of love

CORE BELIEFS:
- I have to take care of others first.
- The needs of others come first.
- I have to earn love.

TYPE TWO: THE HELPER
THEME: "It's my pleasure to give. Now what do you need?"

ABOVE THE WATERLINE

 When I'm Expansive and at My Healthiest Levels (Gifts and at My Best)

I am empathetic. I can step into other's shoes and connect to them while staying connected to myself.

I am nurturing. I have an innate sense of what others need while staying connected to my own needs.

I am openhearted and warm. My emotional warmth has an embracing quality and allows others to feel cared for.

I am generous in doing sincere good works. I can be selfless in giving to others.

I have unconditional love for others. I give without expecting anything back. There are no strings attached.

I extend the same generosity and love to myself as I extend to others.

I find meaning in my own life. I find joy in being alive and paying attention to my own needs.

I am gracious and humble. I recognize that life incorporates graciousness in both giving and receiving.

Awakened Capacity: Creativity through Humility

I recognize that everyone has needs, including me. The distinction between my needs and those of others melts away, and the needs of others are neither more nor less important than mine. As I let my whole self with my interests, needs, joys, and hurts into my heart, I experience the authentic love that I had previously worked hard to get from others. My creative voice has space to shine through and be expressed.

Distinguishing Characteristics When the Personality Has Its Grip on Me

I am a people pleaser. I try to get people to like me through my giving behavior.

Approval is important for me to receive and to give. I look to others for their approval and use my approval as a way to unconsciously manage the behaviors of others.

Others may see me as a rescuer. I tend to attract people into my life who, from my perspective, need rescuing. This is also known as codependency.

I can be possessive of others, wanting their attention and closeness. Other people may see me as being intrusive and trying too hard to get close and personal with them.

I like to feel that I'm important in other people's lives. I sometimes think, "Where would they be without me?" I like being a special or privileged friend.

I can be a martyr for others. I sacrifice myself to meet what I think are the ever-present needs of others.

Where I Put My Attention When Identified with the Personality (Focus of Attention)

I put my attention on relationships with others. I focus on what I could be doing to help other people out and to show them that I care. As the needs of others take precedence, I lose contact with my own needs and deny having needs. To have needs would be selfish. I look for cues from others to assess the degree that they appreciate me. When I don't receive the feedback that I indirectly look for, I feel resentful and taken advantage of.

Impact on Others

+ Positive

Others feel embraced and honored by the genuine warmth and caring of the Two.

Others are inspired by the Two's genuine and unconditional love.

- Negative

Others feel guilty and unable to keep up with the giving of the Two.

Others feel smothered by the overgiving and underlying neediness of the Two.

BELOW THE WATERLINE

The Ego Code's Inner Logic

Core Belief

I believe that I have to take care of others first before I can be loved and accepted.

The needs of others come first.

I have to earn love.

≋ Coaching Cue::

Examples of what you might hear your clients say or do/not do:

- *I really don't know how to say no to others. It feels like they know what will push my guilt buttons.*
- *I carry a lot of guilt. I just can never do enough for others.*
- *I often give compliments to others and tell them they should be proud of themselves. Doesn't that put me in a good light with them?*
- *I sometimes extend myself to others with the secret hope that they will show their appreciation for my generosity.*
- *How will I ever have time to do everything that I've promised others? I'm tired but will figure out a way.*

△ Triangle of Identity

What I Pursue: The Experience of Love
I define love as reaching out and doing something for others to feel a connection. I do a lot for others with the hope of having my loving nature affirmed.

What I Avoid: Being Seen as Selfish
I avoid directly acknowledging my own needs. I never want to be seen as selfish because that would mean that I'm not a loving person. To acknowledge or put attention on my own needs feels threatening and irrelevant; they are not even on my radar. Putting attention on myself and asking for what I need is the most difficult thing to do in life.

My Core Coping Strategy: Putting Attention and Energy into the Lives of Others

I attend to and put my energy into other people. The lives and needs of others feel far more important, interesting, or urgent than what is happening in my own life, so I leave myself and jump into their lives. Yet, through giving to others, I try to provide indirect hints about what I would like from others.

I see that much of my life has been organized around getting people to like me and, really, to accept and love me.

Sense of Self ("I Am . . .")

I see myself as loving, caring, and selfless. These are positive characteristics; however, they become limiting when I feel obligated or compelled to be this way.

If I see myself acting only in helpful ways, there are many other qualities that I don't allow myself to experience or express. Always feeling that I must help leads me to feeling resentful of others, especially if they don't express enough appreciation for what I do.

 ## Fixation of the Personality (Habit of the Mind)

I give a lot of what I consider positive attention to others in the form of flattery. I want to be seen as a good person and unconsciously think that by flattering others, they will see me in a positive light.

 ## Where I Miss the Mark (Passion)

I have a lot of pride. I secretly may feel that I'm better than others or that I can do things better. Since I don't recognize my own needs easily, I do not take good care of myself. I feel that I'm above having the needs that others have.

 ## What the Inner Critic Insists Upon

I'm not valued or loved if I don't put others' needs ahead of my own.[4]

My inner critic has rules upon which to evaluate how others treat me. For example, if someone doesn't give me a big enough smile, it is the inner critic's evidence that I'm not loved and that I haven't done enough to be loved. This can lead to a reaction of judging the other person for not being attentive. As long as I'm caught in the inner critic's web, I will continue to sacrifice my own needs to others, maintaining a cycle of resentment and avoiding living my own life.

What Causes Me Stress

I feel stressed when I feel obligated to take care of too many people and, simultaneously, I resent them for not appreciating me enough. When I try my best to take care of others, and they back away from me, I feel abandoned.

I can also feel stressed when people tell me to take care of myself. I don't quite know what they mean nor how to do any better than I am.

When I'm Most Constricted and Inflexible

I manipulate others to think they can't do without me.

My tendency for worry becomes exaggerated and turns into overbearing self-importance.

I have a condescending, patronizing attitude toward others and instill guilt into them for not doing enough for others or for me.

I wear myself out because I don't take care of my own health needs.

Lines of Access

Type Two shares a line with both Types Eight and Four. Below are just a few ways that the characteristics of either of these types might show up or the reactions I might have to these characteristics in others. Refer to the discussion of these two types for further insight.

At Type Eight: I can become bossy, aggressive, and angry. The gift of the Eight is that I can speak up and make my wants known.

At Type Four: It's hard for me to admit, but I can become depressed and filled with jealousy. I can be very critical of others who display these characteristics. With greater awareness and presence, I begin to experience a deeper connection to my authentically creative nature.

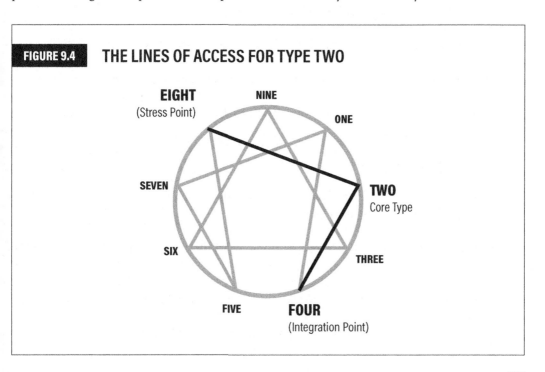

FIGURE 9.4   **THE LINES OF ACCESS FOR TYPE TWO**

Type Two Case Study

Sonja came to coaching providing the following information:

I'm on the cusp of retiring from my position as the founder and longtime executive director of a community nonprofit. The organization has gone through some extremely difficult economic times trying to meet the expanding health needs of the community, but I've led it back to a more solid financial footing with the help of the board.

The staff works hard but has needed a lot of support and guidance from me. It's not unusual for me to work 60–70 hours or more a week, and many of the staff do the same. There's never enough time to meet the needs of our clients.

A succession plan was developed, and the transition has been in the works for several months. The new executive team is expected to begin in a month, and now I feel like the board is anxious to have me step down. Still, I'm concerned how the board, the staff, and the clients will fare. I've been the initiator, leader, problem-solver, and mentor, among the many roles I've fulfilled. That's what is needed in a small nonprofit, isn't it? It's just hard for me to let go.

Sonja is a warm, caring, and action-oriented woman. She also revealed that she is exhausted and a little scared.

Her initial intentions for coaching were:

- Reduce her level of worry for the community of people involved with the organization

- Learn how to step back and let go of the organization

- Explore retirement—what it would mean for her, along with next steps

- She was also curious about how the Enneagram could be of use to her.

The following are among the Type Two patterns that Sonja recognized in herself:

- I'm stunned to learn that my focus on everyone else is related to an Enneagram type and not just the result of leading a nonprofit.

- I have worked so hard to please everyone: board members, staff, clients, and their families. No wonder I'm so exhausted.

- I often have felt resentful because I don't think others truly appreciate how much of myself I have given them, year after year.

- I really don't know what I want. Needs? What does it feel like to have needs?

- I have no idea how to slow down. All I know is how to give, give, give.

An early theme of coaching centered around recognizing and celebrating the good work she had contributed to her organization and the community, as well as identifying the personal costs of extending herself to a great many people.

As Sonja began to be more reflective and curious about her own life, more time was devoted to slowly discovering what was under the drive to give so much of herself. She voiced concern that if she wasn't focused on others, she would lose the caring, loving, and warm qualities that she so valued, and she would lose approval from others. With attention focused on gently connecting with her own heart, waves of grief poured forth at different times. She was also able to tolerate the darker emotions that she had denied. She experimented with specific practices that gave her the opportunity to discover what it felt like to let herself into her own life.

SUGGESTIONS FOR COACHES WORKING WITH INDIVIDUALS WHO IDENTIFY WITH TYPE TWO

Acknowledge Their Inner Experience

I believe that I must do for others before I can do anything for myself. I believe that it is selfish and unacceptable for me to take care of myself first. I work hard to earn love from others because that is what is necessary.

I don't think that I have any needs that deserve attention. My job is to help other people because they have so many needs of their own. Who am I to have needs?

I often feel underappreciated but don't share this with others. I sometimes feel resentful because others take advantage of me and don't give back to the same degree that I give to them.

≋ Coaching Cue::

> *It may take a long time before your client can acknowledge this, but the heart of a person with a Type Two personality hurts. The feeling of unlovability has a long history, so the heart is tender territory. Meeting the client with warmth, openheartedness, and acceptance can be extremely supportive.*

Offer Counterintuitive Questions/Comments

What is scary about having needs?

What if you didn't have to do anything more for this friend other than simply be with him, just be present?

What is happening in your heart right now? What feelings or sensations are arising as we explore this topic?

What might be selfish about denying your needs?

Love just IS. You are not in charge of making it happen. It is always available to you and through you. Nothing more is needed. How does hearing this land for you?

Invite into awareness how choices are made.

Issues That May Arise in the Coaching Relationship

- Remember that Type Two clients can easily identify what they believe are the needs of others. Asking what they need for themselves may put them in uncomfortable and alien territory. Don't be surprised if they tell you they feel selfish for spending any time on this question at all. With awareness of their pattern of deflecting attention away from their own needs and the development of their capacity to experience their own sensations and feelings, they may begin to allow themselves the possibility that their needs exist as part of their own humanity.

- The communication style for the average Two personality tends to be warm, positive, and peppered with concerns about how other people are seeing them and how they are being treated by others, as well as references to what they are doing to help others. You might note that these clients sometimes have a restlessness or low-level anxiety around the need to take action. They may express concerns over meditative or reflective exercises being nice but getting in the way of doing what is really important.

- Clients who identify with Type Two may be eager to please you and receive your approval. They sometimes bring or send presents and other symbols of affection. Depending upon the client's level of presence, they may look for frequent acknowledgment, confirmation of their value, or other positive feedback from you.

- Because of their inclination to stay positive and upbeat, it may be challenging for them to acknowledge what they consider negative emotions.

OBSERVATIONS AND WORKING WITH YOUR PREDOMINANT PATTERNS

Below are some of the patterns that are associated with the Type Two personality constellation. The process of working with these patterns in order to gain more emotional health and an increased sense of inner peace includes the steps outlined below.

1. Become a detective and recognize when the pattern shows up.

2. Create a little distance between yourself and the pattern as you normalize it.

3. Be with the experience of the pattern and its associated sensations.

4. Allow the experience with compassion and nonjudgment.

5. Acknowledge and accept what is showing up.

Refer to appendix F for an expanded version of this process.

Indirect Communication

Notice the tendency to go around an issue and not directly ask for what you need.

You may think that others should be able to read your mind about what you want or need. However, that generally is not the case.

Notice if you tend to act as if you are just fine and have no needs or wants. It is likely that this is what others will think. They won't have a clue unless you communicate more directly.

Self-Sacrifice

Notice when you feel that you have to reach out and give. Others always come first. This is a sign of people pleasing.

People who identify with Type Two often feel that they have to sacrifice themselves by forgetting about their own needs. If this is a strong pattern for you, you may notice some related patterns:

–   You have a lot of people in your life who depend on you. Some of those people might seem like they are needy—that is, needing a lot from you. You are likely seen as a rescuer. This is immensely draining. And this pattern tends to act as a magnet to attract people who are needy. This sets up a pattern known as codependency.

–   Some people distance themselves from you. They might be experiencing you as quite needy or intrusive. This may come as quite a surprise for you. This is the time to use the process outlined above to be both observant and compassionate with yourself.

–   You deny having needs, yet there is something nagging you. It is likely that it is your needs that are nagging, as what is denied tends to get bigger (much to your dismay). You may also find yourself feeling underappreciated and resentful.

The Centrality of Relationships

Notice if you feel that your life is suspended if you are not currently in an intimate relationship.

How much of your attention and energy is focused on being with others, creating a sense of close association with others but not really letting them into your life?

The Type Two personality is the embodiment of having warm relationships that is part of being in the human family. When that focus takes most of your energy, however, you can lose a sense of self.

Notice the tendency to flatter others. Observe what you are trying to achieve through flattering another. The initial response is to believe that flattery is an expression of your generosity. In-depth exploration may identify your desire to receive positive attention from the other person. This can be difficult to acknowledge, so both honesty and compassion for yourself is vital.

Because flattery is an exaggerated expression of complimenting another, it may feel false to the person who you are trying to please through your flattery.

FIELDWORK PRACTICES

1. What are your needs?

This can be a tricky question, as taking action such as getting a massage or taking a long bath may actually turn out to feel more self-indulgent than truly nurturing for you. True self-care starts with embracing your own humanity and includes recognition of your right to being self-accepting. Then, taking a bath might be exactly what will support you. See what feels right for you in the moment.

Having needs is part of being human. If it feels selfish to have needs of your own, recognize this as a pattern of the Two's personality constellation. Can you accept the possibility that it simply is not true that having needs is selfish?

Let your attention move into your heart space, in the center of your chest. What arises for you? If you're unclear as to what you need, slow down, go look in a mirror, and sincerely ask, "What does my heart need?"

Consciously work with bringing your attention back into your own life. Allow it to return back home. While it will feel very awkward to experiment with this, you will come to see just how much energy you make available for everyone else. It's your turn.

2. Experiment with nurturing yourself.

What would it look like to nurture yourself? Let go of any reasons for not doing so at the moment and reflect on what would most replenish your soul.

This is one of the hardest things for people with a Type Two personality to learn because it feels so counterintuitive. But here goes: as you nurture and give to yourself, the more you will experience your genuine gifts of unconditional love, and your authentic relationships with others will be based on a true connection of your heart to the hearts of others.

3. Create a practice for quieting the mind.

Developing a witnessing, observant mind—an awareness that simply notices the mental chatter or anxiety rather than feeling compelled to act on the inner activity—moves you toward greater liberation, health, and emotional intelligence.

Practice dropping into and sitting in the silence of your heart.

4. Find support for opening your heart to yourself.

Identify people who can support you in the practice of being in your own heart. This may be a spiritual teacher, coach, or a group that focuses on the practice of presence that includes connecting with the heart.

Read books or other positive literature that support your practice.

5. Practice showing your love for others by simply being with them.

If you are likely to show your love for others by doing something for them, try something new—just showing up.

What most people really want from others is someone to listen deeply, to appreciate them for who they are. Sometimes loving by doing can get in the way of having a real relationship.

Movement to Highest Levels of Health

To move toward the highest levels of health, people who identify with Type Two must eventually:

- "Let go of the belief that they are not allowed to care for themselves. Thus, they can own their feelings and needs and are free to love others without expectations."[5]

- Open their hearts to themselves.

- Explore what has true meaning in their own lives.

- Be willing to deeply love and accept themselves.

TYPE SIX

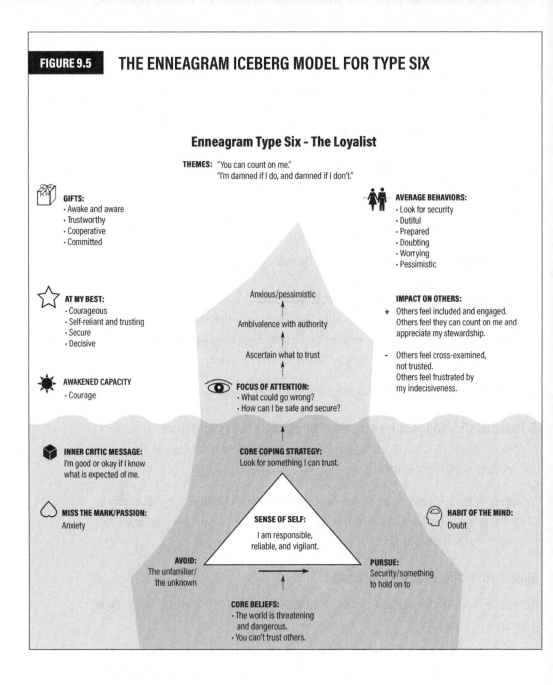

FIGURE 9.5 THE ENNEAGRAM ICEBERG MODEL FOR TYPE SIX

Enneagram Type Six – The Loyalist

THEMES: "You can count on me."
"I'm damned if I do, and damned if I don't."

GIFTS:
· Awake and aware
· Trustworthy
· Cooperative
· Committed

AVERAGE BEHAVIORS:
· Look for security
· Dutiful
· Prepared
· Doubting
· Worrying
· Pessimistic

AT MY BEST:
· Courageous
· Self-reliant and trusting
· Secure
· Decisive

AWAKENED CAPACITY
· Courage

Anxious/pessimistic

Ambivalence with authority

Ascertain what to trust

FOCUS OF ATTENTION:
· What could go wrong?
· How can I be safe and secure?

IMPACT ON OTHERS:
+ Others feel included and engaged.
Others feel they can count on me and appreciate my stewardship.

− Others feel cross-examined, not trusted.
Others feel frustrated by my indecisiveness.

INNER CRITIC MESSAGE:
I'm good or okay if I know what is expected of me.

CORE COPING STRATEGY:
Look for something I can trust.

MISS THE MARK/PASSION:
Anxiety

HABIT OF THE MIND:
Doubt

SENSE OF SELF:
I am responsible, reliable, and vigilant.

AVOID:
The unfamiliar/
the unknown

PURSUE:
Security/something
to hold on to

CORE BELIEFS:
· The world is threatening and dangerous.
· You can't trust others.

TYPE SIX: THE LOYALIST

THEME: "You can count on me." "I'm damned if I do and damned if I don't."

ABOVE THE WATERLINE

 When I'm Expansive and at My Healthiest Levels (Gifts and at My Best)

I am awake and aware of what is happening in the external environment—both positively and negatively.

I am trustworthy. I am steadfast and responsible and can be counted on.

I am cooperative. I see others and myself as being equal contributors to efforts that benefit all.

I am committed. I take my commitments seriously and follow through.

I am self-reliant and self-trusting. I pay attention to my inner knowing and use that to guide my decisions.

I am secure within myself and as part of the groups and organizations that I choose to participate in.

I am decisive. I take different perspectives into account, then make a firm decision.

I am attuned to and can take a stand on behalf of the greater good.

Awakened Capacity: Courage

Courage comes from trusting that I am supported in taking on whatever challenge is mine to meet. I am grounded in my belly. Courage also means to stand by my heart. As I listen to what my heart knows, I can take appropriate action or take no action at all, depending upon what is needed in the moment.

My courage is supported by my trust in the unfolding of the universe.

Distinguishing Characteristics When the Personality Has Its Grip on Me

I look for security. I want to make sure I find something outside of myself that I can trust.

I am dutiful. I try to determine what's expected of me, then fulfill my obligations.

I always try to be prepared for whatever may come my way. I try to cover all the bases as a way of being safe.

I am in constant doubt. I ask, "What if?" and vacillate between choices, second-guessing myself.

I am a worrier. I anticipate all the things that can go wrong, and these become impossible obstacles to overcome, even before I take any action.

I tend to be pessimistic and can move into seeing things as catastrophic. I focus on what is not working and magnify the negative possibilities and outcomes.

Where I Put My Attention When Identified with the Personality (Focus of Attention)

I am concerned about what could go wrong, so I put a lot of energy into developing plans and systems that create safety and security. I can be hypervigilant about my environment and look for cues regarding whether I can trust myself or others. While I want to believe some source of authority outside myself, I may question or even become suspicious of authority. My anxiety feels ever-present and overwhelming.

Impact on Others

+ Positive

Others appreciate the loyalty and the stewardship of the healthy Six toward issues that they care about.

Others feel taken care of and included in group or social environments.

- Negative

Others can feel confused or frustrated by the indecisiveness of the Six.

Others can feel hurt or angered by the doubting mind and suspicion of the Six.

BELOW THE WATERLINE

The Ego Code's Inner Logic

Core Belief

I believe that the world is full of threats. I can't trust the world or others and I can't trust myself to make the right decisions or do the right things. I need to be prepared to protect myself or my family from these threats.

 ## Coaching Cue::

Examples of what you might hear your clients say or do/not do:

- *I don't know what to do next. It's so hard to make a decision. I want to decide, but then I doubt and second-guess myself.*

- *Who will listen to me? You say I need more self-confidence? What self-confidence? I have little to none.*

- *I'm worried sick that those I care about won't be okay. They could be at risk.*

- *Sometimes, when I rely too much on the suggestions of others, I get disappointed in the outcomes and start questioning if I can trust them.*

△ Triangle of Identity

What I Pursue: Security and Support That I Can Hold on To

I pursue experiences or structures where there is something secure to hold on to so that I can feel supported or safe. I look for something solid that gives me a sense of guidance and direction. I want to know that I have covered all the bases and know what is expected of me.

What I Avoid: The Unfamiliar and the Unknown

The unfamiliar and unknown come with risks. I don't know where to find a sense of solidity or safety and feel unmoored. I don't like surprises. The unfamiliar always brings up fear and anxiety, and I don't know what is expected of me.

My Core Coping Strategy: Looking for Something to Trust Outside of Myself

I keep looking for something outside of myself to believe in and to put my loyalty on. This could be a belief system; a group oriented to a particular social cause; a civic, political, or religious group; a job; or a teacher that I can trust.

Sense of Self ("I Am . . .")

I see myself as being responsible, reliable, and vigilant. I also see myself as likable. While these are all positive attributes, they become limiting when I feel compelled to be this way.

If I see myself only with these qualities, my ability to acknowledge and express my emotional or spiritual dimensions is restricted. My sense of self is dependent on what responsibilities I take on and how well I fulfill my obligations. This undermines my own authority for my life. Always feeling that I must be responsible leads me to eventually feel resentful and caught between a rock and a hard place because I create multiple responsibilities that often conflict with one another.

Fixation of the Personality (Habit of the Mind)

I am filled with doubt and worry. I often feel pulled between polar opposite responses to situations that arise in my life. I don't trust my own thinking and worry that I'm making the wrong decisions. The lack of trust is a constant source of anxiety.

I look for ways to create stability from external sources, but I end up changing my mind about how to move forward. The opposite stance is to disregard my worry and barge ahead.

Where I Miss the Mark (Passion)

I feel and identify with enormous fear and free-floating anxiety. I either become paralyzed by my fear and fail to take the necessary steps to move in the direction that I want to go, or I try to blast my way through fear and can end up bullying my way through uncomfortable situations.

What the Inner Critic Insists Upon

I do what is expected of me.[6] When I let my inner critic have free rein, I am constantly trying to identify what is expected of me and fulfill those expectations. It is exhausting to be so vigilant, to figure out what I think the expectations of others are, and to try so hard to fulfill them.

The inner critic always points my attention to the outside world. When I follow this course and get caught in the inner critic's web, I forget what it is that I want in my own life and lack trust in my inner knowing.

What Causes Me Stress

I feel stress when I have made commitments to more people than I can deliver. My stress increases when I am forced to make a decision and feel unprepared. I may feel that I haven't collected enough information to make a good decision or that I am being rushed.

When I'm Most Constricted and Inflexible

I trust no one. I am deeply suspicious and paranoid.

I hang out with people or groups that are bad for me.

I am unreliable.

I am emotionally all over the map, lacking stability.

I am paranoid, feeling that others are out to get me.

Lines of Access

Type Six shares a line with both Types Three and Nine. Below are just a few ways that the characteristics of either of these types might show up or the reactions I might have to these characteristics in others. Refer to the discussion of these two types for further insight.

At Type Three: I can become competitive, driven, and oriented to getting things done quickly without thinking through implications. The gift of the Three is that I become decisive.

At Type Nine: It's hard for me to admit, but I can numb out and get distracted by insignificant distractions. I can be very critical of others who display these characteristics. With greater awareness and presence, I begin to experience a deep sense of relaxation and presence with ground to stand on. My fears subside.

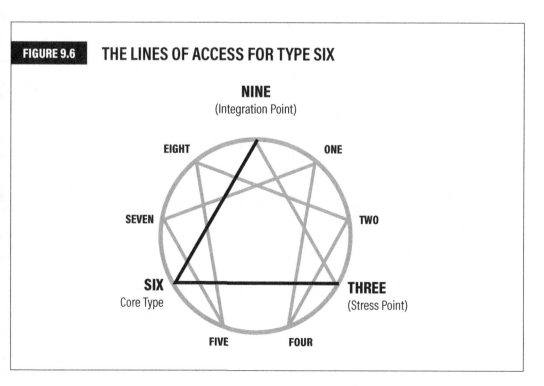

FIGURE 9.6 **THE LINES OF ACCESS FOR TYPE SIX**

Type Six Case Study

Selene came to coaching providing the following information about herself:

I've been in a several-year relationship that has become completely unsatisfying. My partner always thinks she knows what is best for me and doesn't listen to me. We've been to therapy, but nothing has changed. I feel like I've lost my voice and my confidence. I also get quite emotionally charged whenever we interact. Now, I want to focus on myself.

I'm terrified of leaving the relationship and I'm terrified of staying in it. I feel paralyzed.

I'm in the clothing design profession. I sometimes don't trust that my designs are marketable, but it turns out that I am quite successful, so that has helped build my confidence in that part of life. I also find that colleagues at work tend to come to me as I can help solve problems.

My home life is in one box, and my work life in another. I'm a different person at work than at home.

As is true for many coaching clients, the sessions took place over Zoom. This required special attention on the part of the coach to create a welcoming, warm, and safe virtual environment to establish trust.

The early coaching conversations with Selene revealed a lack of confidence in herself.

Her intentions for coaching included:

-   Gaining clarity on what to do about her relationship

-   Developing a stronger sense of confidence and having less fear

-   Getting clear on her own needs and life interests, rather than having so many obligations to others

She also expressed her aspirations for living a happier, more balanced life.

Selene recognized, among others, the following Type Six characteristics:

-   A feeling of being pushed and pulled in different directions that overwhelmed her, especially related to agreeing to many commitments

-   Her frequent disappointment in others

-   Fear that showed up in different ways, such as doubt or anxiety, or as confusion

-   Always anticipating the problems that could pop up and not being able to relax

One major theme of coaching centered on developing a relationship with her body, despite being physically active. With consistent and varying practices in discovering sensations, she found that connecting to her belly grounded her and offered her insights. Whenever she allowed her energy to drop from her mind into her body and heart, she would relax. She began to trust herself more.

Selene courageously initiated discussions with her partner about their next steps and offered the possibility that she would leave the relationship if nothing changed.

She enrolled in embodiment work with a somatic coach facilitating a small group and is learning to feel her fears without them becoming an insurmountable obstacle.

SUGGESTIONS FOR COACHES WORKING WITH INDIVIDUALS WHO IDENTIFY WITH TYPE SIX

Acknowledge Their Inner Experience

I experience enormous self-doubt and anxiety about my decisions. I often feel torn between two or more options. I just don't trust myself to make the right decision.

I'll ask a number of people their opinion on what I should do. It seems like I have a number of conflicting inner voices also telling me what to do.

I believe that it's important to create safety and security in the world because the world is such a dangerous place.

It's important to be prepared for the worst-case scenarios, so I try to figure out everything that can go wrong.

Offer Counterintuitive Questions/Comments

Tell me about a time that you trusted yourself (your instincts or your intuition).
    Help your client remember a previous experience of self-trust.

What factors were present that led to self-trust?
    Experience the sensations available in your body.

What is it that you do know about yourself in this situation?

What do you trust right now?

What do you trust about yourself?

What is arising in your heart? Any feelings or sensations? What does your heart want for you?
The mind moves at a far faster rate than the wisdom of the body and of the heart. As you guide your client into contact with the body's sensations and with what is arising in the heart, it is essential to provide a spacious and unrushed pace. This allows the client time to have a direct experience of these sources of intelligence, which may feel quite foreign to them.

What is it like to allow the anxiety that you experience and not judge it?

Invite into awareness how choices are made.

Issues That May Arise in the Coaching Relationship

- Remember that clients who identify with Type Six tend to believe that their fears and suspicions are true. Support the client in recognizing that fears come from the mind, and when believed, continue to live in the mind. Mindfulness and meditative practices can help clients become more observant.

- The communication style of the average Type Six client often involves inner contradictions and the inclusion of varying perspectives on any given issue. You might hear, "Well, I could do plan A, but then I tell myself if I take that approach, this result could happen, so maybe I should take this other approach, but then that result could happen. I go back and forth between the two, and oh, I just don't know what to do. What do you think?"

- Some Type Six clients may be heavily reliant on the coach's perspectives and input. Other Type Six clients tend to be skeptical and questioning or even demanding that the coach performs in a particular way. Both types of clients have challenges in accessing and trusting their own guidance.

- Anxiety is a significant internal experience for these clients, regardless of external circumstances. What is your client's experience of anxiety?

OBSERVATIONS AND WORKING WITH YOUR PREDOMINANT PATTERNS

Below are some of the patterns that are associated with the Type Six personality constellation. The process of working with these patterns in order to gain more emotional health and an increased sense of inner peace includes the steps outlined below.

1. Become a detective and recognize when the pattern shows up.

2. Create a little distance between yourself and the pattern as you normalize it.

3. Be with the experience of the pattern and its associated sensations.

4. Allow the experience with compassion and nonjudgment.

5. Acknowledge and accept what is showing up.

Refer to appendix F for an expanded version of this process.

Diminished Self-Confidence

Those in the throes of the Type Six patterns are challenged by a lack of self-confidence. It may show up in some of the following ways:

They are apt to diminish their accomplishments or, more likely, forget them altogether. What accomplishments have you had in life? What are you forgetting?

Do you ask others for advice on what to do? Notice how many people you ask for advice about any one situation. What are your inner rules for accepting or ruling out the advice of others? Do some people carry more weight with you? What are you looking for when you ask for advice?

Notice what is under your request for advice.

Do you tend to change your mind frequently? Do you notice that you sometimes feel pulled between diametrically opposed answers, such as yes and no?

If you notice this tendency, be an observer the next time it happens. Can you name what part of you is tugging in one direction or another?

What role do fear and doubt play in your decision/indecision?

What leads you to your final answer?

Exploring Fear and Anxiety

What conditions or situations tend to ignite fear or anxiety for you?

Get to know these experiences more directly.

What does fear or anxiety feel like in your body?

How do you know that you are experiencing fear? Where is your breath when you are fearful? Do you remember having a breath?

Can you move your fear into a part of your body, such as your left foot?

What would it be like to let your anxiety exist—that is, not try to push it away or make it bad?

The Reign of the Inner Committee

The inner committee is a source of confusing mental chatter and indecision. It is composed of any number of members, and each thinks they have something to contribute to your decision. Each member typically represents a particular viewpoint, some of which you learned as a child. For example, you may have an internal unruly uncle, a prissy cousin, a boss, a mother, a scholar who expects perfection, and a counterculture teen.

Who sits on your inner committee? Do they have names?

In what ways does the committee serve you? In what ways does it undermine you? What are the costs and benefits of investing time and energy in listening to these different voices?

Your Belief System

What do you believe? Identify some of your most influential beliefs.

What is the source of your beliefs? Can you identify their origins?

What are the criteria for trusting or not trusting a particular belief system?

What are you looking for from people or organizations you associate with?

How do your beliefs support you in making decisions? Do you carry any beliefs that you may have outgrown without realizing it?

As you explore your beliefs, what is happening in your body? What sensations are you noticing? What is happening in your heart?

Overcommitment

Those who identify with Type Six tend to overcommit themselves, thus jamming up their lives and creating stress.

When is the last time you overcommitted yourself? What were the consequences of saying yes to more things than you realistically can do? What did this do to your stress level?

How did it impact your relationships? How did you get out of the bind?

Compassionately notice what is underneath this pattern of overcommitment. What problem are you trying to resolve?

Worry and Pessimism

You may notice being consumed with worry about what might happen in the future, with a bias for a worst-case scenario.

Notice the circumstances that capture your energy in worry and pessimism about the future. Do you notice that both of these mental activities are pointed toward the future?

How pervasive are these mental activities? How often do the things you worry about come to fruition? Can you notice these as patterns and not as the truth about life?

FIELDWORK PRACTICES

1. Discover practices that allow your mind to become more spacious and clearer.

You may have noticed how many of your type's patterns are connected to unrelentless mental activity. There are a number of strategies available to allow your mind to quiet.

Find your way back into your body. Become attuned to having a direct experience of sensations in your body. It can be helpful to begin your awareness with your feet and toes, as these are the farthest distances from your head. Experiencing the life in your body and settling into all the cells and your physical structure can shift your energy downward. Remember that this isn't thinking about your body but experiencing sensations that are available to you in the here and now.

Commit to a meditative practice. A practice that can be very helpful is a sitting meditation with your eyes slightly open and focused on one point in front of you. Some people find that this helps them to stay connected to their bodies while consciously breathing and allowing their mental energy to quiet.

2. Acknowledge fear, befriend courage.

Fear and insecurity exist. Fear is a natural response to moving into unknown territory. They are a part of life, especially in confusing and unpredictable times.

Get to know fear through your expanding capacity for observation. Recognize it as a pattern.

It often helps to take one step at a time when moving into new territory. Allow in and celebrate your successes along the journey, even if they seem small.

Experiment with feeling your anxiety and fear in your body. Perhaps you'll experience shakiness or interior movement that feels like electricity coursing through you. Put your attention on whatever is showing up. Sensations can also signal the aliveness in your body.

Honor the courage that you already have. Your courage and strength ultimately are required for exploring your own self-development. Find a coach or therapist whom you trust or become engaged in a trusted spiritual group. Allow yourself to take in the support you need.

Reclaim faith in yourself and in the universe. Look for signs that the universe works. They abound.

Look for what is working in your life. Express gratitude for the many gifts you have in your life. Acknowledge every time that you can trust yourself.

Spend time in nature, appreciating the serenity, the natural cycle of seasons and of life, using nature as a great teacher.

3. Acknowledge your inner authority.

Catch yourself wanting to figure out how things will be in the future. Come back to the present. Come back to experiencing your breath and sensations in your body. When you experience yourself in your body, you can ask yourself, "What do I know to be true in this moment?" Wait for your body to answer. Listen to what arises. That is all you need to know at this moment.

4. Acknowledge the insight that has been made available to you.

If this information guides you to some action, take it.

Listen to your inner knowing and follow through with whatever step is asked of you. Often, it will not be a big outer step, but an inner letting go or recognition.

Over time, you will come to experience more and more of your precious inner authority.

5. Look for the positive aspects of a situation.

People who have Type Six patterns are easily attuned to the negative dimensions, skewing their perceptions. Notice what is working, what is possible, what is inspiring, what is uplifting.

Movement to Highest Levels of Health

To move toward the highest levels of health, people who identify with Type Six must eventually:

–   "Let go of the belief that they must rely on someone or something outside themselves for support; they discover their own inner guidance."[7]

–   See through their fears and fearful thinking and trust their inner knowing.

–   Experience the courage of following through on their convictions.

–   Discover their own inner authority and begin to recognize that the support they have been seeking is everywhere and is always available.

The Deep Work
of Coaches

10

PRESENCE AS THE BASIS FOR REAL CHANGE IN DEEP COACHING AND FACILITATION

THE PRACTICE OF PRESENCE

Developing the capacity for presence is one of the most potent practices for creating real and sustainable change. In having the repeated and embodied experience of being present, we enter into a totally new relationship with ourselves, with others, and with our environment. We realize that there is far more to us and life itself than what our egos would have us believe.

Practicing presence allows us to become acutely observant just in this moment of what we resist, where we hold tension, the internal contributors to our struggles, and compulsions that create difficulties in our lives. We are able to create distance from our habitual (mis)interpretations and engage in healing as we see ourselves and others more clearly and objectively. The practice of presence loosens the grip of the personality and allows our authentic gifts to be expressed and our truer nature to shine through. This is why we engage with the wisdom of the Enneagram.

In this third section of the book, we expand on the coaching and facilitation processes that further build the capacity for presence. In our professional work, we do our best to live and model presence for our clients.

Appendix I offers a worksheet with considerations for meeting your client with presence. You may find it helpful in preparing for client sessions, as it highlights many of the principles included in this book.

THE POWER OF DIRECT EXPERIENCE

When people have a direct experience of themselves in the moment, they gain information that is real, not simply theoretical. As we learn to pay attention to present-moment experience, our constructs gradually give way to the truth of our experience. Direct experience allows us to feel through subtle shifts in sensations. It also allows shifts to actually happen, and with those, we recognize that something is different.

Interestingly, most people do not have a direct experience of their own life. Instead, objective or real experiences get lost in inner stories and ideas that are made to fit into one's subjective reality. The inner story revolves around a particular self-image, a mental model of what is happening, automatic emotional reactions, and somatic constrictions. It takes considerable commitment and quiet attention to penetrate through the personality's stories to access one's direct experience. A benefit of doing so is greater intimacy and connection to oneself.

An important element of direct experience is its focus on detail as the basis of change. Direct experience focuses attention on the specific details (e.g., the specific mental message, the specific body sensation, the specific movement of the breath, the arising of a specific energetic quality). Generalities, on the other hand, do little to create lasting change. Generalities are often theoretical and mental. Sometimes they come in the form of platitudes, such as "Just look on the bright side and things will work out." Only direct experience will allow an individual to know what is true about the saying, if anything, and its impact on one's experience.

A direct experience can be noticed fully only in the present moment. It is possible to recreate some aspects of a direct experience after it has happened, and that can be very helpful. This is important in working with clients. For example, a client might be aware of having had an emotional reaction to a situation that was interpreted as either positive or negative, and just let the reaction pass. When attention is not focused on the direct experience of that situation, it almost assuredly will occur again. With reflection and inquiry, the client may be able to recall how that situation played out internally, noticing what triggered the reaction. It is possible to recreate the situation and gain important insight. The process of sensing into that experience in the moment, however, generally provides the most awareness and even healing when there is nothing between the client and the experience.

All of the coaching principles and tools in this book have the element of direct experience in common and build on a basic practice of bringing oneself (and one's clients) back to the present moment. This practice is a powerful antidote to constriction.

THREE AMAZING GIFTS: THE CENTERS OF INTELLIGENCE

The three centers of intelligence provide an anchor for the deep coaching process. We can think of them together as the core principle around which our counterintuitive (e.g., one that does not come from the ego's usual logic) coaching and facilitation revolve, as we deepen our trust in the innate intelligence within our clients and ourselves.

Your clients are wired for presence—for groundedness, for openhearted-ness, and for clarity and insight. Each one has the resources for experiencing profound moments of presence. These resources come in the form of the three centers of intelligence: the belly/instinctual center, the heart/feeling center, and the head/thinking center.[1] While different terms are used to name each of these centers, we will use the following: belly, heart, and head centers.

Developing a greater understanding of the role that the three centers of intelli-gence play in releasing egoic patterns that no longer serve our clients supports our efficacy as specialists in high-level human development. The direct experience of these centers provides access to powerful entry points that advance a client's sense of wholeness, integration, and fulfillment.

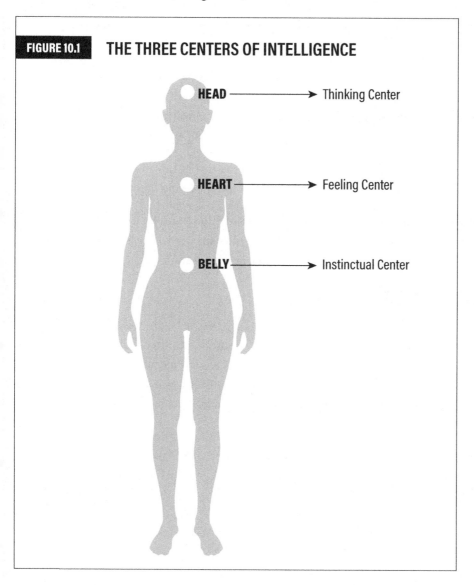

FIGURE 10.1   **THE THREE CENTERS OF INTELLIGENCE**

HEAD ⟶ Thinking Center

HEART ⟶ Feeling Center

BELLY ⟶ Instinctual Center

Being in tune with the strengths of the belly center helps us to fully occupy our bodies, as the body is what exists in the here and now. When we pay attention to this center, we more easily access our innate sense of strength, inner authority, vitality, substance, and groundedness. It is vital to focus on this center as the foundation for opening to the strengths of the other two centers.

The strengths of the heart center help us recognize and identify our feelings; fully open our hearts to ourselves and to others; and experience openness, love without conditions, compassion, and the truth of who we are. From this center, we recognize that we can be a source of genuine kindness in the world.

The strengths of the head center include a mental spaciousness, a quieting of inner chatter, mental clarity, and access to inner and divine guidance. As mental chatter quiets, we have access to a greater level of trust in ourselves and trust in the unfolding of life.

Each of these centers can serve as an entry point for coaching. The specific blessings of each are necessary to embrace in order to experience ourselves as authentic, fully present, and unified. It is rare for people to fully integrate the strengths of these centers in their daily lives without a conscious practice. Thus, the centers themselves offer a focus of ongoing inner work.

Coaches add immense value by being attuned to the distinctions between these different kinds of intelligence and helping their clients focus on accessing their diverse strengths.

The following sections provide a brief overview of intentions behind focusing on each specific center and strategies for building the client's capacity with each center, along with some of the issues that may arise with the center in the coaching process itself.

THE BELLY CENTER

The intention behind focusing on this center is to help people begin to inhabit their bodies—that is, develop the capacity for sensing into direct contact with the intelligence of the body's sensations, find their center, connect with the earth, and land in themselves. The location of this center is below the navel and a couple of finger widths inward. But the sensations that exist throughout the entire body are part of its intelligence.

Coach to the strengths of this center when the client's attention is focused on the past or on the future, when clients are in their inner story (e.g., talks nonstop or is rationalizing behavior), when their energy is scattered, and when they have difficulty moving into positive action.

Support clients in activating this center in a healthy way by engaging them (or suggesting action plans) in purposeful, conscious body awareness.

Examples of strategies for coaching a client to have greater access to body sensations and using the body to become more present:

– Somatic work

– Conscious movement, such as yoga, chi gung, aikido

– Horseback riding

– Massage that strengthens awareness of body

– Giving a voice to the body

– Getting in touch with the natural energy of anger

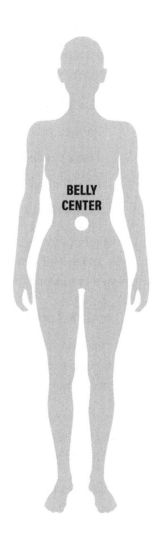

While bringing attention to the body center is essential for all clients, people who identify with Enneagram Types Four, Five, and Nine can particularly benefit from a focus on coming back to their bodies, as they tend to be disconnected from or underutilize this source of strength.

Activating and engaging the body's intelligence brings clients into a direct experience with themselves. Here, the filters formed by one's beliefs, assumptions, and inner stories are decommissioned. The body's intelligence is needed to support the client in embodying desired outcomes.

Coming into contact with one's sensations is very new territory for many people. It does not fit into the customary, familiar way of experiencing oneself. Clients may expect coaching to be based on conversation and be skeptical of the body's role in coaching or if that source of intelligence is even real. The coach's personal experience in developing their own somatic awareness can convey confidence in this center's strengths and value.

≋ Coaching Cue:

It is important to realize that the body remembers everything. It holds memories, both positive and those associated with trauma. It is essential to always check with clients and ask their permission before moving into somatic work. For those who have been impacted by serious trauma, the body likely does not feel like a safe place to explore. If you encounter this, it would be wise to know whether the client has or currently is working with a trauma specialist, and if appropriate, offer a referral. It still may be possible and beneficial to bring attention to sensations in parts of the client's body that are not affected by trauma, such as experiencing the contact of feet to the earth. This takes place on an individualized basis.

Listen for the Client's Metaphors and Somatic Cues

Coaches can listen for metaphors to tap into visual images that have meaning for the client. Images are especially useful in accessing the creative, right brain capacities and bypassing the linear mind.

Metaphors can be conveyed through story, music, poetry, and other artistic forms. They often come in the form of somatic cues. That is, they state or imply an internal or external movement or a relationship to the body.

Here are a few metaphors that you might hear:

- I leaned over backward.

- I have painted myself into a corner.

- I feel the wall between him and me.

- I acted like I'd just been let out of a cage.

Metaphors can be taken deeper when the body is actually brought into play. Having both the coach and client stand while engaging somatically with this material can be useful, whether meeting in person or virtually.

Consider this example:

A client was planning a special event to celebrate a business partner's retirement party. She was concerned about her ability to be graceful at the event, as she noticed, "I feel a barrier between my partner and myself." She noted the distress she was feeling about the barrier.

I asked her to come back to her breath. She identified the barrier as a dense wall. I asked her to sense just where the wall was. When she checked in with herself, she said, "It's right in front of me."

I asked her to allow the wall to be there and to allow it to be as big as it needed to be. She said, "It is heavy and solid."

As she stayed with her experience for a while, she said, with some surprise, "The wall is coming from me! It's not something separate."

We explored what the sensations of the wall coming from her felt like, and as she took the time needed to experience it, it released, and she experienced having a much more open heart toward her partner.

Later, she reported that the event went well, and she was pleased with her ability to be authentically caring and graceful.

Here's another example:

A client was concerned because he was feeling alone and weighed down by all the projects he felt needed to be done to advance his company. He wanted to know how he could stay grounded in the midst of all the demands.

I asked him to let his energy drop down into his body and connect with his breath. Once he was grounded, I asked what it felt like to be weighed down. Immediately his body sank beneath the weight of a large boulder that he was trying to push up a staggeringly high hill. I asked the client to move into the physical position he was experiencing energetically, so he initially crouched. Then he continued holding and pushing the boulder, fully experiencing its weight and what it felt like to put all his energy into pushing it up this impossible hill.

He decided to leave the boulder on the ground where it could be seen more clearly. He realized that he held the belief that he needed to figure out in advance what to do with the boulder before he could ask members of his team for help with it. He discovered that his default was to tackle the boulder solo. He realized how unproductive and exhausting this default had become for him.

As he experimented with the boulder, he realized that he could change the size and shape of it. The boulder shifted to a small pebble that contained the seeds of an idea.

He reported recognizing a familiar pattern of making small things into big and heavy objects, even before there was any real substance to them. By letting the project idea be what it was—small and flexible—he was able to approach his work with more equilibrium and ease. He could invite his teammates to collaborate with him or to give him support where needed.

≋ Coaching Cue:

Listen carefully for body or movement-related words or phrases from the client. These can be translated into a more body-based (and often more powerful) approach to coaching.

THE BODY AS A SOURCE OF INFORMATION

The body offers profound information on what is happening in the present moment.

Two fundamental body-based strategies are:

– Teaching the client to tap into body-based sensations

– Using the client's somatic experiences as integral to coaching

Teaching the Client to Tap into Body-Based Sensations

As strange as it may seem, given cultural messages that emphasize physical health, most people are out of touch with actual sensations in their bodies. While pain calls attention to the body, a first response is to medicate the pain. We tend to think about the body rather than actually experience it, so in day-to-day life, the body is often relegated to taking me where I want to go and doing what I want to do.

DEVELOPING LITERACY AROUND BODY SENSATIONS IS VITAL TO IDENTIFYING AND RELAXING PERSONALITY PATTERNS, RECOGNIZING THE EXPERIENCE OF CONSTRICTION AND EXPANSION, AND ENJOYING TRANSFORMATIVE SHIFTS.

Coaching to body awareness may feel foreign to the client (as well as to coaches who have not trained in somatic work). Developing literacy around body sensations is vital to identifying and relaxing personality patterns, recognizing the experience of constriction and expansion, and enjoying trans-formative shifts. Literacy includes being able to describe and name sensations as clearly as possible.

Using the Client's Somatic Experiences as Integral to Coaching

As clients become more attuned to their physical substance, the coach can ask about any sensations they may be experiencing while exploring tender or other important topics. Staying with sensations that may be uncomfortable can often lead to a more expansive experience. (Refer to appendix F for a description of the process.)

Many of the coaching cues and suggestions in section 2 provide questions or guidance in bringing attention to this center.

Increasing somatic awareness and intelligence provides a necessary foundation for another essential key dimension of presence: an expansive heart.

THE HEART CENTER

The intention behind focusing on this center is to support clients in identifying and discerning feelings, as well as experiencing truthfulness, compassion, openheartedness, authenticity, and love without conditions. Bringing attention to this center includes attending to emotions and to the somatic sensations around the heart. Invite clients to put their fingers or hand gently on the heart center, in the middle of the chest.

Coach to the strengths of this center when the client is having a hard time getting in touch with feelings, appears overly emotive, has experienced changes that involve a loss, and is having trouble hearing their inner truth.

Support clients in activating this center in a healthy way by encouraging them to become more open and receptive and less emotionally defended.

Examples of strategies:

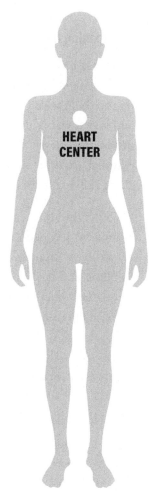

HEART
CENTER

–   Listening with compassion and acceptance
    (with an open heart)

–   Somatic work, or putting conscious attention
    on the sensations and posture associated with
    the emotional state

–   Encouraging the client to stay with the experience
    of receiving and allowing in

–   Yoga or other body-oriented techniques with a specific
    focus on physically opening the heart

–   Giving a voice to the heart

–   Writing, painting, or any conscious personal expression
    that is not focused on outcome or product

While focusing on the heart center is essential for every client, people who identify with Enneagram Types Three, Seven, and Eight can particularly benefit from consistently bringing attention to their hearts and inviting themselves into their hearts, as they tend to be disconnected from or underutilize this source of strength.

〰 Coaching Cue:

Coming into direct contact with one's own heart energy can be frightening for some people, even those who are warm and caring and who would seem to have a well-developed heart center. It is important to recognize that this is a place of great tenderness and requires compassion, a slower pace, and sensitive attunement on the part of the coach.

Keep in mind that opening to one's great heartfulness means that one is simultaneously letting go of something.

Metaphors associated with the heart abound. Listen for your clients' use of metaphors that can also be the basis for somatic work:

- I was heartsick/brokenhearted.

- My efforts were halfhearted. Or I put my whole heart into it.

- My heart was in my throat/in my stomach/on my sleeve.

The Opening Heart

How easy it is to armor our hearts. The hectic pace of life, the flooding of senses with information, the stresses of life, and the multitudes of distractions that call for our attention piled on top of unhealed hurts can leave little space for nurturing tenderness, caring, generosity, and love toward ourselves and others. Common unconscious strategies for distracting and distancing oneself from the heart include staying busy, being overly focused on goals or external activities, and being overly involved in the lives of others or on ideas. Whenever a client is living in an internal story, the contact with the heart has diminished.

Through the ages, teachers from across every spiritual tradition (and more recently, neurobiologists) have contributed to the teaching that our hearts are the central powerhouses of our lives. An open heart is the guiding force behind our ability to meet and engage in a fulfilling and healthy life. When the intelligence of the heart is lacking, there is an innate sense that something important is missing in life, even if the person cannot state what it is. Some clients may resist tapping into this part of their lives, perhaps fearing what they will or will not find. It is not unusual to hear a client say, "I don't think I'm going to find anything there." Thus, the inquiry into the heart is done with patience, right timing, spaciousness, compassion, and honesty.

〰 Coaching Cue:

Coaches can encourage clients to relax the armor around their hearts by asking them to notice with tender awareness and acknowledge their emotions without getting swept up by them. The capacity for noticing is required. And in any moment when clarity is clouded, coach to the open, loving heart… the greatness within the heart. You might ask: if you responded with the openness or greatness of your heart in this moment, what would that experience feel like?

Building the Capacity for Gratitude

Authentic gratitude is one of the great gifts of an open, generous, and receptive heart. Clients often report that they have experienced significant expansiveness when they have practiced building the capacity for this quality.

Coaching to gratitude involves a series of practices:

- A recognition of specific aspects of life for which the client is grateful. For example, setting aside several times a week to reflect on and write about what one is grateful for. It's especially valuable to take time to sense into the importance of each gratitude and its impact.

- A present-moment awareness of what a client is grateful for about themselves, about others, about their opportunities, about their lives. For example, when in a coaching conversation, you could ask, "What are you particularly grateful for about this situation in this moment?"

- Expressing gratitude to others. Coach the client to identify ways to express gratitude to specific people.

- Finding the gifts in difficult circumstances or difficult relationships and being grateful for those gifts. For example, seeing a person perceived as being the source of difficulty or of pain as a teacher of something that the client is learning.

- Being a person of gratitude. Living with gratitude as an embodied experience.

≋ Coaching Cue:

Coaching to gratitude, as is true of so many other aspects of coaching, involves:
- *Bringing awareness to the quality*
- *Identifying and acting on strategies that enhance the experience of this quality*
- *Expressing this quality to others*
- *Recognizing gifts that can arise in unexpected times and places*
- *Shifting into an experience of being and living from this spiritual quality*

This continuum of recognizing to acting upon to being/living from involves a process of opening that leads to increasing expansiveness. Each step in the process may be explored somatically, and each may have a different impact on the client's heart.

What Has Heart for Your Client?

The heart center is the channel for connection: a deeper connection with oneself; connection with others, including those who appear to be different than oneself; connection to animals; connection to the aliveness and intelligence of the earth; connection to the divine.

A lack of experienced contact with the heart leads to feelings of aloneness, alienation, loss of hope, and depression, among other isolating states.

≋ Coaching Cue::

Sometimes clients express a desire for a particular outcome but lack the momentum to put energy into it. You might ask: Is your heart in it? What does your heart have to say about this desired outcome? You might suggest that the client puts a hand or even a couple of fingers gently on their heart as they allow for some information to arise. Allow the client the time that is needed. Tears may not be far behind.

The heart can hold or repress many feelings, especially sadness and grief. Shame may also show up. This very tender part of the human experience requires our kind and compassionate attention in order to heal and release pent-up emotions that do not serve.

Bringing attention to the heart offers a powerful source of coaching. It is where an individual's truth lives.

THE HEAD CENTER

The intention behind focusing on this center is to support the client in accessing the quieter mind that is clear and spacious as attachment to outcomes is decreased.

The strengths of this center are heightened when the client's attention is brought to the belly and heart centers. This shift in attention can increase the awareness of the mind's activities when caught in a lot of mental chatter, anticipation or unnecessary planning, doubt, or judging. The shift in attention serves to interrupt mental activity.

Support clients in activating this center in a healthy way by guiding them to allow their mental chatter to decrease, giving way to mental clarity, openness, and trust.

Examples of strategies:

– Mindfulness meditation practices, such as focusing on an object or mantra, somatic-based meditation that focuses on the movement of the breath or other aspects of the body, and emptying of the mind, which is related to contemplative practices

– Present-moment awareness

- Listening to and being curious about themselves with neutral acceptance and nonjudgment

- Somatic work that includes bringing awareness to the sensations of the neck, head, skull, face, mouth, and eyes

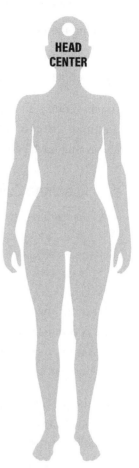

HEAD CENTER

(Note: many of the strategies listed under the belly and heart centers also help quiet the mind.)

While focusing on the head center is essential for every client, people who identify with Enneagram Types One, Two, and Six can particularly benefit from allowing their minds to quiet, as they tend to be disconnected from or underutilize this source of strength.

Metaphors associated with the mind also abound. They can be incorporated into somatic work. Here are some examples:

- My thoughts are going in twenty directions.

- I can't make up my mind.

- I was taught to mind my manners.

- I've been absentminded.

Since the busy mind is a well-rehearsed and automatic way of living in many parts of the world, it represents the path of least resistance and is what most people resort to under most life circumstances. Yet when most clients experience a break from the constant mental chatter, they feel relieved.

It is not unusual for clients to voice concern that a quiet mind is fine for coaching sessions but impractical for life. Remind clients that these practices are immensely practical, as they will not diminish their intelligence but will provide increased clarity and perspective.

≋ Coaching Cue:

As a reminder, it is counterproductive to directly attempt to get the mind to quiet. That only reinforces the mind's busyness.

Disabling the Inner Critic Mechanism

While the inner critic is also expressed in emotional dynamics and somatic discomfort, many people at least initially find that its messages are experienced as mental dictates.

Coaches often find themselves working with a client around inner critic messages. The inner critic or judge is an outgrowth of messages received from a child's authority figures that have been internalized and maintained into adulthood.

〰️ Coaching Cue:

For those clients who have an ego-inflating orientation, the inner critic may seem irrelevant, but it is as problematic as for other people. The inner critic is more apt to act as a pushy cheerleader or a performance manager, insisting on how great the person is and how they must continue being great and even greater than before.

Some of the messages of the inner critic are loud and obvious, and the intrusion of the inner critic is unmistakable. But the inner critic can also exist at a subtle, nearly inaudible level. Yet its intrusion is no less pervasive and deadly. It is as if a low-level, but irritating, background noise constantly persists in our head.

The inner critic is a centerpiece of the architecture of the personality. (Note: Look at where it is located on the iceberg model. It is right under the waterline, as it oversees the other dynamics of the personality. No wonder it is also referred to as the superego.) It helps keep the ego in power by undermining the individual's trust in self and in the divine. The inner critic, when believed, serves to take people away from their true nature. Through listening to, believing in, and identifying with the inner critic, one loses connection to their soul.

Thus, the capacity to identify and observe the workings of the inner critic is vital to disengaging the power of the ego to run rampant. Since the critic's activities often take place below the waterline, the client is often unaware of its impact.

As noted in the type description chapters, each Enneagram type has a specific inner critic rule. It is important for the coach to be aware of each of these type-specific messages because they are so central to shaping the psyche of the client.

Remember being graded in the classroom? Your work was evaluated against certain criteria that were determined by the teacher. Sometimes you were aware of the standards against which you were being measured; often, you probably were not aware.

That's basically the way the inner critic works. It grades the individual. When the dictate of the critic is followed, the individual gets the equivalent of an A and momentarily is off the hook. When and if the dictate is disregarded, the result is an F. The person is pummeled by the inner critic for failure.

There are two major problems here. First, the inner critic changes the rules, willy-nilly. What was acceptable one time is devalued at another time. Generally, the inner critic's standards keep getting higher and higher.

The second problem is that people are not even aware that they are in this game. This leads to feeling miserable.

There's no winning in this game with the inner critic. And there's nothing to win. So, the coach can support the client by being on the lookout for signs that the inner critic is running the show and creating strategies for noticing and disidentifying with this fundamentally useless psychological mechanism.

> "THE ONLY REAL ALTERNATIVE TO SELF-JUDGMENT IS KNOWING THE TRUTH ABOUT WHO YOU ARE . . . ONCE YOU KNOW DEEP INSIDE YOU, WITH A DIRECT AND FELT SENSE, THAT YOU HAVE INHERENT VALUE AND ARE FULLY ACCEPTABLE TO YOURSELF, THEN YOU WILL BEGIN TO FREE YOURSELF."
>
> —Byron Brown[2]

One of the most impactful strategies to deactivate the inner critic is to bring attention back to the heart with compassion. This direct contact with the heart creates the entryway into a deeper truth and a higher degree of presence.

〰 Coaching Cue:

You can use a framework suggested by Julio Olalla, founder of Newfield Network Coaching, to discern between assertions and assessments.[3] The capacity to discern between assertions and assessments can assist in relaxing old personality patterns.

An assertion is a statement of truth. It is a declaration of an objective reality that can be agreed upon. It can serve as feedback and can be used as a basis for making useful adjustments.

An assessment is a statement of judgment. It is a subjective assessment and is generated by the inner critic, and it goes much further than a source of feedback. The underlying message of an evaluation is a devaluation of one's worth. Seldom can we thrive under the consistent rule of evaluations.

When the client is unaware of the distinction between the two, an evaluation can feel like a declaration, and subsequently it becomes an internal statement of fact. And it can become the basis for a limited self-identity.

You can add value by being attuned to client statements of assertions.

*Chapter 17 of **Deep Living with the Enneagram** is devoted to changing one's relationship to the inner critic.*

ENGAGING THE THREE CENTERS

Gestalt work and certain improvisational activities, such as speaking with presence and in the presence of a group of nonjudgmental people and improvisational expression/theater, provide integrative experiences that tap into each of the centers simultaneously.[4] Thus, these activities can generate powerful shifts for clients.

Any of the above strategies can be used as appropriate in addition to powerful coaching conversations. Ultimately, it is a gift to help people experience themselves in an entirely new way.

> WHEN ALL THREE CENTERS ARE ENGAGED IN WHAT THEY WERE DESIGNED TO DO, WE ARE MOST OPEN, RECEPTIVE, FLEXIBLE, HEALTHY, AND EXPANSIVE.

When all three centers are engaged in what they were designed to do, we are most open, receptive, flexible, healthy, and expansive. It should be noted that this is a rare experience in daily life and is part of the life journey to spiritual awakening.

Further transformative work often involves the focused deepening of contact with each of these centers. This is often best experienced in a group environment.

Chapter 11

A COUNTERINTUITIVE APPROACH TOWARD EXPANSIVE OUTCOMES

CREATING THE CONDITIONS FOR MEANINGFUL OUTCOMES

A fundamental principle of deep coaching is that the consciousness that we bring to the coaching relationship is more important than what we actually do as a coach. Yes, models and tools are useful in their place, but it is presence that most matters. Deep coaching is not about *making* something happen.

Rather than efforting to reach some goal, what we can do is create conditions that allow the client's personality structure to relax and invites their spaciousness and essence to arise in their own timing. In truth, it is presence that opens the doors to insights, realizations, and new choices that cannot be predetermined. This counterintuitive approach to coaching strengthens our attunement to the client's internal movement toward their truer nature and represents a shift from an ego-driven approach. Yes, it takes courage, and it takes trust.

SPACIOUS INQUIRY: A WAY OF BEING WITH YOUR CLIENTS

Our clients are more inclined to experience a softening of their egoic defenses or protections and open to new alternatives when met with a spaciousness. "The Guiding Principles for Supporting the Experience of Presence" presented in chapter 4 may land more deeply now. When we inhabit and express our own presence-based capacities for noticing, curiosity, radical compassion, honesty, and courage and we trust in the process, we offer our clients an open door into the same qualities and into their more expansive nature.

Spacious inquiry is rooted in being authentically open to the client's direct experience, which is beyond conceptual knowing. It provides room for in-the-moment exploration and for the fascinating process of making connections that integrate pieces of the client's puzzle into a new perspective, sometimes even into a coherent recognition of their life's path. Through a counterintuitive (again, one that does not come from the ego's usual logic) approach, intentions rooted in three-centered awareness lead to meaningful outcomes.

CREATING THE CONTAINER

Regardless of the setting in which we provide service, the foundation for our work with clients revolves around creating a safe container, or holding environment. This pivotal process helps establish the parameters of the client-professional relationship, as well as a safe and trustworthy environment.

The three primary functions of this container are based on object relations theory, which identifies the building blocks of the egoic system. (Note: The functions are referred to as archetypal figures and are beyond the scope of this book. For more on object relations, refer to *Finding Freedom in Authentic Relationships: A Life-Changing Exploration of the Enneagram and Object Relations* by Belinda Gore.[1])

In chapter 2, we noted that it is rare for children to be raised in an environment that reflects the totality of their nature and that meets their unique needs for nurturance, structure and guidance, and a sense of belonging. The child naturally develops an egoic sense of separation and of inadequacy.

Now, we arrive at the present moment with our clients who carry this internal (false) sense of separation and inadequacy, even though it is likely hidden under a mask. As coaches, we can create a healthy experience of the following three functions to support our clients' positive development as they engage in growth work. The three functions are:

– **The nurturing function:** The purpose is to provide physical, emotional, and spiritual nurturing, attunement, and mirroring of the client's innate preciousness and essential quality. The coach or facilitator contributes to this function through being a warm, welcoming, caring figure who reflects back the client's full nature. Other qualities include compassion, respecting clients and their priorities, deeply listening, and seeing each person without judgment.

– **The guiding function:** This function is to provide structure, direction, clarity, and guidance, with a focus on supporting the client's confident movement into the world. The coach or facilitator embodies this by offering clear agreements about the relationship, including the scheduling and cost of sessions, and expectations of the client and the coach at the front end of the relationship. Other qualities include the capacity to co-create fieldwork and a system for whatever degree of client accountability is appropriate.

– **The belonging function:** Clients may come to coaching with an existing sense of alienation or aloneness. Being engaged in one's personal development can often feel lonely, as well. This function offers the client the experience of being integral to something beyond themselves, including being part of a valued social support system or a larger purpose shared with others. The coach or facilitator contributes to creating the sense of belonging by indicating that they are walking with the client on their journey by offering written, visual, virtual, and in-person resources that can help bring clients into the journey shared by many, as well as through other ways of enlarging the client's circle.

Together, these three functions of the holding environment create a sense of safety that provides a context for clients to feel safe enough to be self-observing, honest, and willing to try new experiences. They also help develop trust and rapport between the coach and client, allowing the client to explore areas that have been hidden away. These functions also support the coach in holding the full nature of each client.

≋ Coaching Cue:

Like most of us, you likely prioritize one or two of these three functions, with one or perhaps two receiving limited attention. Review how you create a holding environment for your clients and determine which functions you have underutilized. From there, you can develop those areas so that your containers do not have holes.

While these three functions are integral to any holding environment, also consider the relevance of the holding environment for a diverse clientele. It's important that it be responsive to a client's cultural, racial, or ethnic experience.

BUILDING THE CAPACITY FOR SELF-OBSERVATION

How do you support the client in developing greater awareness? Below are some of the key points that can guide the inquiry process.

Self-observation includes a focus on a client's habitual thought processes, attitudes, emotional patterns, somatic experiences, defenses, and external behaviors. Providing a strategy that allows clients to step back from being thoroughly engrossed in this complex set of reactions helps clients see themselves more honestly, without the many layers of illusion.

An executive client who was considering a career move talked about his penchant for adapting to whatever he thought a situation needed from him. He mentioned that he constantly assessed the moods and needs of others in senior management to determine what he should say and do and what tone of voice to use. He said, "That behavior totally describes me. I do it all the time." Then, he asked somewhat incredulously, "Doesn't everybody do that?"

He was stunned to learn that this approach to interacting with others is related to a particular personality pattern and is not commonly experienced by everyone else.

This initial awareness allowed him to begin seeing his inner activity as a pattern—not just who he is—and slowly he began to create a little distance between himself and the pattern. In time, his entire sense of himself shifted, and he was able to focus on making decisions based on his priorities within the context of the organization.

Shifting the Focus of Attention

Recall the focus of attention introduced in figure 2.9 and the brief descriptions for people who are dominant in each of the nine types. The more active the personality structure, the more that a person's focus is habitually narrowed to a specific perceptual field. This reduces the person's perception of available choices. One reason people often feel disconnected from themselves is that a large part of their experience occurs without their awareness.

> ONE REASON PEOPLE OFTEN FEEL DISCONNECTED FROM THEMSELVES IS THAT A LARGE PART OF THEIR EXPERIENCE OCCURS WITHOUT THEIR AWARENESS.

An astonishing dimension within the human experience is the capacity to change where a person places their attention. This capacity is key in the deep coaching inquiry process. The following section identifies approaches to guide clients in the essential practice of focusing inward as the foundation for inner guidance.

THREE AREAS FOR OBSERVATION

As coaches, we can support a client's capacity for self-observation by helping them discern among these three developmental levels of observation.[2]

THE WHAT OF EXPERIENCE

Most of us learn to put attention on the what, or content, of our experience. This includes not only the activities and interactions of our day-to-day life, but also the dissatisfactions, struggles, and frustrations that accompany the activities.

Focusing on the what of experience keeps our already busy minds busier and can distract from the deeper experiences that we most desire and do not know how to access.

≋ Coaching Cue:

Content is interwoven in most coaching conversations. If clients have sufficient presence, we can encourage them to step back from their focus on the content and engage a broader perspective about the situation.

Notice recurring themes (and stories) of struggle, turmoil, and dissatisfaction that your clients bring to sessions. Perhaps your clients are even getting bored with familiar experiences recurring over and over. This can be a signal to look deeper with inquiry. Perhaps there is something helpful to discover here.

THE HOW OF EXPERIENCE

What is harder to notice is how we approach or interact with the content of life. Our ideas about our behavior often do not line up with the actual behavior. Bringing attention to the how offers a deepening of self-awareness.

≋ Coaching Cue::

Bring curiosity and nonjudgement to this inquiry: What personal behaviors does the client observe? What are they saying or doing? What state of mind does the client bring to the content or interaction? Do any of these behaviors or attitudes seem to relate to an Enneagram type?

A statement posed for every Enneagram type in section 2 that reflects inquiry into the how of experience was "Invite into awareness how choices are made."

THE INNER EXPERIENCE OF EXPERIENCE

Below the what and how lies the world of emotions, memories, feelings, motivations, and sensations, many of which are tied directly to what is below the iceberg model waterline for a particular Enneagram type. The less awareness clients have of these dynamics, the more power the dynamics assume. By developing the capacity to notice and observe the specifics of the inner world, the client can begin the process of making new choices.

≋ Coaching Cue::

With your own experience in noticing and addressing sensations, you can support the client in bringing the capacity of self-observation to their sensations. Sensations carry useful information and serve as a path to deeper healing. Chapter 10 includes considerations and cautions when bringing the body's intelligence into coaching sessions.

Noticing

In deep coaching, we help shift the client's focus of attention to what lies below the waterline. This is integrated into the counterintuitive approach and addresses the experience of the inner experience discussed above. Clients may prefer to try to think their way through a situation to arrive at a resolution. The coach's trust in the nonlinear process is pivotal in providing a safe container for the client. Clients often find it a great relief not to rely on automatic ways of efforting to arrive at a satisfying result.

Noticing provides an entry point into the unknown. As the coach, you will not know in advance what the client is noticing. Even the process of taking a few breaths together at the session's beginning may bring up information. Offer inquiry as a way to deepen noticing of sensations, feelings, images.

〰 Coaching Cue:

Noticing can be integrated at any point in the coaching session, even in the discovery of the client's intention for the session. Ask, "As you talk about your intention, what are you experiencing internally?" Emotions may well arise here. Checking in with the internal world of the client helps them develop trust in their own inner knowing. It also helps the client to discern the alignment or truth of the intention for the session.

Inquiring may include questions such as: What are you noticing now? What is arising for you? I notice some tears. What is happening for you internally? What sensation(s) are you noticing? Where is this sensation? Can you describe it—its weight? Its density? Any color? Is it still or is it moving?

Acknowledge, Allow, and Accept Whatever Shows Up

When a client comes into contact with sensations and feelings around the session topic, they may also feel a resistance to experiencing what is here. There is no doubt: it can be uncomfortable to allow our experiences to actually exist. Allowing is not an interior action that has been taught or valued in many cultures and represents another counterintuitive process.

Allowing in one's direct experience involves the tender territory of the heart center. The pace and rhythm of the heart are slower than that of the mind, so it is a great gift to provide the necessary time and space for the client to enter into this experience that is neither logical nor linear. As clients develop the capacity to be more open, receptive, and welcoming to what is showing up in the moment, they begin shaping a new relationship with themselves. Imagine the impact of welcoming the full experience of oneself into one's life.

> AS CLIENTS DEVELOP THE CAPACITY TO BE MORE OPEN, RECEPTIVE, AND WELCOMING TO WHAT IS SHOWING UP IN THE MOMENT, THEY BEGIN SHAPING A NEW RELATIONSHIP WITH THEMSELVES.

Paradoxically, we unsuspectingly give energy to those areas of our lives that we do not want to acknowledge through denial or avoidance. Those issues, feelings, or experiences that we actively avoid will continue to lurk, grow even larger, and pop out when least expected.

It is helpful to tune into the many habitual ways that clients may try to avoid allowing in their in-the-moment experience. A few avoidances you may notice include:

– **"It's not supposed to be this way":** The experience is not in sync with the client's expectations or ways of thinking about how life works.

- **Judgment:** This is a common and often subtle reaction. For example, clients may feel that they don't have a right to a certain emotional reaction, such as anger, grief, envy, disappointment, or even joy. Remind the client that emotions just are. Having an emotion doesn't mean they need to act on it. Emotions do not define the person. You can support a client in recognizing an emotion that exists in the moment and sensing into it without becoming it.

- **Dismissing the importance of the issue:** Clients may downplay or ignore aspects of themselves that fall outside of their self-image or sense of self. Distinctions need to be made between those issues that do not need to be addressed and patterns of dismissal around certain kinds of situations. Interestingly, dismissal often shows up in connection to one's strengths, contributions, or successes, as well as in our limiting patterns. Some people habitually undervalue themselves through dismissing their innate gifts.

- **Fear:** Sometimes clients may fear that acknowledging a certain experience or truth in their lives may jeopardize them in some way. For example, they may believe that acknowledging and allowing a feeling such as resentment will strengthen it. Most often, acknowledging the seemingly unacceptable feeling or experience provides relief and diminishes rather than magnifies it.

- **Sense of inadequacy:** Clients may carry the belief that they are not capable or worthwhile enough to have certain experiences, such as the respect of others or being loved.

Each of these avoidances (and there are others) reflects a part of the personality structure that obstructs a direct experience with the deeper nature of the person.

The experience of acknowledging what is actually here is often very significant for the client. When the client accepts the experience, the aha moment becomes a more powerful lever for change.

Acceptance is one of the paradoxes of Enneagram-based coaching and is one of its most profound teachings and practices. When any part of us is denied or judged, we create a war within. We become divided against ourselves and create an obstacle to our growth and development. When we reject the objective reality of a situation, we fight against life itself, which creates further struggle.

Acceptance is less something we do and more a willingness to consider the possibility that what we were convinced was unacceptable is, in fact, what is. Perceiving more clearly the truth of what is present opens us to acceptance. Acceptance can create an inner movement that allows our whole perspective to shift. How we relate to a situation shifts. When our energy is not put into fighting reality, we create a greater clarity of mind. Here, the thinking/head center is involved.

≋ Coaching Cue:

When all three centers are awakened through the inquiry process, a client feels an increased sense of presence. With that process, aspects of a client's experience that felt separate and even opposite of each other proceed to weave together. This internal integration is not something that you can make happen, but you can support your clients as they experience it. Ask: Does this experience feel familiar? Is there a connection between this experience and the experience you talked about earlier? What might this be showing you? What are you learning? How does this inform the intention you brought to the session?

WHAT'S NEXT? DISCERNING ACTION OR NONACTION

I urge you to take a few moments to consider this question. Can you imagine the difference that a counterintuitive change process can make for clients who are arriving at their next step after:

– Having been met in an expansive, nonjudgmental field with a coach committed to the practice of presence

– Having an increased capacity to shift their focus of attention from content to observing their behaviors, attitudes, and motivational factors more clearly and compassionately

– Learning to be curious, noticing their direct experience and what is calling their attention from within

– Allowing a fuller range of their experiences without judging themselves and acknowledging a truth that was not accessible previously

– Accepting a reality that they had not seen or had been fighting

With the client's belly, heart, and head centers more activated and aligned, they can see a greater degree of choice and assess different options. A client still needs courage to take the selected next step, but that courage can seem much more available. It is highly likely that the client's next step may not have appeared as an option to either the coach or client prior to engaging in this process.

The client has experienced, at least momentarily, a shift in consciousness toward more expansiveness.

≋ **Coaching Cue:**

Sometimes the next step involves not taking an external action. The client might need to slow down, or rest, or wait. What is most needed typically reveals itself.

An exciting aspect of this process for most coaches is that they are not responsible for figuring out a solution. Being as present as possible to the client's experience along with being willing to inquire and be in the unknown alongside the client is a rare privilege and a profound gift to the client. It can be thrilling to witness the declaration of the often unexpected next step that is perfect for this client at this time.

ADDITIONAL COUNTERINTUITIVE STRATEGIES

The Impact of Language: Powerful Questions

Asking powerful questions and making well-crafted and well-timed comments are key to the coaching process. Powerful questions and comments tend to have these qualities in common:

- They are simple.

- The coach does not already know the answer to the question.

- They are anything but obvious to the client. They are counterintuitive and usually don't appear on the client's radar screen. They can stop clients in their tracks rather than prompt an automatic or "appropriate" response.

- They interrupt an internal story.

- They ask for the truth of the situation.

- They are likely to come from the coach's intuition or hunch. They are not analytical in nature, but more instinctive.

- They connect to a hidden, inner intelligence, opening the door to a transformative shift.

The type-specific coaching considerations for each of the nine personality types in section 2 include examples of questions that may be particularly powerful for people who are engaged in the clutch of a particular personality pattern. Appendix G provides suggestions for potential questions or comments that you might find helpful when coaching in certain situations, regardless of the personality type. These questions take the focus off the client's particular situation and identification with their story and put the focus on the client.

For example, a client comes to the session with: "I've been struggling over what to do about my colleague. He is always bringing up the negative aspects of a project. He takes away from everything else we're doing."

You might ask, "What about this situation makes this a struggle for you?"

A follow-up question might be: "Does this experience of struggle feel familiar to you?"

Note that the focus is shifted away from the colleague to the client.

≋ Coaching Cue:

It's vital for you to stay observant and not get caught in the drama of the client's story. It can be tempting to get involved, but this is not in service to your client. Remember to coach the client and not the story.

Intended uses of questions are:
- *To identify and interrupt a current internal story*
- *To encourage curiosity and wonder*
- *To recognize that a personality pattern is just a pattern and does not define the person*
- *To develop and expand the client's perspective*
- *To challenge the client's self-definition*
- *To plant a seed*
- *To point the client in the direction of an unacknowledged strength, hidden intelligence, inner truth, or the inherent mystery of life*

THE PATTERNS OF EACH PERSONALITY TYPE PLAY A PROFOUND, IF OFTEN CHALLENGING, ROLE IN THE COACHING PROCESS. CLIENTS UNCONSCIOUSLY SENSE THAT THEIR PATTERNS ARE THE FOUNDATION UPON WHICH TO MAKE CHANGES, NOT THE BASIS FOR CHANGES THEMSELVES. THE COACH'S ABILITY TO HELP A CLIENT RECOGNIZE A PATTERN FOR WHAT IT IS—JUST A PATTERN AND NOT ME—PROVIDES THE CLIENT A THRESHOLD INTO A TRANSFORMATIVE EXPERIENCE.

The Counterintuitive Coaching Request, or Making a U-Turn

The patterns of each personality type play a profound, if often challenging, role in the coaching process. Clients unconsciously sense that their patterns are the foundation upon which to make changes, not the basis for changes themselves. The coach's ability to help a client recognize a pattern for what it is—just a pattern and not me—provides the client a threshold into a transformative experience.

It is a natural human tendency to push away or deny that which we anticipate will cause discomfort, whether that dis-ease be emotional or physical. We typically meet discomfort with resistance. So it is completely counterintuitive to invite in the discomfort. This involves taking a step that is opposite of our natural tendency.

The counterintuitive nature of this inquiry is paramount to going seventy-five miles per hour on an interstate across the country with a sense that there is something following us very closely. Suddenly stopping, we turn around and come face to face with the dreaded monster. Often, we don't even know what it is that we're dreading. That is the nature of working with relaxing the personality. It often feels foreign, causing us to feel vulnerable and out of control. All we need to do is be with what arises in the moment. This is having a direct experience with oneself.

I use U-turn questions with clients who are at a point in the coaching process where they will begin to interrupt their patterns. I ask them to begin recognizing the early signs that their typical pattern is kicking in, stop and breathe, sense whatever sensations are present, and notice their feelings in order to relax and unhook from that pattern. Clients often report they feel a physical urge to move into a habitual reaction. This information from the body can provide just enough space to stop, breathe, and interrupt the usual reaction.

I then ask the client to metaphorically turn around and go in the opposite direction of the pattern. Refer to the Triangle of Identity for each type to become more familiar with what a client may automatically pursue, then look at what is avoided. The area of avoidance is one reflection of the opposite direction.

This request typically elicits a look that questions my sanity or brings with it a yikes! As we coach around the U-turn, exploring what it would look like to make the U-turn, I typically hear: "This is really scary." "I don't know what this means." "I don't know where I'm going with this or what I am doing." "This is hugely uncomfortable." "WHY???"

This can be a good place to incorporate a somatic exercise. Ask a client to walk in one direction that represents their default or automatic pattern, then reverse direction, walking toward the area of avoidance.

As we continue being in this unknown territory, clients often simply stop ... and then experience an inner shift, followed by "I sense that this is going to be freeing. Is it really okay to do this?" It's an indication that we have struck gold!

Taking the U-turn is a technique in raising awareness and challenging restrictive internal habits. Coaching with this model provides a window into the great and small paradoxes of life. One of the paradoxes is that the U-turn generally increases the stress level until the new U-turn action has been taken. Then a significant measure of stress dissolves, and the client experiences a new sense of freedom. After having the experience of behaving in a substantially different way, clients often observe that this is both delightfully subversive and a secret they wish that they would have known about long ago.

Table 11.1 identifies one characteristic pattern of each type and pairs it with a U-turn. Note that U-turns are typically introduced after a strong trust has been forged between the coach and client.

TABLE 11.1	SELECTED PATTERNS OF CONSTRICTION AND EXAMPLES OF SUBSTANTIAL U-TURNS	
Personality Type	**A Characteristic Pattern of Constriction**	**Example of Making a Substantial U-Turn**
ONE	Continuously trying to improve things	Leaving something to be fixed alone and appreciating it as it is or enjoying another experience
TWO	Overextending themselves in trying to help others	Acknowledging and attending to their own needs first
THREE	Striving in every part of life and needing people to recognize how well they've done	Engaging in an experience for its own sake with no outcome/product necessary; not telling anyone about their experience
FOUR	Living in a dream world of how the ideal life could be	Taking specific steps toward tangible desired outcomes
FIVE	Withdrawing into mental preparation mode	Getting into and having direct contact with their own body
SIX	Looking for information on their decision-making from numerous external sources	Following their own inner guidance
SEVEN	Trying to have it all or do it all	Slowing their level of activity and taking in one experience at a time
EIGHT	Being overly self-reliant and strong	Experiencing and expressing caring, vulnerable feelings
NINE	Avoiding conflict by trying to figure things out in their own minds	Staying engaged in conversations, including difficult ones, even when there is no predetermined solution

Taking a conscious U-turn is not a one-time action. Building reminders about exploring alternative actions into the coaching process eventually helps the new approach become more real, conscious, and sustainable. The client's sense of new options deepens.

≋ **Coaching Cue:**:

Sometimes clients can become self-judgmental when they forget to act on the new information and experiences that they are learning. It helps to remind them that historic patterns are insistent; they can be expected to surface as the default mode. That's why increasing consciousness is so vital. You add value by being as conscious and present as possible and by offering strategies and reminders to your clients to do the same.

Conscious Breathing

The starting place for supporting an individual in relaxing the personality is through the conscious use of breath. Fortunately, conscious breath is always available to the client and is always just one moment of awareness away.

When a client brings their attention to their breath, breath becomes a powerful tool that helps them become more grounded in their body. Breath can also be directed to the heart and head centers. A client can bring breath to an experience of being in this space and place now. Working with the breath often is beneficial within sessions and as fieldwork.

≋ **Coaching Cue:**:

Have clients practice bringing their attention to their breath and noticing what happens as they continue to observe the movement of their breath in and out of their bodies. Encourage the client to allow the breath to move more deeply into the body and slowly into the belly.

The impact of sustained conscious breathing is that the client is reminded, or perhaps experiences for the first time, a different sense of themselves. Clients often remark that they feel lighter, more spacious, more aware, and more present. By entering into a relationship with their bodies, clients have a direct experience.

It is not unusual for people new to conscious breathing to be surprised by what they find out during the process of breathing. They may initially feel very little, or a lot of information may flood their awareness. Breathing is the fundamental step in relaxing patterns of constriction and accessing increasing degrees of insight and expansiveness. Breath, as a movement of energy, can also support the experience of connectedness with what lies beyond one's physical body.

Bringing Attention to Choice

"The day I discovered real choice was the day my life changed."
—From a conversation with a colleague.

The recognition of choice is one of the great aha moments for people. That the client is making choices may be obvious to the coach and completely unseen by the client. This is true for both choices that lead toward dissatisfaction and those that lead toward health, ease, inner peace, and effectiveness.

Throughout the coaching relationship, bringing attention to the choices the client makes and their impact expands and affirms the client's consciousness of their role in the new behaviors, thoughts, decisions, and emotional states.

For example, a coach may say:

- I recognize that you made a choice to say no when you really meant it. How was that for you? Notice what is happening within you now.

- Congratulations on your choice to take the initiative on this matter. What was the impact of your choice—for you? For others? What is arising within you as we talk about this? What sensations are you noticing?

- You made a choice to stand up for yourself. Wow! That's a significant step. What difference did that make for you? Notice how this is landing in you.

Without the conscious affirmation of choice, it can easily go unnoticed or be dismissed as unimportant by the client when, in fact, it was a significant step. Every conscious choice is important.

UNRAVELING THE INNER STORY: AN INTEGRATIVE TOOL

The purpose of the inner story process is to allow inner stories and patterns that people carry to come to light. These inner stories carry our limiting beliefs, our messages to ourselves, our motivations, and the dramas that shape our lives. The inner stories are evidenced in our physiological, emotional, mental, and behavioral responses to our environment. The word response might be more accurately termed reaction, as our stories are reactive in nature. The degree to which we react to what is otherwise a neutral, objective event or situation is the degree to which the inner story has a hold on us.

Fundamentally, the inner story process is a discovery tool designed to dissect a recurring and often bothersome reaction. Using it as a coaching tool allows clients to:

- Develop insights rather quickly into a previously unquestioned pattern

- See the story's elements more vividly as they are brought into visual awareness

- Identify cues or signals that allow clients to catch themselves in the act at different points in the story's cycle

- Become aware of choice points in the story where the cycle can be interrupted

- With help, begin seeing the catalyst to the activation of the pattern as a neutral, objective situation. The process of unraveling the inner story also increases the sense of hope on the part of the client.

As clients gain familiarity with their stories, the seemingly disparate patterns seem to fit together in a more organized or coherent way. That is, clients are able to recognize the relationship of different issues to one another in their lives. A common response is: "I've known most of this before, but I never saw it as part of a pattern. Now it makes more sense."

This tool seems to work best when clients identify a sense of stuckness in a familiar and unsatisfying pattern and have sufficient capacity for curiosity, compassion, and honesty.

Elements of the Inner Story Process

The elements of the inner story process presented in figures 11.1 and 11.2 are incorporated into this exploration process. The elements are the same across Enneagram types and are posed as questions to help clients realize how the pattern plays out in their life.

As you introduce this process, you'll find it important to be in tune with your client's responses. You may need to change the suggested order of the questions offered below. What is important is to ask the questions so that the mental, emotional, physiological, attentional, and behavioral reactions are addressed.

The necessary starting point for the process is being curious about the information that shows up. Clients often report feeling that holding a space for curiosity gives them permission to be nonjudgmental and more open to discovery.

FIGURE 11.1   ## ELEMENTS OF THE INNER STORY PROCESS

The issue that keeps tripping up the individual

This is the beginning of the story's cycle.

What situation or event tends to create the pattern that is troubling you?

First sign

What is the first thing you notice that is happening for you?

What is the first indication that you are in this pattern?

The mental story

What do you tell yourself when you find yourself in this situation?

The emotional story

What are you feeling at this point?

The somatic story

Describe the sensations you are experiencing in your body in the midst of this situation. Where are you feeling the sensations?

Focus of attention

What are you looking for? What are you listening for?

The behavioral story

What do you actually do? How are you behaving?

Outcomes

What are the consequences of this pattern? How is the situation resolved?

Then what?

What happens next?

Usually, this relates to the repetition of the cycle.

Name the pattern

What name could you call this pattern in yourself?

Giving a name to the pattern seems to help make the underlying dynamic clearer.

You may repeat questions that refer to different dimensions of the story a number of times, depending upon the client. Some questions may be much more difficult for people from certain types. Some questions will bring a significant amount of awareness and information to the client.

FIGURE 11.2 **THE VISUAL COMPONENT OF THE INNER STORY PROCESS**

The "Triggering Situation"

FIRST SIGN:
1st thing you internally notice?

THEN WHAT:
What happens next?

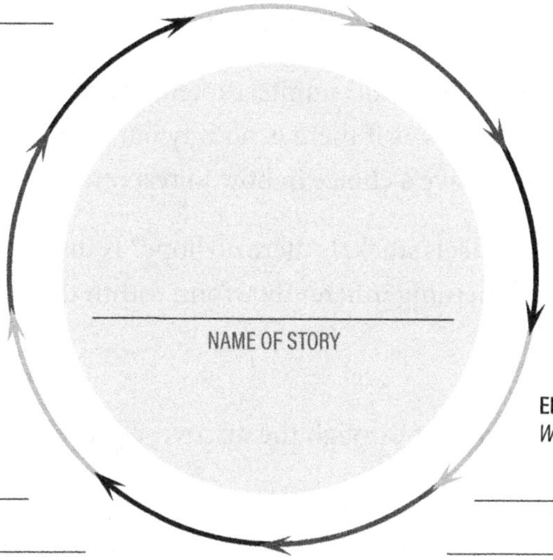

_____

OUTCOMES
What are the consequences?

_____

_____

NAME OF STORY

MENTAL STORY:
What do you tell yourself?

_____

_____

BEHAVIORAL STORY:
What do you do?

_____

_____

EMOTIONAL STORY:
What are you feeling?

_____

_____

FOCUS OF ATTENTION:
What are you looking or listening for?

_____

_____

SOMATIC STORY:
What sensations do you notice?

_____

_____

General Observations about the Patterns

How the uninterrupted storyline works:

- From the first hidden and charged reaction to an otherwise neutral condition/situation, an old storyline gets activated and recreated. It becomes the client's reality and, once they are caught in the dream of the story, it can continue spiraling out.

- The story is reinforced by all the conditioned reactions: mental, emotional, physiological, attentional. The nervous system cooperates, and the story "feels like who I am" to the client. We see that many channels of the client's reaction are activated. Thus, the story is holographic.

- In many cases, the client may experience an emotional (or neural) hijacking that Daniel Goleman describes in this way: "A center in the limbic brain proclaims an emergency, recruiting the rest of the brain to its urgent agenda. The hijacking occurs in an instant, triggering this reaction crucial moments before the neocortex, the thinking brain, has had a chance to glimpse fully what is happening, let alone decide if it is a good idea. The hallmark of such a hijack is that once the moment passes, those so possessed have the sense of not knowing what came over them."[3]

- Unidentified, unrestrained, and uninterrupted, the story continues to reappear, reactivating responses. It feels as if there is no way out. Mostly, the story is so real that the client feels they don't have a choice in how to respond.

- The awakening client feels stuck. Is there no hope? Is there any way out? Often the client feels that there is something inherently wrong within their being.

The story gets found out:

- As the story comes to light through the discovery process, the client takes another step in the awakening journey.

- As they identify points in the cycle, the client can notice where the cycle can be interrupted: prior to falling into the pattern, at any time during the pattern, or when feeling the consequences of the pattern. We can coach the client to observe the signals (mental, physical, etc.) that are markers of being in the pattern.

- The client, with intentionality, observant practice, and the use of the inner observer, begins to notice the subtle intricacies of the pattern and where they are likely to get stuck.

≋ Coaching Cue:

The inner stories use well-laid neurological tracks. They are what we rely on when we are on automatic. Waking up to our inner stories is a humbling process requiring patience, compassion, and humor because we are often not even aware that we're in the story until well after it has completed its cycle. (Refer back to Goleman's description that people may not know "what came over them.") Remind clients that every time they see the pattern in action, it is significant. Every time they make a different choice, it matters. Neurobiological research tells us that a moment of consciousness develops a neurological pathway that can create new, healthful brain patterns. This is called neuroplasticity.[4]

Now what? How to work with the story:

– There are many possible strategies for relaxing the typical reactions and patterns of the story. When clients can see the story play out in a visual format, they usually can gain some distance from the story and more easily shift from the emotional or energetic entanglement of the story to curiosity and choice. I have found it useful to ask the client: Where in this inner story cycle could you interrupt the story? What is happening at that point in the cycle that would allow you to interrupt it? What specific steps can you take? What cues or signals can provide feedback that you are in the story? As the coach, you are providing an anchor for the client to become more present to their experience.

– Selecting an appropriate strategy for interrupting the story's hold likely will depend upon the client's Enneagram type. Suggestions are offered under the "Observations" and "Fieldwork Practices" sections for each type in chapters 7, 8, and 9. Any of the specific coaching strategies discussed in section 3 may also be useful. Appendix H offers some examples of using this inner story process in a coaching situation.

– If a client displays a high degree of attachment and physiological or emotional involvement in the story, a referral to another practitioner may be advised.

Chapter 12

COACHING AS AN INNER PRACTICE

THE CALL TO COACHING, REVISITED

In the opening lines of the first chapter, we are reminded that:

"As coaches, we have the unique opportunity to be with human beings who are engaged in the life-altering work of committing to and realizing their desires for a fulfilling life, and at a deeper level, living with true authenticity. We do our best to show up so that our clients can do the same, meeting somewhere in the client's familiar inner world and traveling together to new territory that yields both remarkable possibilities and realities that, at one time, seemed but a distant dream."

Whether you are a new or seasoned coach, coaching (and other growth-oriented professional practice) is no small undertaking.

With an increased knowledge, appreciation of, and compassion for the nine variations of the human condition and the associated patterns of each, along with access to an array of approaches and tools to support clients, you might wonder, "How can I best serve?"

Remember the five pillars of deep coaching:

- The Enneagram is a profound map for understanding the full range of the human condition.

- Presence is the basis for coaching.

- The counterintuitive change process itself is understood to be informed by presence.

- We orient clients toward self-acceptance, love, and interconnectedness.

- Fundamentally, it is our inner work as coaches that allows us to best serve.

It is exhilarating, sobering, and a bit breathtaking to accept that, we too, are on our own journey as we move into unknown territory with presence every time we are engaging with our clients. We are given the opportunity to live with more expansiveness. Meeting clients with spaciousness supports their own spaciousness and the experience of belonging and interconnectedness.

NEXT STEPS FOR YOUR OWN TRANSFORMATIVE WORK

The importance of doing your own inner work is undeniable. As emphasized in chapter 1, I strongly recommend that you first explore what Enneagram type or types most resonate for you, then engage in inquiring and discovering how this awareness impacts you. Consider the following questions:

– How has this type limited your experience of life?

– How does it illuminate some of the perplexing issues you've faced?

– What are you beginning to see about what has caused you to struggle or suffer?

– What beliefs has it brought to the surface?

– How has it served you in the past?

– What gifts has it shown you?

– What do you most love about this type?

– What quality or experience might you be afraid of losing if you were to become more present?

– What is supporting you through this process of discovery?

If these questions do not seem to resonate for you, there's a good chance that you have not yet landed on your core type.

Remember that the more active and engaged the personality is, the less present we are. Certainly, a coach's Enneagram type can have a profound impact on the coaching relationship, especially if the coach is unaware of patterns associated with the type.

There is an enormous body of literature on the Enneagram that can help strengthen our understanding and knowledge. The key to change and transformation with the Enneagram is to engage in the practices that help us recognize, heal, and release obstructions to presence. The ego is persistent in trying to convince us that we are already present, and it is only with humility that we slowly come to see how not present we are.

Just as we are compassionate with our clients as they become aware of their own interferences to presence, it is vital we are compassionate with ourselves. This is not about being perfectly present, as that is only an ego wish and doesn't exist. The spiritual journey back to ourselves is lifelong.

STAYING WITH OURSELVES AS COACHES

The teachings from Diamond Heart, founded by A. H. Almaas, encourage the practice of keeping at least 70 percent or more of our attention on our own inner experience—on the direct experience of the three centers.[1] Thirty percent of attention is on the client. This is a reversal of other teachings that encourage coaches to get in there with the client. We've already seen that paradox is integrated into the Enneagram, and this is another example. So let's explore the purpose of the 70/30 ratio in the coaching relationship.

When we lose contact with our three centers, the personality takes over. This is true in both life and coaching. It's very easy to get caught in our own agenda of the moment, as well as in the client's dilemmas and their perceptions. Consider the dynamics that are under the iceberg waterline—beliefs, the agenda illustrated by the Triangle of Identity, the energetic patterns of the mind and heart, and the inner critic. These are some of the obstructions that can interfere in coaching. If we are not present, then it is our personality that is coaching to the client's personality. The results, then, are likely to be unsustainable, even if they are satisfying to the personality.

> IF WE ARE NOT PRESENT, THEN IT IS OUR PERSONALITY THAT IS COACHING TO THE CLIENT'S PERSONALITY.

Another benefit of staying present with our inner experience during a coaching session is that we may have a sudden insight or sensations that can be reflected back to the client to see if they resonate. For example, as a client talks about a struggle, you might notice a knot in your solar plexus. You can breathe into it and be curious, asking the client, "What are you experiencing as you talk about this? Are any sensations arising?" Or you might share with the client, "I'm experiencing a hard knot right below my rib cage. I'm curious if this is something happening for you. Or perhaps it's just my experience."

The point is that you don't need to be right. The client may not be having a similar experience, but they might. Being curious with the client provides spaciousness and room for further inquiry.

Working with this inner practice is just that—a practice. We learn to notice where the urgings of our particular personality style tend to interfere in the coaching process. For example:

- Do I have an unspoken agenda for the client? Do I believe I know what's best for this person?

- Do I put pressure on myself to know the answers or solutions to the client's questions?

- Do I try to make their discomfort disappear?

- Do I tend to push or rush through a session, not giving time for the client to arrive at a sensation, an insight, or a knowing?

Coaches do have internal responses to their clients' appearances, their behaviors, their patterns, and sometimes to the content of what they bring to the session. Bringing these internal responses into awareness so they can be seen for what they are (reactions) can further minimize the mental clutter that can distort the coaching process.

Table 12.1 identifies examples of personality biases for coaches.

> WITH A CLEARER INNER SPACE WE BECOME MORE OF A REFLECTIVE MIRROR TO OUR CLIENTS AND THEIR EXPERIENCES.

We notice our personality's inclinations, take a moment to breathe into spaciousness, then return to the grounded body, open heart, and curious and quieter mind. With a clearer inner space, we are apt to be more present to clients. We become more of a reflective mirror to our clients and their experiences.

The questions we ask, the feedback we offer, and the insights we share come from our more authentic nature.

| TABLE 12.1 | **EXAMPLES OF UNCONSCIOUS PERSONALITY BIASES IN COACHING INTERACTIONS** |

If you have a lot of this Enneagram type within you:	Be aware of an unconscious tendency to:
ONE	Have a strong opinion about client behaviors or thinking processes that may not fit your perception of what is good or right. Want to tell clients the right way to fix whatever doesn't seem to be working.
TWO	Want the client's positive regard, thus, being averse to offering truthful feedback. Try too hard and try to make things good or take responsibility for the client.
THREE	Avoid the emotional dimensions of the client's experience. Skirt the truth in order to be what you think the client wants you to be.
FOUR	Get hooked into the emotional element of the client's situation. Get overinvolved in the story itself.
FIVE	Remain emotionally cool or distant from the client. Feel the need to show your own mastery of the situation.
SIX	Not trust your responses to or questions of the client. Avoid encouraging the client to take appropriate risks.
SEVEN	Short-circuit the time spent on processing particular (especially sad) emotional states. Stay focused on future goals and activities.
EIGHT	Move quickly to the bottom line of the coaching conversation with little time spent on the steps or process. Distance yourself from heartful engagement.
NINE	Overidentify with the client or the client's story and lose your objective clarity. Avoid difficult conversations.

See appendix J for an overview of additional patterns that can impact your coaching.

≋ **Coaching Cue:**

Becoming aware of our personality's biases is one of the important tasks facing coaches.
The following suggestions can help you bring these biases into your awareness:

- *As you prepare for an upcoming session, notice your internal responses to this client. Is there something that creates a sense of discomfort? Is there something that you haven't said that needs to be said to this client? Be aware of anything that doesn't feel internally clean or clear for you and work with that yourself before the session.*

- *During this preparation, notice if there is something about the client that you have not yet personally acknowledged. Perhaps the client reminds you of a favorite cousin or a boss that was dismissive. The issue that the client brings forth may relate to something similar going on in your life. What will support you in recognizing those potential interferences and allow them to drop away during the session?*

- *Spend time after the session reviewing your interactions with the client.*
From your perspective, what aspects of the session were most truthful? Most powerful? Most clean? Most transformative? Most exhilarating?

- *In what ways, if any, did unhelpful personality patterns show up on your part?*

WHAT TYPE OF CLIENTS ARE YOU ATTRACTING?

If you are an experienced coach, you may have noticed that you regularly attract clients who share similar behaviors or challenges. It is fascinating and useful to pay attention to any clustering of clients with the same Enneagram type in your practice. You may discover that there is a mirroring taking place of a particular strength, quality, belief, or behavior that you have not yet recognized in yourself.

For example, if you regularly attract people with Type One personalities, it may be an opportunity to examine where you hold your own previously unperceived judgments. Simultaneously, you may have not yet recognized your own access to wisdom, a gift of that particular type at the higher levels of health.

≋ **Coaching Cue:**

When you notice that you have several clients with the same Enneagram type in your practice, it is an opportunity to look at that particular type within you. What have you not previously recognized in yourself? What patterns? What gifts?

You might notice what personality types are missing in your practice.
What would that suggest to you?

CALLING UPON YOUR MASTERY

Those who love coaching recognize this field to be as great a gift for the practitioner as it is for the client. As coaches, each of us is called to embrace the more powerful, unlimited, and healing aspects of our own nature. In our own inner work, we are asked to heal and release constricting ideas and beliefs, to challenge the behavioral and emotional patterns from our life history that no longer serve us or our mission, and to acknowledge that our lives make a contribution that only each one of us can make.

The Enneagram provides a map that points us to our greatest gifts as human and spiritual beings. These gifts are not ones that we can make happen but are available the more we release the tensions, constrictions, and patterns of our personality.

As we access, appreciate, and embrace these gifts, it is reflected in the positive impact of our coaching. The configuration of our gifts contributes to the unique relationship we have with our clients, and how we support our clients in particular ways. However, these gifts also provide a mirror for clients. What we express through our lives and through our interactions help our clients see this dimension in themselves. Under the best of circumstances, these gifts are brought to life in our clients.

Table 12.2 provides a glimpse into the gifts of coaches based upon the higher levels of health and presence for each personality type. It is important to remember that none of us are influenced only by our core type. Thus, you will likely recognize your particular gifts in several of the descriptions below, but know that all the gifts are available to you. Even if your gifts are not as developed as you would like (and for most of us, this would be the case), you can practice the tools and perspectives available for relaxing what hinders the expression of your gifts. Although our coaching focuses on the client, it is important to remember that the client gets who we are and what we have to offer as human beings.

> "LET YOUR PRESENCE LIGHT NEW LIGHT IN THE HEARTS OF PEOPLE."
>
> —Mother Teresa

TABLE 12.2	**CALLING UPON YOUR MASTERY AS A COACH**
Core Enneagram Type	**When You Are in Your Mastery**
ONE	– Your orientation toward mission and purpose can help your clients identify their own purpose and what has meaning and significance in their lives. – Your discerning wisdom creates a refined clarity, helping your clients experience more objectivity. – Your serenity provides an environment of calm strength.
TWO	– Your empathy helps others truly feel understood and cared for in your presence. – Your unconditional generosity and genuine warmth allow others to experience a deep level of support and love. – Your gracious humility allows you and your clients to have a true partnership where they are freed to assume responsibility for themselves.
THREE	– Your ability to inspire and uplift others creates a relationship that is motivating and empowering for clients. – Your commitment to excellence challenges clients to strengthen their resolve and willingness to do what it takes to realize important outcomes. – Your authenticity supports clients in exploring their own truth, integrating their heart's desires, and bringing those into the world.
FOUR	– Your sensitivity to the emotional experiences of others creates an environment of depth and understanding. Others learn that their emotional life is safe with you. – Your focus on creativity inspires others to explore and express themselves in original ways. – Your equanimity helps others to recognize emotions for what they are, helping them not to become overly attached to them, and to balance emotions with physical engagement.

FIVE	– Your curiosity inspires others to be curious about themselves and life and to arrive at new understandings. – Your objectivity and ability to see with a clear mind help others develop new perspectives unclouded by drama or entangled stories. – Your playfulness provides clients a nonthreatening way into addressing seemingly difficult situations or innovative ideas.
SIX	– Your cooperativeness and orientation toward teamwork help clients step into their own power as equal partners. – Your trust in your inner authority helps your clients develop and access their own varied and unfamiliar sources of intelligence. – Your faith in how life works inspires your clients to explore the unknown with more courage and trust in themselves and in the universe.
SEVEN	– Your love of life is awe-inspiring, helping others to appreciate what they already have. – Your spontaneity and versatility allow you to support your clients in diverse ways and stretch them to develop their own flexibility. – Your capacity to slow down, be patient, and stay the course inspires others to produce real outcomes.
EIGHT	– Your capacity for being visionary challenges others to recognize a bigger, bolder vision of themselves and of their future. – Your confidence and courage inspire others to develop, access, and embody their own confidence and courage in the face of obstacles. – Your magnanimous heart opens others to their own hearts as they are challenged to show up in life.
NINE	– Your receptivity and openness help others feel deeply accepted and met, allowing them to see themselves from a more liberated perspective. – Your unpretentiousness and natural presence create an environment in which others can experience their own genuineness. Clients learn that it is a relief to be themselves. – Your ability to be touched by whatever life brings and to stay engaged inspires clients to expand their presence.

THE GREAT WORK

When a core Enneagram pattern is recognized for what it is—a deeply ingrained pattern that has been the basis for one's self-identity, but not the truest nature of the individual—it lifts a veil of untruth. People typically experience this new awareness with amazement and shock, with a sense of having crossed over a deep ravine into entirely new territory, or with a sense of liberation. Clients have shared that inner shifts feel akin to spiritual chiropractic adjustments. Others noticed that their shifts were redirecting the course of their inner lives, and while little changed on the outside, it felt entirely different because so much had changed on the inside. Here, more paradoxes are revealed.

Our own shifts are a result of engaging in our inner work over time. For many committed practitioners, the Enneagram becomes integrated into our lives over decades, and perhaps for a lifetime.

On one level, the Enneagram is a map of the truth of life. At some point in inner work, the deeper truths underlying our core type become apparent. Below is a brief statement of truth that transcends the patterns of each type. When the ego is activated, these statements sound absurd. When read with presence, the statement associated with our type may resonate or may send a chill up the spine. Each of these grand statements challenges a core rule of that Enneagram type's personality.

- Type One: It is not my responsibility to fix everything.

- Type Two: I ask myself "What do I need?" and I ask for help.

- Type Three: How other people see me is none of my business and inconsequential.

- Type Four: The beautiful quality of my life is based on the small, ordinary moments.

- Type Five: It is safe to be in the world.

- Type Six: My security lies within me.

- Type Seven: My fulfillment exists in experiencing the exquisiteness of the here and now.

- Type Eight: Being vulnerable is the source of my true strength.

- Type Nine: My presence matters.

To accept and experience this truth requires trust, courage, acceptance, and love.

LOVE IN ACTION

Why would we be coaches if we did not love life, love learning, love inspiring others toward their greatness, and love the opportunity to serve? There is nothing more powerful, more healing in the entire world than loving presence. Through our being, we can be the messengers and the channels for loving presence.

The Enneagram is a map of love in action. It teaches us to love ourselves enough to take the journey toward the healthier and more expansive levels of our own truer nature. As coaches, it is hard to ignore this journey. The Enneagram also teaches us to be in loving presence with others, with the earth, with all of life because there is no separation. Everything is interconnected. As we serve one person or a team or a community or people around the globe with loving presence, boundaries dissolve. This powerful healing force broadcasts much farther than we can know. We can trust the mystery.

My greatest wish for all who read this book is that you will continue to experience increasingly authentic love and presence in your life and in your work. The world needs it, and the world needs you.

From the sign attached to the door of my coaching office: "Something wonderful is about to happen."

ACKNOWLEDGMENTS

The soul of the second edition of *Deep Coaching* has been nourished, informed, and supported by many significant influences. I have learned and been changed myself from my conversations with the early adopters of the original edition that participated in my 2007 and 2008 virtual courses and those who have engaged in integrating this work into their professional practices over the last fifteen years.

It was through the International Enneagram Association in 2007 that I met Belinda Gore, PhD, who spurred further conversations about this work and helped bring it to life in our early in-person retreats. Our collaborative teaching led to us form the Deep Coaching Institute, which attracted Diana Redmond as a trusted colleague and partner. *Deep Coaching*, the book, carries the imprints of both of these cherished friends with their grounded capacities, great hearts, unique gifts, willingness to live with the unknown, and depth of wisdom.

I've been profoundly inspired by too many students (now colleagues) to name as they approached each newly discovered presence-based paradox with commitment, courage, and an emerging trust in the counterintuitive approach of deep coaching. I especially want to thank a group of coaching colleagues who studied with me almost monthly for seven years, integrating the deep coaching principles into their professional work, offering questions and profound insights, and influencing my own understanding. My deep gratitude goes to Devon Carter, Susan Hansch, Lara Heller, Ipek Serifsoy, Karen Van Zino, and Irma Velasquez. My gratitude also goes to early coaches Marcia Hyatt, Pamela Johnson, Moira McCaskill, Brian Mitchell-Walker, Samuel Schindler and Katie Gay for their love and ongoing contributions to this work.

Among my many formal and informal teachers, I will always be indebted to the late Don Richard Riso and Russ Hudson for their seminal body of work and for their inspired and profound teachings. Their work provided the foundation upon which the original edition of this book was written, and much is carried through the current edition. Don, who offered treasured mentoring and guidance, asked me to aim high with the first book. I wish I could share this new edition with him.

I have been blessed to work with an amazing production team. Davis Creative Publishing Partners has been my production partner for years. I'm especially grateful to Cathy Davis and Missy Asikainen for their dedication, breadth of experience, professionalism, and design expertise in bringing this complex project to completion. Jeanie Williams is also a longtime collaborator. Using her vast experience in the book world along with her natural capacity to resonate with my work, she brought her eye to every tiny detail as my proofreader.

The most influential person in my life is Dr. Jim Murphy. It is inconceivable that this book could have been published without his ongoing support, patience, and love. It was Jim who encouraged me for years to consider writing this second edition. No words suffice for how grateful I am for his wise spirit and for having him as my husband and life partner.

APPENDIXES

APPENDIX A: Dynamic Nature of the Personality along the
Continuum of Constriction and Expansion

APPENDIX B: Enneagram Interview Process™

APPENDIX C: Dynamism of the Personality: Lines of Access

APPENDIX D: Social Style Somatic Coaching Exercise

APPENDIX E: The Triangle of Identity for Nine Personality Types

APPENDIX F: Presence as a Basis for Transformation

APPENDIX G: Examples of Potentially Powerful Questions and Comments

APPENDIX H: Example of Inner Story Process

APPENDIX I: Worksheet: Considerations for Meeting Your Client with Presence

APPENDIX J: Examples of Personality Patterns That Can Unconsciously Undermine
or Bias Your Work as a Coach

APPENDIX A

Dynamic Nature of the Personality Along the Continuum of Constriction and Expansion

Healthy Attributes: Expansive

Expansive	I have my personality	Observant of patterns and nonattached	High level of inner freedom and choice	Curiosity about what I'm experiencing	Broad range of perspectives	Receptive, transparent	Most available to possibility	Flexible, responsive	High degree of ease	Energetic lightness	Most positive impact on others	High level of emotional intelligence
....	....	....	....	....	....	....	....	....	....	....	....	....
Highly constricted	Personality has me	Highly attached to my patterns	Imprisoned/ no true choice	Certainty that how I am is who I am	Narrowing of perspective	Closed off/ closed to input	Most unaware of alternatives	Inflexible, reactive	High degree of tension	Energetic denseness	Most negative impact on others	Low emotional intelligence

Unhealthy Attributes: Constricted

NOTE:
Your clients are unlikely to be at either end of the continuum because there are many shades or degrees of attachment to the personality that lie in between these two polarities. On the other hand, most of us have at least glimpsed into our most inflexible nature and have tapped into our healthiest qualities.

APPENDIX B

Enneagram Inquiry Process™

STEP 1

Set context of Enneagram and why one would want to know their type (using your own words):

- The Enneagram is a profound and practical map of consciousness that has spanned many traditions and combines psychological and spiritual understandings of the human condition.

- The Enneagram helps us understand precise ways that we disconnect through our ego or fixated personality from our deepest nature and potential; it opens new ways of seeing ourselves, others, and life.

- Sometimes there is a disparity between how we want to see ourselves or how we want others to see us and how we are. Find what is most true for you.

- No type is better than another, and with each type there is the good news and bad news. It can be difficult in the beginning seeing how much our fixated personality runs our life, but if we stay with it, there is an abundance of possibility and liberation on the other side.

- It's best when finding your type to think about yourself in your late twenties or early thirties if you are older than that now.

STEP 2

Say the first things that come to you and don't overthink:

- Name several adjectives that best describe you.

- How would a best friend or partner describe you?

- What would you describe as a challenging quality about yourself (in work or relationships)?

- What are your greatest strengths? What comes easily to you?

STEP 3: NARRATIVES OF ENNEAGRAM TYPES

We're going to go through a brief narrative of all nine Enneagram types so that you get a flavor of each and see how different they are. After each narrative, let me know what resonated with you and what didn't. I may ask a few more questions before going on to the next one. Some people know right away what their type is, and others make this discovery over time. Although everyone has just one core type, we access other types at different times; it's a complex and dynamic system. There is no rush, and the process can be as valuable as the actual discovery. (Note to coach: use a moniker like A, B, C to distinguish the types rather than using the actual type number to prevent possible bias.)

Type Eight (A)

People say that I'm bold, strong, decisive, and sometimes a bull in a china shop. Well, I definitely wouldn't call myself delicate or touchy-feely, and weak is not in my vocabulary. I'm direct, honest, and forthcoming and look for the same in others. Everyone expects me to be the strong one, the rock, and I am. At the same time, I've been called a Mack truck filled with marshmallows and that's not far from the truth. I protect those I care about but don't have much time for people who don't put out effort. I always make sure people are treated fairly and justly, especially those that can't stand up for themselves. I can hold my own in any situation and I'm glad I'm so capable. I make things happen, I'm assertive, and I like to take the lead, so I often find myself in charge—the boss. I've been told that I'm "too much" sometimes, but I'm just who I am, no need to apologize for that. Life is here to be lived fully, the more and bigger the better.

Type Nine (B)

People always tell me how easygoing and easy to get along with I am. Plus, I'm relaxed, calm, and a good listener. This is mostly true. Although sometimes, especially when I feel like someone is trying to push me into a decision or urge me to do something I'm not certain about, I can be quietly stubborn and resistant. This is a part of myself I don't really like to dwell on though, as mostly I think I am a pretty go-with-the-flow type of person. It takes a lot to ruffle my feathers. Those who know me well have also called me a peacemaker or mediator. I think it comes from my desire for wanting everyone to feel good and people to live together harmoniously. When that happens, I feel content; I really don't like discord of any kind. Why should there be—we're all in this together. Why not get along? One downside of being able to see everyone else's perspective is that it can be hard for me to know what I want and express my own opinions. Sometimes it's as if what I want or what I have to say is not so important, almost like I don't matter. But all's good—everything comes over time.

Type One (C)

I like to think of myself as conscientious, hardworking, reliable, and a person with high standards. A person of integrity! Some tell me I am a perfectionist, and I can understand that because I do like things to be done a certain way. I can get very frustrated with others' lack of attention to detail and commitment to doing the right thing (sometimes people are so irresponsible and inappropriate!). In most cases, I do think there is a better way to do things and I have a gut sense of that. I'm aware of what isn't as good as it could be—about what I haven't done well, what others haven't done properly, what needs to be done and isn't being done. As a result, there's always more to change, to improve. If you really want to know what I see, just ask me, I'm a natural-born teacher. People often appreciate my efforts but sometimes they tell me that I'm too judgmental or critical. This feedback is hard for me to hear. I really don't like to be criticized or corrected (I don't think anyone would believe how hard I am on myself already). Frustration can be a common experience as I tend to feel it is my responsibility to fix what's not working and there is much that needs to be made right. If only the world was as glorious, perfect, and wonderful as I know it can be!

Type Two (D)

Mainly I'm interested in connection and being kind and loving. And I have lots of energy for it! I mean, isn't that why we're here—to take care of and support one another? I don't want to sound conceited, but I excel at that, I must admit. I can sense what others need almost better than they can. Sometimes I think if someone would care for me as well as I take care of others, I'd have it made! But that is a selfish thought. My goal, my gift, is in giving and helping, and I derive incredible satisfaction from it—it's how I find fulfillment. True, sometimes if my efforts aren't noticed or appreciated, I can get snippy. All I need is for you to tell me what you love and appreciate about my efforts and to acknowledge me. Then we're good. Indeed, people call me sensitive and empathetic, and I think that's true. I've always been that way, as far back as I can remember.

Type Three (E)

"I'm on it," you'll often hear me say, because I am. In my worldview, life often seems like an endless list of to-dos, and more than anyone else I know, I have the ability to check off my list with the best of 'em. I have been called an accomplishment machine and I can see why. I am usually very busy and rarely take a break to catch my breath. It's like I have this inner drive that compels me to keep moving, doing, and getting things done. But I am grateful for that drive because it has helped me become very successful at almost anything I want to achieve. Sure, it would probably be good to learn how to slow down and turn my drive down, but I don't know who I'd be if I wasn't moving, doing, and accomplishing all the time. (Don't tell anyone but, honestly, that sort of bothers me. I have a hard time just sitting on the couch without jumping up to do one more thing.) People say I'm competitive, and I guess I am, but I don't usually think of it that way—I just want to be the best at whatever I do, and I know I can as I am capable and confident. I do have a bit of a weakness for wanting to impress others and have them think well of me and I guess you could say that I "work it" pretty well in a room, but doesn't everyone? I mean, who doesn't want others to respect and admire them?

Type Four (F)

"Who am I?" "What gives meaning and purpose to life?" These are a few of the questions that consume me, that I must understand and answer. Don't bother me with the mundane, with the common. I seek passionately and deeply to understand why I'm here. I want to know myself to the depths and often I feel that it'll never happen because something is missing, or worse, there's something intrinsically wrong with me. Others seem so clear about who they are, and their life seems so perfect. Sometimes I'm envious of them, and I spend a lot of time wondering why I feel so lost on my own path in life. I know I have gifts and that I possess something unique—something special. But I don't think anyone, including myself, has really seen the real me in all my glory. I long and yearn for that. You might say that I'm overly sensitive or dramatic; I do have a love of melancholy, but please don't ask me to conform. The ordinary is my death knell. I long for deep, authentic connection with others and with myself. Sometimes I have difficulty appreciating present relationships as I yearn for what could be better. So let me live. Let me feel. Feelings tell me that I'm alive and real.

Type Five (G)

I don't like to talk about myself that much, but if I had to sum it up, I'd say I'm smart, innovative, and focused. I love to learn and am almost compulsively curious about all kinds of different things. I thrive on understanding what I study and not just skimming the surface. I can spend hours, and in some cases decades, delving into the depths of something that fascinates me. Some people think I'm a little over the top in my passion for learning, but that's just the way I've always been—I am voraciously curious and have a strong drive to understand the complexities of how things work. In a way, my knowledge and perspicacity give me a feeling of safety and security, and that must be important to me. I wouldn't consider myself much of a people person; I definitely need lots of time on my own and a place that is just for me. Too many demands on my time and energy overwhelm me, and I withdraw. Sometimes I wish I didn't have to deal with as many people as I do. I'd be happy to spend much of my time on my own, although I will say a part of me knows connection with others is important.

Type Six (H)

It's hard to describe myself really, but people say I'm dependable, thoughtful, trustworthy, and a good team player. I'm motivated by my need and desire for others to feel safe and secure. So I pay attention to potential danger or hazards, things that could go wrong. I watch for them and devise strategies to protect against them. I'm well prepared in that sense. Often when the path forward isn't clear, I can become anxious and indecisive, seeking the opinions of others (sometimes valuing them more than my own). Usually I'm best at playing defense, although I sometimes take the offensive to eliminate potential threats—meeting them head on, without fear. Loyalty is also big for me. I don't trust easily or automatically, particularly people in positions of authority—I am always assessing whether others are trustworthy. It's just plain smart. If you do earn my trust, I have your back, and my support is solid and consistent. Same with organizations: I might challenge the leadership to determine if they are the real thing, but again, when I find an organization or a cause that is dependable, I'm committed. People say I have a good sense of humor and I can make light of myself. This helps me a lot when I get into difficult spots.

Type 7 (I)

I have a sense of boundless possibility. I'm optimistic, enthusiastic, and upbeat, and I live for new experiences and opportunities. Others think that I'm constantly planning for the future. But my plans are mere sketches. Rather, I anticipate. I constantly think of what could be, might be, that which might bring joy and freedom to life. And in the process, I avoid anything that might limit my options. And because I don't want to miss out on anything that might be glorious and exciting, my plate is always full. My calendar is often double-booked. I have lots of energy and enjoy starting new projects, but implementing them, doing the nitty-gritty, can be a challenge, especially when doing so becomes tedious or boring. So I prefer to let others finish things. I'm happy creating. And I have the wonderful ability to think big, to see connections that others do not. One thing I'm clear about is that I never want to lose my sense of freedom. Therefore, commitment can seem tantamount to death. So, if you join me in exploring new possibilities and don't get stuck in painful or unpleasant emotions or experiences, we'll get along just fine. Life is supposed to be enjoyed, so let's put our energy in the right direction!

STEP 4

- Ask your client: What types resonated most for you and why?
- Use the key issues notes below to delve more deeply into themes of those types that they recognize.
- Identify at least three types for them to explore further.

A few sample key issues and questions for each type:

TYPE 8 Challenger

Strength
How often do you feel you need to be the strong one?
How easy is it to show vulnerability—when and with whom?

Big, bold energy
How often do you get feedback that your energy is too much or too forceful?
Or that you need to tone it down?

Protectorate
What about fairness/justice? What does protection mean?
(This is not about the letter of the law.)

TYPE 9 Peacemaker

Receptive/mediator
How good are you at seeing other people's perspectives?

Easygoing/complacent
How important is it to keep things comfortable? How do you handle conflict?
Energy level?

Other Themes
How good are you at staying focused, staying on task?
In a group, how easy is it for you to express your own opinion?

TYPE 1 Reformer

Hardworking
How easy is it to fit pleasure into your schedule?
Do you tend to work before you can play?

High internal standard
How good are you at seeing better ways of doing things?
How often do you notice errors and tend to want to fix things?

Principled/moralistic
How often do you tend to follow rules or think you know the best rules
to be made and followed?

TYPE 2 Helper

Attuned to others' needs, empathetic

Do you take special pride in being able to sense what other people need
and what they are feeling?
How easy is it to be aware of and express your own needs? To ask others for help?

Relationship oriented

How important are relationships to you?

Generous

How do you feel if people are not appreciative of your generosity?

TYPE 3 Achiever

Compulsive accomplisher

How easy is it for you to stop—for example, take a vacation?
Do you bring your computer with you?

Image-conscious

How important are other people's perceptions of you?

Confident and competent

How impatient do you find yourself with people who appear to be slow at making
decisions or appear incompetent?

TYPE 4 Individualist

Attuned to inner emotional world

Would people describe you as being even-keeled with your emotions or more like
a tidal wave? What is your experience?

Authentic

How important is it to create deep, authentic relationships?
What makes a relationship authentic to you?

Beauty/creative

How important is it to have beauty in your environment?
What role does creativity play in your life?

TYPE 5 Investigator

Perspicacity/astute observer

Would you describe yourself as perceptive and a good listener?

Do you tend to be more an observer or a participator? Why?

Thought focused vs. feeling focused

When are you most comfortable expressing your feelings?

Is it easier to identify how you feel after giving it some thought?

Secretive

How easy is it to share personal information about yourself with others?

TYPE 6 Loyalist

Loyal

On a scale of 1–10, how loyal would you consider yourself?

Vigilant

How good are you at anticipating problems? Do you notice what might go wrong?

Trust

How comfortable are you in deeply trusting your own wisdom?

What is your relationship to authority figures? Do you tend to push against, be dutiful (compliant), or want to be the authority?

TYPE 7 Enthusiast

Optimistic

How often do you take on the roll as the optimistic and enthusiastic one in your circle of friends or with your family?

Stimulation, anticipation

What is your experience of boredom? How important is having stimulating experiences in your day-to-day life? In general, how full is your calendar?

Keeping options open

How often do you start things that you don't finish? How easy is it for you to make a commitment and stick with it?

APPENDIX C

Dynamism of the Personality: Lines of Access

→→→→ Movement to "Integration" Point →→→→
←←←← Movement to "Stress" Point ←←←←

Levels of Attachment/ Identification with personality*	TYPE NINE: The Peacemaker	TYPE THREE: The Achiever	TYPE SIX: The Loyalist	TYPE NINE: The Peacemaker
"Hold personality lightly": Living with presence	- Present - Self-remembering & determining - Inclusive/receptive - Comforting/healing - Unpretentious	- Authentic - Heartful - Outstanding - Communicator - Uplifts others— helps them to become "stars"	- Courageous - Inner knowing - Trusting and secure - Community-builder/ the "glue" - Dependable steward	- Present - Self-remembering & determining - Inclusive/receptive - Comforting/healing - Unpretentious
Moderately attached to personality: Moving toward presence	- Self-effacing - Acquiescing - Avoid conflict - Checked-out/ auto-pilot - Passive-aggressive	- Image and status- conscious - Performer - Competitive - Overly-adaptive - Self-promoting	- Lacking confidence in Self - Indecisive - Doubting/pessimist - Worrier/anxious - Looks to others for answer	- Self-effacing - Acquiescing - Avoid conflict - Checked-out/ auto-pilot - Passive-aggressive
Deeply identified and involved with personality	- Unresponsive - Numb - Dissociates/denial	- Unprincipled - Deceptive - Opportunistic	- Unreliable - Cynical - Paranoid	- Unresponsive - Numb - Dissociates/denial
Passion	Sloth	Vanity	Fear/Anxiety	Sloth
Virtue	Engagement	Authenticity	Courage	Engagement

* Based on the work of Don Riso (1977)

Roxanne Howe-Murphy, 2008

→→→→ *Movement to "Integration" Point* →→→→
←←←← *Movement to "Stress" Point* ←←←←

Levels of Attachment/ Identification with personality*	TYPE EIGHT: The Challenger	TYPE TWO: The Helper	TYPE FOUR: The Individualist	TYPE ONE: The Reformer
"Hold personality lightly": Living with presence	– Magnanimous – Heroic Protector and champion – Self-reliant – Decisive leader – Action-oriented	– Unconditionally loving – Self-nurturing – Compassionate & caring – Dedicated – Generous and supportive	– Life-enhancing – Original/Personal Creativity-universal – Equanimity/ emotional strength – Intuitive – Inner-directed	– High purpose and mission – Highly principled – Integrity – Wise – Discerning
Moderately attached to personality: Moving toward presence	– Assertiveness becomes aggression – Intense/big energy – Dominating – Territorial – Confrontational/ intimidating	– People-pleasing – Flattering – Self-sacri- ficing/rescuer/ co-dependent – Self-important – Intrusive	– Moody & dramatic – Takes things personally – Envious – Strong inner fantasy – Feels uniquely flawed	– Responsible for "fixing" things – Afraid of making mistake -perfectionist – Judgmental – Rigid
Deeply identified and involved with personality	– Violent – Abusive – Raging	– Hypochondriac – Manipulative/ desperately needy – Entitled	– Depressed – Alienated – Hopeless	– Dogmatic – Absolutes – "Holy war"
Passion	Lust/Intensity	Pride	Envy	Resentment
Virtue	Innocence	Humility	Equanimity	Serenity

* Based on the work of Don Riso (1977)

Levels of Attachment/ Identification with personality*	TYPE ONE: The Reformer	TYPE SEVEN: The Enthusiast	TYPE FIVE: The Investigator	TYPE EIGHT: The Challenger
"Hold personality lightly": Living with presence	– High purpose and mission – Highly principled – Integrity – Wise – Discerning	– Filled with awe of life – Truly joyful – Enthusiastic and free spirited – Curious/fast learners – Generative and passionate	– Profound Vision – Pioneering and revolutionary thinking – Perceptive – Smart – Focused	– Magnanimous – Heroic Protector and champion – Self-reliant – Decisive leader – Action-oriented
Moderately attached to personality: Moving toward presence	– Responsible for "fixing" things – Afraid of making mistake -perfectionist – Judgmental – Rigid	– Acquisitive – Sensation-seeking – Scattered and distracted – Self-centered – Excessive	– Conceptualizing – Preparing – Detached and private – Provocative/ intell./ arrogant – Stingy	– Assertiveness becomes aggression – Intense/big energy – Dominating – Territorial – Confrontational/ intimidating
Deeply identified and involved with personality	– Dogmatic – Absolutes – "Holy war"	– Escape artist – Insatiable – Out-of-control	– Eccentric – Dark fantasies/focus on dark side – Hallucinationss	– Violent – Abusive – Raging
Passion	Resentment	Gluttony	Avarice	Resentment
Virtue	Serenity	Sobriety	Non-attachment	Serenity

* Based on the work of Don Riso (1977)

Roxanne Howe-Murphy, 2008

273

APPENDIX D

Social Style Somatic Coaching Exercise

Here's an exercise to offer your clients. Be sure to read through the description first before introducing the exercise to clients.

Begin with asking your client to identify a challenging interpersonal situation. When they have one in mind, invite them to sense into what is arising within in that moment—for example, sensations, emotional reactions, or thoughts.

Then, guide the client with the following somatic directions, asking them to allow the identified situation to drop away for now.

Ask the client to stand in a neutral position with their feet shoulder-width apart. Then ask them to:

- Sense into the felt connection of their feet with the ground

- Bring attention to their breath and allow it to move more deeply within

- Bring attention to three important areas: the belly area, the heart, and the head (Note: these are called the centers of intelligence and are addressed in chapter 10.)

Read selected characteristics from the following page of each of the social styles. Share characteristics of one social style at a time.

Ask your client to bring the challenging interpersonal situation back into their awareness as they explore each social style. Read through the characteristics slowly, giving your client the time needed for sensing into the characteristics, and then ask them to move into the position, posture, and/or internal experience that their bodies would take if they were using that style. Take some time to explore this experience with the client. Examples of guiding questions that you can ask are included.

Start with the private/introspective types.

Ask the client to move into the position or posture that their body would take if they were using this style.

Ask: How are your feet placed? Does one foot carry more weight than the other foot? How does your body move—backward, forward? Do you notice movement in your chest, such as becoming more concave or more expansive? What other observations do you have about your experience in this moment? How familiar or comfortable is this position for you?

Have your client take a deep breath, shake their body out, then return to the neutral position.

Continue this process with the assured/confident style, then again with the service-oriented, responsible style.

What is your client taking away from this experience? Was one of the three styles more familiar? Was there a negative reaction to any of the styles?

As the client kept the challenging situation in mind for the three styles, what would have been their default approach to this interaction? How does that style serve them? How does it interfere with realizing a beneficial outcome? What options are available to them through the other styles? What happens when they approach the situation with more neutrality, not dependent upon any one of the styles?

Of course, all the styles have value in certain situations, and it is valuable to be able to call upon any of them.

If your client is in the self-typing process, you might encourage them to read about the three types that are included in the style that feels the most natural or familiar to them.

1. Personality Types Relying on Private and Introspective Strategies

- I tend to withdraw or even avoid active social, physical, emotional, spiritual, or intellectual engagement.

- I have an inner sanctuary or inner world that provides what feels like safe space in order to avoid external demands that may feel too overwhelming for me.

- I can disappear, whether physically, emotionally, or energetically.

- I can easily go into fantasy or resort to mental intensity.

- I sometimes secretly feel that I don't belong or don't fit in with other people or with groups.

- I tend to pull back from engaging if it feels like the situation or others are demanding too much of my attention.

2. Personality Types Relying on Assured, Confident Strategies

- My attention is external, outwardly focused.

- I communicate directly and clearly and look for others to do the same.

- I'm used to going after what I want and can be insistent or demanding.

- It feels natural to be at the center of attention.

- Things happen when I'm around, and I often initiate the action.

- I tend to keep others at a distance emotionally.

3. Personality Types Relying on Service-Oriented, Responsible Strategies

- I need to know what the rules are and what is expected of me.

- I carry an inner sense of responsibility for the safety of others and of my surroundings.

- I sometimes feel burned out because of the never-ending list of things that need to be done. I keep busy.

- It's really hard for me to take care of myself.

- My mind goes nonstop. It's difficult to have my mind become still.

- I become anxious when I don't know what to do next.

APPENDIX E

The Triangle of Identity for the Nine Personality Types

OVERVIEW OF THE TRIANGLE OF IDENTITY

We have all these human experiences within us, but one will be most distinct. While these structures are not who we are, our core personality type's structure "feels like me."

Types by Social Style Cluster	What I Pursue	What I Avoid	Major Coping Strategy
Using Private/Introspective Strategies			
FOUR	Sense of identity	Being ordinary	Being emotionally intense
FIVE	Knowledge/making a contribution	Being ignorant	Being mentally intense
NINE	Harmony	Loss of connection	Accommodating others
Using Assured/Confident Strategies			
THREE	Being seen as successful and valued	Being seen as a failure/ worthlessness	Adapting, performing, producing
SEVEN	Open-ended freedom	Being caged in	Not missing out
EIGHT	Being powerful and in control	Showing vulnerability	Imposing my will
Using Responsible/Service-Oriented Strategies			
ONE	Doing and being good	Being wrong or bad	Being on a mission
TWO	The experience of love	Being seen as selfish/ unlovable	Putting attention/energy into others' lives
SIX	Security/something to hold on to	The unfamiliar/unknown	Looking for something I can trust

Copyright Roxanne Howe-Murphy, 2009

APPENDIX F

Presence as a Basis for Transformation

CREATING SPACIOUSNESS, RELEASING INTERNAL EMOTIONAL PATTERNS, AND HEALING

This guide is an application of the principles and strategies included throughout the book to support clients in creating sufficient internal spaciousness to meet and heal some aspect of a troubling pattern with the power of presence. Use this guide with great care and while in contact with your own three centers of intelligence. There is no goal or expectation associated with this process. You are not trying to get somewhere. With presence, you are walking with and being with your client in the unknown, and sometimes uncomfortable, territory.

Introduce this process when the client has sufficient presence and trust in the coach-client relationship to be able to enter into the sensations of their deeper inner territory. When you've noticed that a client is having a reaction to a topic, you can start the process by simply asking, "What's happening for you now?" or "Would you like to check in with your heart right now? What are you noticing?"

This process is written in the second person to encourage you, the coach, to practice it for yourself before using it with clients. You are welcome to use the language associated with each of the steps with your client.

1. BECOME A DETECTIVE AND RECOGNIZE WHEN THE PATTERN SHOWS UP

You or your client may recognize a behavioral or emotional pattern that no longer supports the client's development and causes pain or trouble. (See the descriptions of Enneagram types delineating many patterns in section 2.) Noticing when a pattern is triggered is a major step in beginning to relax its grip. Most people go through their lives with little awareness that certain patterns are shaping their self-identity and limiting their freedom or that such patterns developed as coping mechanisms but soon become unconscious, habitual, and overutilized, even when not beneficial. Remember, you are conditioned to think your reactions are caused by someone or something outside of you.

Detecting such patterns can initially be difficult because they may feel like your second nature, so you must become a pattern detective. Each pattern offers cues that can get your attention, increasing your awareness of it. Cues can be found in a number of experiential channels, such as thoughts, emotional experiences, attitudes, bodily sensations, or behaviors. Cues from some channels might be easier for you to recognize. For example, you might notice that you have a recurring thought or an emotional experience that's associated with a statement made by a colleague or loved one. Or you might notice a faint but familiar body sensation resulting from your reaction to a situation, such as finding you're snarly with someone and then feeling tightness around your head. Or you might feel apprehensive and have a thought such as, "I'm going to get hurt if I say something." Or you might notice that you feel justified in reacting to a situation in a certain way, saying to yourself something like, "He deserved that from me" or "I deserve to do that or have that because I've worked so hard." Or you might notice yourself feeling tense, irritated, rigid, angry, depressed, or even emotionally flat. At first, you may not be aware of a pattern until after you've had an experience of it. But after you've become more familiar with a behavioral, emotional, or sensate pattern, you may notice when you are in it. Consider this real progress!

2. CREATE A LITTLE DISTANCE BETWEEN YOURSELF AND THE PATTERN AS YOU NORMALIZE IT

Becoming aware of patterns often elicits embarrassment or shame.

Remember that having automatic patterns is completely normal and that, unfortunately, most people spend a great deal of energy expressing themselves through patterns. Realize that you are among the fortunate people becoming aware of the painful effects of patterns that do not yield beneficial outcomes and that you are on a courageous journey to these patterns having less power over you.

Creating a little distance between yourself and the pattern means that the pattern does not define you. With presence, you can notice the pattern's existence as part of your human experience, recognizing that there is far more to you than the pattern.

3. BE WITH THE EXPERIENCE OF THE PATTERN AND ITS ASSOCIATED SENSATIONS

Behavioral, emotional, and attitudinal patterns are innately connected to sensations in the body. Once you have recognized a pattern, work with the following steps of the healing process to guide you into its underlying sources.

Consciously breathe and ground.

Breathing and sensing into your feet on the ground or your body in a chair helps you notice that there is much more to you than the pattern, though it can feel like it's taking up your whole life while you are experiencing it. The felt contact between your body and the chair (or floor/earth) supports becoming present, which is essential in this practice. Your body is in the here and now and is an important source of support.

For this process to be most beneficial, it is important to experience these inner sensations as fully possible. This means breathing into the sensations with a relaxed and focused attention.

Notice the various facets and dimensions of your sensations.

Inquire into the specifics of the sensation, such as: Where is it located in the body? What is its dimensionality, its size? Does it have a color? A temperature? A weight? Is it still, moving, increasing or decreasing in size?

Approach your sensations with a curious, open mind, even if it feels strange. Try saying, "Isn't that interesting? There it goes again," perhaps even finding humor in it. Clients and students often say that curiosity is very helpful because it lightens the load and keeps them from taking their patterns too seriously. This process can create distance between you and the sensations, and you notice that you begin to see the sensations as separate from you. You are having an experience, without it having you. You shift from identifying with the pattern to inquiring about it.

4. ALLOW THE EXPERIENCE WITH COMPASSION AND NONJUDGMENT

Recognize that the pattern has existed for good reasons, even if it no longer serves you well. Remember that you did not actively choose this pattern but that it comes with the territory of your particular Enneagram personality type and is part of the human condition. Judging yourself is a basis for great suffering, is one of the most damaging aspects of the personality's structure, and has little value for adults. Invite your fair witness—that aspect of yourself that is simultaneously observant and nonjudgmental—to be your ally. Ultimately, being nonjudgmental will allow you to experience more freedom in your life. In being compassionate with yourself, you are using your heart's intelligence for support.

While focusing on inner sensations, you may feel emotional or physical pain, such as a tight knot that extends from your stomach to your ribcage or a constriction in your throat. In such instances, just keep breathing and staying with your sensations, even if you don't understand why they are occurring.

Because this is a new and challenging approach, it's natural to:
- Repress sensations, which leads to exaggerated internal tension.
- Numb yourself so that you don't feel.
- Act out pain that you may be feeling.
- Short-circuit the experience, too rapidly determining that you've done enough.

However, being with the uncomfortable experience allows you to fully experience what is showing up and allows something new to arise that often feels like an opening. This process may take a few minutes on one occasion or longer periods on many occasions. Just through noticing, it is likely that something about it will shift, especially if you don't try to make anything happen.

As you continue breathing and focusing attention on sensations, you'll eventually notice more shifts accompanied by a little more ease. You may actually feel tired, though rejuvenated.

IMPORTANT NOTE: If you experience too much discomfort or the sensations bring up past trauma, stop the process, reground, and spend a few moments breathing with gratitude for yourself. Alternatively, you could focus on a neutral object in your environment, noticing its characteristics while continuing to breathe.

5. ACKNOWLEDGE AND ACCEPT WHAT IS SHOWING UP

Acknowledge that this process, though simple, is not easy and that it calls upon several major things from you: a strong commitment to become freed from the compulsion of personality patterns, a radical new orientation toward compassion, and a high level of courage that you may not have known before. However, with every use of this process you will discover something important about yourself and will in some way be changed beneficially. You will come into deeper contact with your inner truth.

From a psychological perspective, your patterns are associated with your particular neurological system, and your neurology and brain structure are changed when you bring such consciousness to your inner work. Old neural connections are shaken up, and new neural pathways are created.

From a spiritual perspective, the power of presence is at the core of this process. Many people feel that through being so connected to their inner experience they have been touched by an invisible, beneficial force—by grace. They realize that they didn't have to fix themselves or make something happen; rather, when they showed up, the universe extended a helping hand. In doing this, they are being supported by presence, the great field of inexplicable spaciousness and being that holds us all.

RECOGNIZE THE MYSTERY OF ALCHEMY

As many early spiritual mystics knew, combining curious attention and loving compassion with awareness of breathing and bodily sensations when addressing difficult inner experiences can have the effect of changing the heavy lead of psychic suffering into the precious gold of freedom. Pain does not get resolved by judging, denying, or avoiding ourselves or by identifying with and reinforcing it. Your reactions to pain provide the basis of your personality's patterns, and those patterns are what lead you to think there's something wrong with you. But using this process—which highlights the integration of breath and attention with nonjudgment, curiosity, and acceptance—is a powerful vehicle for transformation and will lead to greater compassion for yourself and others who have troubling patterns they may not understand cognitively.

It is a privilege for coaches to guide and be with their clients through this process. If it is integrated into coaching sessions often enough, some clients may have the capacity to use it for themselves. It is reassuring to know that each of us carries within us the capacity for turning our psychic suffering into freedom, ease, and lightness.

APPENDIX G

Examples of Potentially Powerful Questions and Comments

On the way to a client realizing their intentions, the client will face numerous obstacles that reflect their inner landscape.

Below are examples of questions or comments that have been used with clients so that they could see their less helpful behavioral, thought, and feeling patterns more clearly and claim that part of themselves that is beyond personality. These questions offer only a fragment of the entire coaching conversation.

The questions are offered here only as examples and for study, and they should be used with right timing, context, and purpose. No question is ever powerful or even appropriate under all circumstances, so caution is urged. And there are many better questions that could be asked that didn't make their way onto this page. Perhaps what is offered here will spur your own creative process when coaching a client from presence.

When a client introduces situations in which they experience a struggle:

What does it mean to struggle? What is your experience of struggle?

Why is this a struggle?

Does your experience around this situation feel familiar? In what way?

This is coaching the client around the experience of struggle, not the situation. The awareness of an underlying pattern or story could emerge, helping the client see that the situation is not necessarily the cause of the so-called struggle. Perhaps the client will notice that the situation is not a struggle after all.

In what ways does being in a struggle serve you? Not serve you?

What are you resisting?

When working with a client's self-identified troublesome behavior (e.g., procrastination, anger, dismissing another person's perspective, judging self or another person):

What are the clues/indicators/markers that you are in this pattern?

The markers can be emotional, physical/somatic, mental, or behavioral, so take the time needed to identify all the markers.

How do you experience this pattern in your body?

How are you judging yourself for experiencing this behavior?

How has this pattern served you?

It is often useful to incorporate somatic work into coaching when working with patterns. The inner story process can also be beneficial here. See chapters 10 and 11 for more information.

When a client is making a decision:

After the client identifies the options, explore each one.

- *Take on this option as your chosen answer.*

- *Notice the sensations in your body. What are you experiencing?*

- *Does this choice feel more expansive or more constrictive?*

- *Where/how are you experiencing this state of expansiveness or constriction?*

Somatic work can be very powerful when coaching around making big decisions.

When a client is in a habitual troublesome pattern (e.g., fear, anger, frustration, sleepiness):

What part of you is not in this pattern?

This can help clients recognize that there is more to them than this pattern. Coach around that recognition.

What action would this freer part of you take?

What would the more expansive, freer part of you say to the restricted part?

When you hear a client say, "I'm so ___" (fill in the blank with some self-defining adjective that reflects a repetitive pattern: boring, hurt, busy, resentful, envious):

Ask the client to change the language pattern to:

Up to now, I've been _____.

Working somatically, ask the client to heavily exaggerate the feeling and experience and express it through their body. Have the client stay with the experience until it shifts (or until you both explode in laughter).

What if you are not what you are telling yourself?

What part of you is ready to choose something more fulfilling?

When a client refers to experiencing a particular repetitive state (e.g., moody, sad, cantankerous, lonely):

What is your experience of that particular state or emotion?

What do you know about this state?

Encourage the client to be curious about this state. This can lead to amazing shifts. Clients often say, "It's not what I thought it was."

When a client is agitated about a specific experience they have had or anticipate having:

What is the story you are telling yourself about this experience or about this person?

This question supports the client to listen in to the inner dialogue and develop perspective around it.

What strengths of your Enneagram type (or any Enneagram type) could you bring to this situation to lead to a desired outcome?

When a client says "I'm stuck":

Explore the Triangle of Identity associated with the client's core Enneagram type. What feels familiar to the client? Coach around what they are pursuing and what they are avoiding.

What makes you believe you are stuck?

Describe your experience of this state.

What if being stuck is a lie you are telling yourself?

What is working well?

This can be a mental model blowout question if a person is consumed with all that is wrong with them. Remember that some clients will focus on troublesome behavior because they are identified with the need to fix themselves.

With clients who have unconsciously committed themselves to a self-identity of being flawed or stuck, challenging the self-identity is a great example of coaching the person and not the situation.

When a client is focused on what is not going well:

Tell me what is going well.

What skills, gifts, and resources are available to you right now?

When a client complains about a situation:

What are you not accepting about this situation?

Bring your strengths to this situation. What is the situation now? What does it require of you?

When you experience that a client is emotionally closed:

Help the client open their heart by saying:

Witness what happens to you and to the situation when you consciously change the way you hold (are willing to perceive) the situation.

What would allow you to approach this situation with openness?

What allows you to open your heart to this person?

What happens when you let down your guard, even just a little?

And the biggie:

What happens when you open your heart to yourself?

How can you meet those situations that are calling upon your greatness of heart?

As we talk about your greatness of heart, what is your experience of your heart right in this moment?

APPENDIX H

Example of Inner Story Process

Here's an example of the inner story process.

You may make copies of figure 11.2 to use with a client or you can draw a circle out on a flip-chart or board and use the following questions to lead the client through this process. This can be done in virtual formats as well as in person. You'll notice that some of the questions are repeated or slightly changed in order to be responsive to the client.

This client came to the coaching conversation frustrated that she didn't seem able to make progress on decluttering. Procrastination is an issue that shows up often in coaching conversations. Clients with different Enneagram types may well have different inner stories that accompany this issue. Here's how this client's inner story process went.

The issue that keeps tripping up the individual
What situation or event tends to create the pattern that is troubling you?
I have an extremely messy office, and I just can't face cleaning it up and organizing.

First sign
What is the first indication that you are in this pattern?
I'm upset because I need access to certain information that I can't get to.

The mental story
What do you tell yourself when you find yourself in this situation?
I tell myself that I don't have any time.
(Then, laughing, "Where do I think I'm going?")

The emotional story
What are you feeling at this point?
I'm disappointed in myself. I'm not fulfilling my expectations of myself.

The mental story
What do you tell yourself now?
I tell myself that I'm lazy and running away from responsibility.

The somatic story
Describe the sensations you are experiencing in your body in the midst of this situation.
Where are you feeling the sensations?
I'm tense. I feel a knot in my stomach.

The behavioral story
What do you actually do? How are you behaving?
I have small starts. I throw away a few papers and create a couple of new files. Then I stop.

The mental story
What do you tell yourself now?
I tell myself that I'm not doing enough and that the task is insurmountable. It's more than I can deal with.

The emotional story
What are you feeling at this point?
I want to cry. I'm so sad as I look at all the projects I started and never finished.

The mental story
What do you tell yourself now?
I question myself. I ask myself what is wrong with me that I didn't finish. I wonder why I'm not perfect.

Focus of attention
What are you looking for? What are you listening for?
I don't want to experience any pain. I'm looking for evidence that I did things well. All I'm getting back is how inadequate I've been.

Outcomes
What are the consequences of this pattern? How is the situation resolved?
I keep distancing myself from what I need to do. I carry a huge amount of unfinished business within me, and I see how tense it makes me.

Then what?
What happens next?
I judge myself relentlessly. Then, I don't go back into the office for days. The process starts all over again when I do go back into the office.

Name the pattern
What "name" could you call this pattern in yourself?
The client called this pattern "The Lack of Forgiveness."

Through this process, the client faced the sadness and self-diminishment she had around the unfinished projects in her office. She recognized the loss of ideals that she had held about herself and how she had been nearly paralyzed by a strong inner critic.

After we allowed space for her grief, she was able to connect more with her heart. Then, we talked about the action-oriented options available to her (e.g., getting help from an organizer, spending a certain amount of time each week on decluttering). She elected to give herself permission to take the time she needed to go through the materials herself, feeling that it would be a healing adventure. She also reevaluated what she had accomplished and realized how easily she had dismissed her successes.

The client was quite surprised that procrastination was not what her mind told her it was.

APPENDIX I

WORKSHEET: Considerations for Meeting Your Client with Presence

Especially if you are new to coaching and/or to the Enneagram, you may find this guide helpful as you prepare for your client sessions. Feel free to make copies of this guide.

Client name: _____

Enneagram type, if known: _____

Client's primary goals or intentions for coaching:

1.

2.

3.

What is specifically possible for this client?

Healthy (expansive) characteristics of type:

Awakened nature:

What is the core belief based upon the Enneagram type?

The Triangle of Identity: Identify potential sources of struggle or a sense of stuckness.

CORE COPING STRATEGY

SENSE OF SELF:

AVOID:

PURSUE:

What is the predominant message of the inner critic?

Key processes to support presence:

_____ Meet the client where they are

_____ Create a spacious container

_____ Clarify with clients the intention for current session, asking them to connect
with their three centers to discern the highest priority

_____ Support the client in having a direct experience in the present moment:

_____ Use conscious breath

_____ Invite five presence-based qualities into session (for you and your client):
curiosity
compassion
honesty
courage
trust

_____ Build client capacity for noticing what is showing up in the moment,
practicing noticing, sensing, allowing, accepting
(working with the three centers)

_____ Guide client to become aware of the inner critic activity and engage with processes
to disidentify with it

_____ Normalize, acknowledge, and accept what shows up

_____ Allow space for the client's experience of pain

_____ Bring attention to client choices

_____ Notice what is occurring within you as the coach

_____ Check on the relevance of original intention with client during session

_____ Link intention with what has been learned

Co-create fieldwork and accountability measures. What's the next best step?

A few additional considerations to support presence in virtual coaching:

- With virtual platforms, do you have enough light in your coaching space that the client can see you well? Can the client hear you well?

- Do you have a backup communication platform in case you lose power?

- What is your agreement with clients about their being in transition (in car, etc.) during the session? What is your agreement around multitasking?

- Create a container appropriate for the type of coaching you offer. Pay attention to how you greet and invite the client into the shared space. For example, you might light a candle as the session begins or guide the client through a grounding process.

- Strengthen your capacity to listen with all three centers.

- Remember the client's whole being. Just seeing the other person's face or head can lead both the coach and the client toward leaning into their planning or analytical minds. This can lead to a faster pace with a limited sense of spaciousness. Check in with the client's experience of breath, offer standing/somatic work, invite the client to place their hands on their belly and heart, as well as their head. Do you or the client need to change distance from the camera to be able to see more of each other?

- Clients can have a whole variety of facial expressions, often without being aware of their expressions (e.g., a blank/seemingly unengaged expression, an expression that you might interpret as judging or criticism, a constant smile, an expression that you interpret as anxious or saying "get on with it"). Check in with the client on what is arising for them in the moment rather than interpreting the expression. Note your own facial expression and energy that is being communicated.

Post-session questions to reflect on:

What was your default when you didn't know what to do next during the session?

What seemed to be the most powerful questions or feedback offered to the client?

How did you allow presence to be a guide?

What else did you learn about your use of deep coaching processes through this session?

APPENDIX J

Examples of Personality Patterns
That Can Unconsciously Undermine or
Bias Your Work as a Coach

TYPE ONE
- Being overly concerned about doing it right as a coach.
- Focusing on the rational, objective side of the client's situation and ignoring or dismissing the emotional dimensions.
- Being opinionated about your client's decisions. Being an advice giver.
- Focusing on how to fix things for or with your client.

TYPE TWO
- Looking for signs that the client likes you.
- Being overly indulgent toward the client.
- Not being direct in giving feedback to the client.
- Not setting appropriate boundaries in your coaching relationships.

TYPE THREE
- Having a singular focus on achieving external goals.
- Keeping the conversation fast-paced and action-oriented, while not allowing space for the client to express their heart and emotions.
- Overly focusing on giving advice on best and most efficient steps for success rather than coaching client to an unexpected outcome.
- Finding ways to show the client how successful you are.

TYPE FOUR
- Being overly involved in the emotional aspects of the client's situation.
- Forgetting to ask the client to take specific action.
- Not grounding yourself or your client in reality but getting caught in wishful thinking.
- Comparing yourself to or envying clients who seemingly have more abundant lives.

TYPE FIVE

- Staying focused on ideas, planning, and analysis and forgetting to spend time with the client on the actual implementation.
- Not disclosing anything about yourself in the coaching relationship.
- Not bringing feelings into the coaching environment.
- Finding ways to show the client how smart you are.

TYPE SIX

- Not trusting your intuitions as a coach. Not feeling confident about yourself and anxiously going back and forth between options.
- Feeling overly responsible for the client's outcomes.
- Not asking the client the big questions with unknown answers.
- Not challenging clients to identify big priorities or to take appropriate risks.

TYPE SEVEN

- Feeling antsy or being distracted when coaching. Multitasking when on the phone.
- Rushing the client during the conversation, forgetting to provide space for the client to have their experience.
- Forgetting to follow up in sessions for purposes of client accountability.
- Assuming that it is not necessary to spend time on the client's pain, sadness, or other darker feelings.

TYPE EIGHT

- Telling the client what to do rather than asking and deeply listening.
- Focusing on bottom-line action without considering the process the client will go through to achieve outcomes.
- Avoiding issues that could elicit vulnerability on the part of the client.
- Overly focusing on challenging the client or having the client challenge situations in their life.

TYPE NINE

- Wanting to make sure the client is okay and avoiding truthful feedback.
- Skirting around conversations about client situations involving conflict.
- Not focusing on helping the client clarify important personal priorities and forgetting about the client's next steps.
- Numbing or blanking out during the session while appearing to listen.

NOTES

Chapter 1

1. Parker J. Palmer, *The Courage to Teach: Exploring the Inner Landscape of a Teacher's Life* (San Francisco: Jossey-Bass, 1998).

2. *Deep Times: A Journal of the Work That Reconnects*, https://journal.workthatreconnects.org/.

   This journal is based upon Joanna Macy's use of the term "deep time" to refer to the ways that we can reconnect with ancestors and future beings as guides to experiencing our inherent relationship with all of life. She is the root teacher of the Work That Reconnects.

3. Thích Nhất Hạnh, "Practising Listening with Empathy," *Buddhism Now*, April 23, 2014, https://buddhismnow.com/2014/04/23/practising-listening-with-empathy-by-thich-nhat-hanh/.

Chapter 2

1. Roxanne Howe-Murphy, *Deep Living with the Enneagram: Recovering Your True Nature* (Santa Fe: Enneagram Press, 2020), 45–52.

2. Roxanne Howe-Murphy, adapted from "Patterns to Liberation: An Introduction to the Nine Paths of Awakening through the Enneagram," unpublished manuscript, last modified 2007, Microsoft Word file.

3. Pema Chödrön, *The Places That Scare You: A Guide to Fearlessness in Difficult Times* (Boston: Shambhala, 2002), 17.

4. Byron Brown, *Soul without Shame: A Guide to Liberating Yourself from the Judge Within* (Boston: Shambhala, 1999).

Chapter 3

1. Don Richard Riso and Russ Hudson, *Understanding the Enneagram: The Practical Guide to Personality Types* (Boston: Houghton Mifflin, 2000), chapter 4.

2. Don Richard Riso and Russ Hudson, *Discovering Your Personality Type: The Essential Introduction to the Enneagram*, rev ed. (Boston: Houghton Mifflin, 2003), 78.

3. Daniel Goleman, *Emotional Intelligence: Why It Can Matter More Than IQ* (New York: Bantam Books, 1995).

Chapter 4

1. Howe-Murphy, *Deep Living*, 107.

Chapter 5

1. Diana Redmond and Elizabeth Carrington, "Enneagram Interview Process," unpublished material, last modified 2022, Microsoft Word file.

Chapter 6

1. "What Is Depth Psychology?" WisdomFeed, https://wisdomfeed.com/depth-psychology/.

2. The author wishes to acknowledge the many contributions of Wendy Appel, MA, to the development of the original version of the Enneagram iceberg model in 2003. Together, she and the author used the iceberg image to illustrate the above the waterline characteristics of each personality type and to identify some of the below the waterline dynamics that drive the personality.

3. Howe-Murphy, *Deep Living*, 79–91.

4. Howe-Murphy, *Deep Living*, 127.

5. Howe-Murphy, *Deep Living*, 127.

6. John Chryssavgis, *In the Heart of the Desert, Revised: The Spirituality of the Desert Fathers and Mothers* (Bloomington, IN: World Wisdom, 2008), 53–62.

   In his exploration of the lives of the early Christian desert elders, Chryssavgis offers insights on the connection between passions and the role of wounding and vulnerability in the healing journey.

7. Don Richard Riso and Russ Hudson, *The Wisdom of the Enneagram: The Complete Guide to Psychological and Spiritual Growth for the Nine Personality Types* (New York: Bantam Books, 1999), 353.

   Riso and Hudson discuss the inner critic messages, or what they call the "marching orders" for each of the nine types.

8. Riso and Hudson, *Wisdom of the Enneagram*, 60–63.

Chapter 7

1. Riso and Hudson, *Wisdom of the Enneagram*, 353.

2. Riso and Hudson, *Wisdom of the Enneagram*, 323.

3. Riso and Hudson, *Wisdom of the Enneagram*, 323.

4. Riso and Hudson, *Wisdom of the Enneagram*, 188.

5. Riso and Hudson, *Discovering Your Personality Type*.

6. Riso and Hudson, *Wisdom of the Enneagram*, 209–10.

   Riso and Hudson use the phrases "mental retention" and "retain the material in the mind" to identify the fixation of Type Five.

7. Riso and Hudson, *Wisdom of the Enneagram*, 216.

Chapter 8

1. Riso and Hudson, *Wisdom of the Enneagram*, 353.

2. Riso and Hudson, *Wisdom of the Enneagram*, 161.

5. Riso and Hudson, *Discovering Your Personality Type*.

4. Riso and Hudson, *Wisdom of the Enneagram*, 353.

5. Riso and Hudson, *Wisdom of the Enneagram*, 270.

6. Riso and Hudson, *Wisdom of the Enneagram*, 353.

7. Riso and Hudson, *Wisdom of the Enneagram*, 296.

Chapter 9

1. Riso and Hudson, *Wisdom of the Enneagram*, 353.

2. Riso and Hudson, *Wisdom of the Enneagram*, 114.

3. Riso and Hudson, *Wisdom of the Enneagram*, 106.

4. Riso and Hudson, *Wisdom of the Enneagram*, 353.

5. Riso and Hudson, *Wisdom of the Enneagram*, 134.

6. Riso and Hudson, *Wisdom of the Enneagram*, 353.

7. Riso and Hudson, *Wisdom of the Enneagram*, 242.

Chapter 10

1. Riso and Hudson, *Understanding the Enneagram*, 247–57.

   Riso and Hudson have written extensively on the three centers of intelligence, drawing from the teachings of George Gurdjieff, a philosopher, mystic, and spiritual teacher who introduced the Enneagram symbol to the Western world.

2. Brown, *Soul without Shame*, 23.

3. Anthea Indira Ong, "Words Create Worlds," *Medium*, November 25, 2017, https://antheaindiraong.medium.com/words-create-worlds-439bbf1cc87d.

4. Sara Glickstein, "Relational Presence Increases Speaker Ease through Healing Attachment," Speaking Circles, accessed April 19, 2022, https://www.speakingcircles.com/en/research/attachment.

Sara Glickstein is a neuroscientist who has studied the impact of Speaking Circles®, a process for speaking with presence that was founded by her uncle, Lee Glickstein.

Chapter 11

1. Belinda Gore, "Finding Freedom in Authentic Relationships: A Life-Changing Exploration of the Enneagram and Object Relations," unpublished manuscript, last modified 2022.

   Gore brings her extensive study and teaching about the relationship between object relations and the Enneagram in support of transforming relationships to this forthcoming book.

2. Howe-Murphy, *Deep Living*, 111–13.

   In *Deep Living*, Howe-Murphy describes in more depth three areas for observation that take the reader from the habitual and automatic areas for observation to the deeper and more transformative levels that can escape one's attention if not brought into awareness.

3. Goleman, *Emotional Intelligence*, 14.

4. Kendra Cherry, "What Is Neuroplasticity?" *Verywell Mind*, February 18, 2022, https://www.verywellmind.com/what-is-brain-plasticity-2794886.

Chapter 12

1. A. H. Almaas, *The Unfolding Now: Realizing Your True Nature through the Practice of Presence* (Boston: Shambhala Publications, 2008).

   A. H. Almaas is the pen name of A. Hameed Ali, who has written extensively on the centrality of direct experience to transformation. He is the founder of the Diamond Approach, an integration of depth psychology and traditional spiritual inquiry.

REFERENCES

Almaas, A. H. *The Unfolding Now: Realizing Your True Nature through the Practice of Presence*. Boston: Shambhala Publications, 2008.

Arrien, Angeles. *Living in Gratitude: Mastering the Art of Giving Thanks Every Day*. Boulder, CO: Sounds True, 2013.

Brown, Byron. *Soul without Shame: A Guide to Liberating Yourself from the Judge Within*. Boston: Shambhala, 1999.

Cherry, Kendra. "What Is Neuroplasticity?" *Verywell Mind*, February 18, 2022. https://www.verywellmind.com/what-is-brain-plasticity-2794886.

Chödrön, Pema. *The Places That Scare You: A Guide to Fearlessness in Difficult Times*. Boston: Shambhala, 2002.

Chryssavgis, John. *In the Heart of the Desert, Revised: The Spirituality of the Desert Fathers and Mothers*. Bloomington, IN: World Wisdom, 2008.

Deep Times: A Journal of the Work That Reconnects. https://journal.workthatreconnects.org/.

Glickstein, Sara. "Relational Presence Increases Speaker Ease through Healing Attachment." Speaking Circles. Accessed April 19, 2022. https://www.speakingcircles.com/en/research/attachment.

Goleman, Daniel. *Emotional Intelligence: Why It Can Matter More Than IQ*. New York: Bantam Books, 1995.

Gore, Belinda. "Finding Freedom in Authentic Relationships: A Life-Changing Exploration of the Enneagram and Object Relations." Unpublished manuscript, last modified 2022.

Houston, Jean. *The Search for the Beloved: Journeys in Mythology and Sacred Psychology*. Los Angeles: Jeremy P. Tarcher, 1987.

Howe-Murphy, Roxanne. *Deep Coaching: Using the Enneagram as a Catalyst for Profound Change*. Santa Fe: Enneagram Press, 2007.

Howe-Murphy, Roxanne. *Deep Living with the Enneagram: Recovering Your True Nature*. Santa Fe: Enneagram Press, 2020.

Howe-Murphy, Roxanne. "Patterns to Liberation: An Introduction to the Nine Paths of Awakening through the Enneagram." Unpublished manuscript, last modified 2007. Microsoft Word file.

Kornfield, Jack. *A Path with Heart: A Guide through the Perils and Promises of Spiritual Life*. New York: Bantam Books, 1993.

Ong, Anthea Indira. "Words Create Worlds." *Medium*, November 25, 2017. https://antheaindiraong.medium.com/words-create-worlds-439bbf1cc87d.

Palmer, Parker J. *The Courage to Teach: Exploring the Inner Landscape of a Teacher's Life*. San Francisco: Jossey-Bass, 1998.

Redmond, Diana, and Elizabeth Carrington. "Enneagram Interview Process." Unpublished material, last modified 2022. Microsoft Word file.

Rilke, Rainier Maria. *Letters to a Young Poet*. Translated by Stephen Mitchell. New York: Random House, 1984.

Riso, Don Richard, and Russ Hudson. *Discovering Your Personality Type: The Essential Introduction to the Enneagram*, rev ed. Boston: Houghton Mifflin, 2003.

Riso, Don Richard, and Russ Hudson. *Understanding the Enneagram: The Practical Guide to Personality Types*. Boston: Houghton Mifflin, 2000.

Riso, Don Richard, and Russ Hudson. *The Wisdom of the Enneagram: The Complete Guide to Psychological and Spiritual Growth for the Nine Personality Types*. New York: Bantam Books, 1999.

Salzberg, Sharon. *Lovingkindness: The Revolutionary Art of Happiness*. Boston: Shambhala, 1997.

Scharmer, C. Otto. *The Essentials of Theory U: Core Principles and Applications*. Oakland, CA: Berrett-Koehler, 2018.

Thích Nhất Hạnh. "Practising Listening with Empathy." *Buddhism Now*, April 23, 2014. https://buddhismnow.com/2014/04/23/practising-listening-with-empathy-by-thich-nhat-hanh/.

WisdomFeed. "What Is Depth Psychology?" https://wisdomfeed.com/depth-psychology/.

FOR FURTHER READING

Almaas, A. H. Keys to the Enneagram: How to Unlock the Highest Potential of Every Personality Type. Boulder, CO: Shambhala Publications, 2021.

Maitri, Sandra. The Spiritual Dimension of the Enneagram: Nine Faces of the Soul. New York: Jeremy P. Tracher/Putnam, 2000.

Menakem, Resmaa. My Grandmother's Hands: Racialized Trauma and the Pathway to Mending Our Hearts and Bodies. Las Vegas: Central Recovery Press, 2017.

Pransky, Jillian. Deep Listening: A Healing Practice to Calm Your Body, Clear Your Mind, and Open Your Heart. Emmaus, PA: Rodale, 2017.

Sardello, Robert. Silence: The Mystery of Wholeness. Berkeley, CA: Goldenstone Press, 2008.

Stabile, Suzanne. The Journey toward Wholeness: Enneagram Wisdom for Stress, Balance, and Transformation. Downers Grove, IL: InterVarsity Press, 2021.

Van Zino, Karen. Midnight's All a Glimmer: Poetry, Personality, and the Power to See, An Anthology. Danville, CA: Sassafras Press, 2018.

INDEX

Page locators in *italics* indicate figures.

ABOUT THE AUTHOR

Roxanne Howe-Murphy is an inner adventurer, thought leader, and change agent. She integrates her education, the depth of her personal inner work, and four-plus decades of professional experience in diverse fields—including rehabilitation, higher education, coach training, and retreat facilitation—in the second edition of the pioneering book *Deep Coaching: Using the Enneagram as a Catalyst for Profound Change.* The original 2007 edition has provided guidance to thousands of coaches, therapists, spiritual directors, and other professionals across many disciplines and from around the world.

A longtime Enneagram teacher and global expert in integrating the Enneagram with executive, life, and spiritual coaching, Roxanne also authored the 2020 #1 Amazon bestseller and multiple-award winning book *Deep Living with the Enneagram: Recovering Your True Nature.*

Roxanne founded the Deep Coaching Institute in 2007 and served as senior faculty until 2022. She is the founder and board co-chair for Deep Living Lab, Inc., a nonprofit inviting all people into their inherent wholeness and interconnectedness through a unique framework of transformative experiences rooted in the Enneagram as a vehicle for presence.

Roxanne's radically compassionate style, as well as her attunement to the relationship between the patterns of our egoic lives and the mystery of who we are beyond the ego, inform her breakthrough methods for sustainable transformation.

After living near the ocean for most of her adult life, she and her husband moved to Santa Fe, New Mexico, in 2012, where they live with their cat, Gracie. They enjoy hiking in the mountains and participating in the vast array of multicultural artistic and educational activities.

CONTACT INFORMATION

Roxanne Howe-Murphy, EdD
The author's website includes updates on Roxanne's books, offerings, and upcoming work.
RoxanneHoweMurphy.com
info@roxannehowemurphy.com

Deep Living Lab, Inc.
Founded in 2021, Deep Living Lab (DLL) is a nonprofit whose vision is of being a significant force in healing the inner divide and moving toward a world where people access their deepest sources of wisdom and live with a greater sense of wholeness and interconnectedness. All people are invited to recover their true selves through a unique framework of progressively deeper, transformative experiences rooted in the Enneagram as a vehicle for presence and Roxanne Howe-Murphy's unfolding work called EnneaCrossings™.
DeepLivingLab.org
info@deeplivinglab.org

Made in the USA
Monee, IL
12 September 2022

12840264R00188